Why Do English Learners Struggle With Reading?

Second Edition

Dedication

Dr. Janette K. Klingner

(1953–2014)

 *Janette was a leading researcher, educator, and mentor specializing in the reading education of English learners, with and without disabilities. During her career, she spent ten years as a bilingual special education teacher in California and Florida. She obtained her PhD from the University of Miami where she developed the highly effective reading method for ELs known as collaborative strategic reading (CSR), which is used in many schools nationwide. Among the many grant funded projects that Janette led, the RTI Effectiveness Model for ELLs (REME) and the National Center for Culturally Responsive Educational Systems (NCCRESt) are two that highlight her extensive work in the field. Much of Janette's research was funded by the US Department of Education and many private organizations. Janette received numerous honors and awards throughout her career, including the AERA—American Educational Research Association–Special Education SIG Distinguished Researcher Award. Janette was past president of the Division for Learning Disabilities in the Council for Exceptional Children, and served as vice president of the International Academy for Research on Learning Disabilities. Most recently, Janette was president-elect of the Council for Exceptional Children. Janette's publications include over fifteen books, one hundred articles, and numerous book chapters and practitioner briefs, addressing the topics of reading education, special education, ELs, response to intervention, and culturally and linguistically diverse education. She was associate editor for the* Journal of Learning Disabilities, *on the editorial boards of ten professional journals, and was a past coeditor of the* Review of Educational Research. *Throughout her career, Janette collaborated with many colleagues in the fields of reading, special education, and culturally and linguistically diverse education. Some of her colleagues share their thoughts about Janette and her contributions to the field.*

Dean Lorrie A. Shepard, University of Colorado Boulder

I am pleased to add my words of remembrance and admiration for Professor Janette Klingner's many significant professional contributions. Her scholarship was prolific, her commitment to addressing inequities in educational systems unwavering, but still you would not have the whole picture if you did not understand how smart and insightful she was about particularizing supports for learning at the same time that she attended to the practical realities of classrooms, the professional development needs of teachers, and the demands for rigorous research designs. I commend this book to you, knowing Janette's intentions "to engage all students and provide the support that enables culturally and linguistically diverse students and students identified as having disabilities to thrive and show their strengths."

Sharon Vaughn, University of Texas at Austin

Janette Klingner's passion for students with disabilities who were also English language learners influenced her thinking, writing, actions, and those of others. She launched a series of studies more than 25 years ago that influences research and practice today and the foreseeable future. Janette's generosity in sharing what she knew, interest in including as many folks as she could in whatever problem she was tackling, and commitment to conducting high quality research that mattered to practicing professionals is legend. There simply was no issue related to promoting effective outcomes for students who were English language learners that she would not take on. Whether it was policy development, multi-cultural education, research methodology, syntheses, effective interventions, or school reform. Progress related to educational reform for English language learners will be built on her influential work.

Beth Harry, University of Miami

Janette Klingner's unique contribution to the field of special education was the bringing together of three key strands related to equity in education: Learning disability, language, and racial/socioeconomic bias. Starting off as a specialist in reading issues facing bilingual learners, Janette bravely confronted the myriad ways in which this apparently simple binary was inextricably bound to the confounding of racial, socioeconomic, and language differences.

Diane Haager, California State University, Los Angeles

What is remarkable and unique about Janette Klingner's contribution to education is how fluidly she melded multiple areas of expertise—cultural and linguistic diversity, special education, and reading instruction—into a singular defining research identity. Something that she accomplished with astonishing grace is helping diverse communities of educators who often hold tightly to divergent philosophies and beliefs to see value in opposing views. She was always pushing against boundaries to help us to understand complex educational problems, holding firm to her belief that complex problems would require complex solutions. It was more than a "can't we all just get along" way of being. To Janette, looking at situations and problems from multiple perspectives, listening closely to diverse points of view, and persisting until there was consensus, was the only way to truly impact classrooms and schools. Janette was a brilliant researcher and scholar. Her collective work has led to a deeper, richer understanding of the challenges of meeting the needs of diverse populations in cumbersome educational systems.

Nonie Lesaux, Harvard Graduate School of Education

It was inevitable that Janette and I would cross paths, as two scholars deeply committed to increasing opportunities-to-learn for children whose home language(s) include those other than English—a population of children commonly referred to as English learners (ELs). But I was even luckier than that; I had the privilege of collaborating with Janette on some key projects. Most recently, Janette and I designed guidance, resources, and professional development modules to support educators as they shifted their instruction and assessment practices to fit the Response to Intervention (RtI) approach, using RtI as a platform for increasing learning outcomes for ELs. I hold these memories dear, and am still engaged in initiatives to support the implementation of RtI in linguistically diverse settings, continuing to cultivate the progress toward equity that Janette championed. It is through her example that I continue to facilitate and encourage action-oriented conversations about classroom- and school-level models of prevention to meet the needs of today's diverse populations of learners.

Julie Esparza Brown, Portland State University

Dr. Janette Klingner has touched the lives of teachers, scholars, and especially the students in our schools, most notably English learners and students in special education, who have benefited from her teaching, research, and service to the community. Her academic and scholarly accomplishments in the fields of literacy, English Learners and special education are without question. Yet, I believe her generosity of time and heart is equally profound. As a Latina and emerging scholar with few role models and little guidance in navigating an academic career, I deeply valued Janette's mentorship. Not only did she make an impact with her own research, but there are many others like me . . . [who found that her] guidance and impact on our scholarship have been invaluable.

John J. Hoover, University of Colorado Boulder

Leonard M. Baca, University of Colorado Boulder

Janette was a scholar, colleague, and friend and will be missed by many. In the contents of the second edition of this book her knowledge and expertise prevail, continuing her efforts to inform, educate and prepare high quality educators in the teaching of reading to culturally and linguistically diverse learners, with or without disabilities.

Why Do English Learners Struggle With Reading?

Distinguishing Language Acquisition From Learning Disabilities

Second Edition

John J. Hoover

Leonard M. Baca

Janette K. Klingner

CORWIN
A SAGE Publishing Company

FOR INFORMATION:

Corwin

A SAGE Company

2455 Teller Road

Thousand Oaks, California 91320

(800) 233-9936

www.corwin.com

SAGE Publications Ltd.

1 Oliver's Yard

55 City Road

London EC1Y 1SP

United Kingdom

SAGE Publications India Pvt. Ltd.

B 1/I 1 Mohan Cooperative Industrial Area

Mathura Road, New Delhi 110 044

India

SAGE Publications Asia-Pacific Pte. Ltd.

3 Church Street

#10-04 Samsung Hub

Singapore 049483

Acquisitions Editor: Jessica Allan

Associate Editor: Kimberly Greenberg

Editorial Assistant: Katie Crilley

Production Editor: Veronica Stapleton Hooper

Copy Editor: Patrice Sutton

Typesetter: C&M Digitals (P) Ltd.

Proofreader: Penelope Sippel

Indexer: Judy Hunt

Cover Designer: Candice Harman

Marketing Manager: Jill Margulies

Library of Congress Cataloging-in-Publication Data

Names: Hoover, John J., author. | Baca, Leonard M., author.

Title: Why do English learners struggle with reading? : distinguishing language acquisition from learning disabilities / John J. Hoover, Leonard M. Baca., Janette K. Klingner.

Description: Second edition. | Thousand Oaks, California : Corwin, A SAGE Company, 2016. | Includes bibliographical references and index.

Identifiers: LCCN 2015045170 | ISBN 9781506326498 (pbk. : alk. paper)

Subjects: LCSH: Reading disability—United States. | Learning disabilities—United States. | Second language acquisition. | English language—Study and teaching—United States.

Classification: LCC LB1050.5 .W49 2016 | DDC 371.91/44—dc23 LC record available at http://lccn.loc.gov/2015045170

This book is printed on acid-free paper.

16 17 18 19 20 10 9 8 7 6 5 4 3 2 1

Contents

Preface   xi

Acknowledgments   xiii

About the Authors   xv

Introduction to Second Edition   1

1. **Distinguishing Between Language Acquisition and Learning Disabilities Among English Learners: Background Information**   7

Michael J. Orosco, Estella Almanza de Schonewise, Carmen de Onís, Janette K. Klingner, and John J. Hoover

   EL Demographics   8
   Teacher Shortages   10
   *Students With Limited/Interrupted Formal
      Education (SLIFEs)*   11
   ELs and Disproportionate Representation   14
   The Evolving Learning Disabilities Category   15
   Historical Overview About LD   15
   Contemporary Perspective About LD   18
   What We Know From Research on ELs With LD   19
   The LD Definition and ELs   21
   *Review of Changing Demographics and
      Educational Features*   21
   Summary   22

2. **Multi-Tiered System of Supports (MTSS) and English Learners**   25

John J. Hoover, Laura Méndez Barletta, and Janette K. Klingner

   Vignette: Culturally and Linguistically
      Responsive Multi-Tiered System of Supports   26

   Overview of MTSS   27
   MTSS: A Way of Thinking   29
   Assumptions Underlying MTSS
      That May Be Problematic With ELs   40
      Assumption 1   40
      Assumption 2   40
      Assumption 3   41

Practical Applications   41
     Practical Application 1: Rural School District Model   41
     Practical Application 2: Marble Mountain Elementary School   45
Lessons Learned From Practical Examples for Educating ELs   49
Summary   51

**3. Misconceptions About the
Second Language Acquisition Process**   **57**

*Janette K. Klingner, Estella Almanza de
Schonewise, Carmen de Onís, and Laura Méndez Barletta*

What We Know About Second Language Acquisition   58
Second Language Acquisition Misconceptions   66
     Misconception 1   66
     Misconception 2   68
     Misconception 3   70
     Misconception 4   71
     Misconception 5   73
     Misconception 6   75
     Misconception 7   76
     Misconception 8   78
     Misconception 9   79
Summary   80

**4. Helping Classroom Reading Teachers Distinguish
Between Language Acquisition and Learning Disabilities**   **83**

Janette K. Klingner and Diana Geisler

Vignette: The Changing School Environment   84

Standards-Based Education and Reading   85
The "Five Big Ideas" of Reading   86
     Phonological Awareness   86
     Alphabetic Principle   88
     Fluency   89
     Vocabulary   90
     Reading Comprehension   91
     Two More "Big Ideas"   92
Oral Language   92
Motivation   94
Decision Points When Students Struggle With Reading   96
Summary and a Caveat   100

5. Select Reading Methods for Teaching English Learners   **101**

Amy L. Boelé

Vignette: Examining Effective Reading Curriculum for ELs   101

Method 1: Language Experience Approach (LEA)   103
   Steps/Procedures   103
   Skills Emphasized   104
   Considerations for Use With English Learners   104
Method 2: Repeated Readings   104
   Steps/Procedures   104
   Skills Emphasized   105
   Considerations for Use With English Learners   105
Method 3: Reciprocal Teaching   106
   Steps/Procedures   106
   Skills Emphasized   107
   Considerations for Use With English Learners   107
Method 4: Collaborative Strategic Reading (CSR)   107
   Steps/Procedures   109
   Skills Emphasized   110
   Considerations for Use With English Learners   110
Method 5: Instructional Conversations (IC)   112
   Steps/Procedures   113
   Skills Emphasized   113
   Considerations for Use With English Learners   114
Method 6: Classwide Peer Tutoring   114
   Steps/Procedures   114
   Skills Emphasized   115
   Considerations for Use With English Learners   115
Summary   115

6. Special Education Assessment of ELs   117

John J. Hoover and Laura Méndez Barletta

Vignette: Culturally and Linguistically
Responsive Assessment Procedures   118

What Constitutes an Appropriate EL Referral?   120
EL Test Issues and Special Education Eligibility   123
Linguistic Features   124
Linguistic Misalignment: Assessment Implications for Educators   126
Dialect and Register   127
   Dialect and Language   127
   Register and Language   128
   Assessment Implications for Educators   129
Linguistic Misalignment: Assessment Implications for Educators   130
Experiential Background With Linguistic Features   132
Authentic Assessment   133
   Curriculum-Based Measurement (CBM)   134
   Dynamic Assessment (DA)   134
Summary   139

7. **Data-Driven Decision Making: Distinguishing Language Acquisition and Cultural Behaviors From a Disability** 141

John J. Hoover

Vignette: Culturally and Linguistically
Responsive Data-Based Decision Making 142

Data-Driven Decision Making 144
   Second Language Acquisition (SLA) and Decision Making 145
   Culture-Based Behaviors and Decision Making 150
Cultural and Linguistic Differences
   and Disability Decision Making 150
   Gathering Relevant Student Data 154
Evidence-Based Interventions and Multi-Tiered Instruction 155
Multi-Tier Teams and the Decision-Making Process 158
   Nondiscriminatory Progress Monitoring 158
Summary 162

8. **Conclusion: Putting the Pieces Together** 163

Leonard M. Baca, Todd Fletcher, and John J. Hoover

Summary of Thematic Perspectives 163
   Theme: Multi-Tiered System of Supports (MTSS) 163
   Theme: Universal Screening 164
   Theme: Progress Monitoring 164
   Theme: Formal Assessment 164
   Theme: Evidence-Based Interventions 165
   Theme: Teacher Preparation and Professional Development 165
Practical Applications of Suggested Interventions 165
   Application: Learning Disabilities or
      English Language Development? 166
   Application: Avoiding Misconceptions About ELs 166
   Application: Effective Implementation of MTSS With ELs 166
   Application: Putting Effective Literacy Instruction Into Practice 167
   Application: Role of Data-Driven Decision Making 168
   Application: Problem-Solving Teams 168
   Application: Avoiding Assessment Pitfalls With ELs 168
Putting the Pieces Together 169
Concluding Thoughts on Future Directions 171

References 173

Index 195

Preface

We have each devoted our forty-plus-year careers to trying to improve educational opportunities and outcomes for culturally and linguistically diverse students, especially English learners with or without disabilities. In our years of work as classroom teachers and as professors preparing educators, we have noticed that one of the most challenging aspects of working with English learners is determining why they might be underachieving, particularly in reading. In some cases, it is that they are not being taught in environments conducive to learning or with instructional practices that are appropriate for meeting their needs. Perhaps they are struggling with English language acquisition. Or they might truly have learning disabilities. In fact, all of the above might be contributing to English learners' slow progress.

The first step in providing students with support that is well matched to their needs is determining the possible reasons for their difficulties. Thus, the purpose of this book is to help practitioners distinguish between learning disabilities and other possible explanations for English learners' struggles in school. We provide readers with a wealth of information about different aspects of this important educational challenge. It is our hope that as teachers and other support personnel read through the different chapters of this book, they reflect on their own practices, discuss the content of the book with colleagues, and apply what they are learning with their students. We envision that the reader will become more confident and competent in determining why English learners might be struggling with reading.

Acknowledgments

We wish to acknowledge that this book is written for all the students we had the privilege of teaching who were English learners and labeled as having learning disabilities: Elvia, Jorge, Francisco, Azucena, Veronica, Richard, and Yulexis—to name only a few. Some of these students had learning disabilities, but many did not. It was their challenges and successes, their frustrations and their joys, that planted the seeds for this book so many years ago.

This book was sponsored by the National Center for Culturally Responsive Educational Systems (NCCRESt). There are many individuals along the way who helped with its construction whose contributions we would like to acknowledge. First, we wish to thank Dr. Grace Zamora Durán. It was her expert guidance as the project officer for NCCRESt that provided the impetus for this work. Secondly, we would like to acknowledge the invaluable assistance of Dr. Alfredo Artiles, co-principal investigator for NCCRESt, whose conceptual contributions helped to frame our approach to the book. Next, we would like to thank the authors who contributed to different book chapters and helped make the book a reality: Michael J. Orosco, Laura Méndez Barletta, Amy Boelé, and Todd Fletcher, as well as Carmen de Onís, Diana Geisler, and Estella Almanza de Schonewise. Finally, we would like to show our appreciation for the researchers who coauthored papers presented at NCCRESt's National Research Conference, "English Language Learners Struggling to Learn: Emergent Research on Linguistic Differences and Learning Disabilities," November 18–19, 2004: Jamal Abedi, Alfredo Artiles, Manuel Barrera, Judith Bernhard, Paul Cirino, Jim Cummins, Kathy Escamilla, Richard Figueroa, Todd Fletcher, Margaret Gallego, Eugene Garcia, Michael Gerber, Diane Haager, Beth Harry, Nonie Lesaux, Sylvia Linan-Thompson, Jeff MacSwan, Laura Méndez Barletta, Patricia Newsome, Alba Ortiz, Kathryn Prater, Elba Reyes, Phyllis Robertson, Robert Rueda, Richard Ruiz, Guillermo Solano Flores, Sharon Vaughn, Cheryl Wilkinson, Michelle Windmueller, and Grace Zamora-Durán. Their research served as the foundation for the chapters in this book.

This second edition contains all the excellent material presented in the first edition and builds on those contributions and works of the educational leaders identified above. This second edition expands upon the works that served as the foundation for the first edition by bringing updated research and contemporary insights to the education of ELs who struggle with reading. Finally, we wish to especially acknowledge our late colleague, Dr. Janette Klingner, for her insightful and leading-edge works that masterfully framed *Why Do English Learners Struggle With Reading?* Her contributions live on in this second edition.

PUBLISHER'S ACKNOWLEDGMENTS

Corwin would also like to thank the following for their professional contributions to the book:

Juliana Arazi
ESL Teacher
Urbana School District 116
Urbana, IL

James Becker
ESL Teacher
Saint Paul Public Schools
Saint Paul, MN

Anne Beveridge
Assistant Head and Primary Years
Program Coordinator (Junior School)
Branksome Hall
Toronto, ON

Christine Engel
ESL Teacher
Webster Stanley Elementary
Oshkosh, WI

Christine B. Rodriguez
Elementary School Teacher
Phoenix Elementary School District
Phoenix, AZ

About the Authors

Janette K. Klingner—*See Dedication Page*

 **John J. Hoover** is associate professor of research at the University of Colorado Boulder and a former K–12 special educator, teaching diverse students representing multiple languages and cultures in western, southwestern, and midwestern states. He earned a BA in elementary and special education (intellectual disabilities), an MA in learning disabilities and emotional disorders with an emphasis in reading, and a PhD in curriculum specializing in special education. His research agenda for the past two decades has focused on the topic of culturally and linguistically responsive special education referral and assessment of English language and other diverse learners. He is currently principal investigator/PI on three, multiyear grant-funded projects addressing ELs and multi-tiered supports, special education referral and assessment of culturally and linguistically diverse learners, and graduate-level teacher preparation for teaching English language and other diverse learners with and without disabilities. Select recent or in-development coauthored/coedited books include: *IEPs for ELLs, and Other Diverse Learners* (in development, Corwin); *Linking Assessment to Instruction: Selecting Reading, Writing and Mathematics Interventions* (Pearson); *Differentiating Learning Differences From Learning and Behavioral Disabilities: Teaching Diverse Learners Through Multi-Tiered Response to Intervention* (Allyn & Bacon); and *Methods for Teaching Culturally and Linguistically Diverse Exceptional Learners* (Pearson Merrill). He also is coauthor of a nationally normed reading test, *Early Reading Assessment* (Pro-Ed), and of a research-based educator self-assessment and professional development tool, *Core ESL Instructional Practices (CEIP) Guide.* Recent refereed journal publications include "Increasing Usage of ESL Instructional Practices in a Rural County Elementary School," *Rural Educator* (in press); "Culturally Responsive Special Education Referrals of English Learners in One Rural County School District: Pilot Project," *Rural Special Education Quarterly* (2015), for which he was awarded the 2015 Research Article of the Year Award by the American Council on Rural Special Education (ACRES), and "Reducing Unnecessary Referrals: Guidelines for Teachers of Diverse Learners," *Teaching Exceptional Children* (2012).

Leonard M. Baca is professor emeritus at the University of Colorado Boulder. He earned an EdD from the University of Northern Colorado and has been a professor of education at the University of Colorado Boulder since 1973. He has taught courses in bilingual and bilingual special education and served as the program chair. Professor Baca is founder and executive director of the BUENO Center for Multicultural Education where he has directed and managed millions of dollars in grant-funded projects promoting the education of ELs and students with disabilities. He is author or coauthor of numerous publications dealing with English learners with and without disabilities, including the *Bilingual Special Education Interface* (Merrill) and *Methods for Teaching Culturally and Linguistically Diverse Exceptional Learners* (Pearson).

Introduction to the Second Edition

The second edition of *Why Do English Learners Struggle With Reading?* contains updated and contemporary research-to-practice material about the education of ELs who struggle with reading, and who may also experience misinterpretation of their language acquisition skills and abilities as a learning disability.

NEW TO THE SECOND EDITION

Updated citations reflecting contemporary research and literature about ELs and reading, and ELs and learning disabilities

Inclusion of *Vignettes* in several chapters

Discussion of educational needs of students with limited and interrupted formal education (SLIFE)

Expanded coverage of response to intervention (RTI) to include the contemporary framework of multi-tiered system of supports (MTSS) that combines key features of RTI and positive behavioral supports in the academic and affective education of all students

Theories of second language acquisition discussion and table (Chapter 3)

Addition of *Misconception 9*, which discusses misinterpretations between sequential and simultaneous bilinguals in today's schools

Expanded coverage of cultural diversity and associated behaviors in distinguishing learning differences from disabilities

Addition of a new chapter (Chapter 5) that describes several select research-based reading methods for teaching ELs

Development of a cultural and linguistic diversity reading methods table that summarizes methods appropriate for helping ELs acquire different reading skills (Chapter 2)

Updated select Research to Practice examples

SECOND EDITION PERSPECTIVE

Many English learners (ELs) in our schools continue to struggle with reading. Why? What can educators do? *Why Do English Learners Struggle With Reading?: Distinguishing Language Acquisition From Learning Disabilities (2nd ed.)* provides educators with information designed to help determine whether their ELs are struggling with reading because they may have learning disabilities (LD) or for some other reason associated with second language acquisition. Simultaneously, we attempt to clarify many of the misconceptions surrounding EL instruction and assessment.

The unprecedented growth of the EL population, concerns about the number of inappropriate referrals of ELs to special education, the challenges associated with distinguishing between reading difficulties related to second language acquisition and problems caused by LD, along with the lack of a comprehensive research base on these and related issues, strongly suggest the importance of and need for this practical book. With increased momentum nationwide to provide evidence-based intervention to all students, it is essential to revisit some of the more pressing issues that have challenged educators of ELs who struggle with learning, particularly in reading.

Our goal is to provide solutions to the challenges educators face as they work to address the recurring needs of ELs. In each chapter, we describe a different aspect of distinguishing between language acquisition and LD. Chapters include numerous guides, checklists, figures, and tables for easy reference and use by practitioners. It is our hope that they will facilitate data-gathering and decision-making efforts to provide the most appropriate education to ELs, while simultaneously reducing their inappropriate referral and placement into special education.[1]

US schools continue to be transformed due to diversity of learners and associated learning qualities. The reauthorized Individuals with Disabilities Education Improvement Act (IDEIA; 2004) included momentous changes intended to significantly alter the ways schools support student learning and identify students as having LD. No longer is a discrepancy between intelligence and achievement needed as part of the special education identification process. Instead, educators are encouraged to determine the extent to which students respond to research-based interventions, using data to inform progress, instructional adjustments, and possible referral for special education. Additionally, the reauthorization and restructuring of the Elementary and Secondary Education Act (ESEA), also referred to as No Child Left Behind (NCLB), was recently passed and signed into law. Though specifics are forthcoming, the passage in 2015 of the Every Student Succeeds Act (ESSA) will result in several significant changes in the education of English learners and students with disabilities, as well as teacher preparation. According to the Council for Exceptional Children, the overall impact of ESSA is seen in the transference of authority from the federal government to states and/or local districts in the areas of accountability, school improvement, and educator evaluations. One significant change is that the "Highly Qualified Teacher" requirement has been eliminated. Other key ESSA provisions strengthen teacher preparation education academies and replace adequate yearly progress with statewide accountability systems. Overall, reading education of ELs, including those with disabilities, are impacted by various changes and provisions in ESSA and readers are encouraged to attend to ongoing developments resulting from this recently reauthorized law.

As a result of legislation, school systems nationwide have been initiating efforts to implement multi-tiered system of supports (MTSS) as the primary school and district-wide structures in the comprehensive education of all learners. Although MTSS models may be new to some practitioners and require a paradigm shift in how we think about helping students, some of the same practices and principles previously used as part of the special education process are still mandated by current law (i.e., IDEIA, 2004). It is against this backdrop that we have updated and revised this book. We describe MTSS for diverse schools, identifying best practices, while clarifying which practices and procedures are similar to and different from previous approaches. Specifically,

> *In Chapter 1*, we provide background information intended to set the stage for future chapters. We detail contemporary demographic information about the diverse EL population in the United States and explain what we know about the disproportionate representation of ELs in special education. Then, we present a brief description of LD, finishing the chapter with an overview of what we know from research about distinguishing between LD and language acquisition among ELs.

> *In Chapter 2*, we describe the MTSS model for educating ELs. First, we provide an overview of MTSS; then, we discuss assumptions underlying MTSS that can be problematic when applied in schools with high percentages of ELs. This chapter also illustrates challenges schools may face as they attempt to implement MTSS. For each difficulty, we discuss possible solutions.

> *In Chapter 3*, we focus on the language acquisition process. We pay particular attention to common misconceptions about second language acquisition that can be confusing for educators and contribute to misperceptions about language delay or LD. For each of nine misconceptions, we explain what we know from research about the realities of that aspect of the language acquisition process among ELs in US schools.

> *In Chapter 4*, we tackle the very real challenges classroom teachers face while teaching reading to their ELs. It is classroom teachers who most

often first notice that a child is not progressing, and classroom teachers who may first suspect that a child might have LD. We explain what we know from research about how literacy instruction differs for ELs and focus on helping classroom teachers distinguish between second language acquisition and LD among ELs by explaining some of the struggles ELs face when learning to read in English.

In Chapter 5 (new chapter), we expand our discussions begun in Chapter 4 to include specific evidence-based practices found effective for teaching reading to ELs. We include a summary of the research, an overview of the methods, and detailed steps for easy application in the instructional environment.

In Chapter 6, we outline issues to consider when assessing ELs for possible special education placement. This chapter focuses on referral and assessment for instruction, eligibility, identification, and diagnostic purposes. We discuss the validity of tests for assessing the performance of ELs and point out the impact of regional and dialectal differences on test scores. In addition, the chapter stresses an ecological perspective to assessment, including authentic assessment.

In Chapter 7, we portray data-driven decision making in a multi-tiered model. We discuss factors teachers should consider when their ELs first show signs of struggling, and we provide charts in which we compare and contrast characteristics of LD, cultural diversity, and language acquisition. In addition, we offer practical guidelines regarding what kinds of data to consider when making decisions about students.

In Chapter 8, our conclusion, we focus on "putting the pieces together." Using the analogy of a puzzle, we note how each previous chapter adds to our understanding of ELs who struggle with reading and how to determine whether they may have LD or are simply manifesting expected signs of the language acquisition process or cultural teachings. At the end of our conclusion, we provide a wrap-up of the topics explored in this book and discuss possible future directions for practitioners.

Overall, the text includes thirty tables and figures, and coverage of numerous evidence-based reading practices and other practical instructional suggestions for assessing and teaching ELs who struggle with reading. We hope that practitioners at both elementary and secondary levels of education will find the practical ideas, suggestions, guides, and checklists valuable resources as they continue with their own professional growth to best meet the educational needs of English learners with or without disabilities.

NOTE

1. This book is based in part on a series of research papers presented at a 2004 conference on English language learners. This conference was held in Tempe, Arizona, and was cosponsored by the National Center for Culturally Responsive Educational Systems (NCCRESt) and Arizona State University, with support from the National Association for Bilingual Education (NABE) and the Council for Exceptional Children (CEC). This book is sponsored by NCCRESt. The second edition builds upon these efforts with expanded and updated research ideas, practices, and findings.

1

Distinguishing Between Language Acquisition and Learning Disabilities Among English Learners

Background Information

Michael J. Orosco, Estella Almanza de Schonewise, Carmen de Onís, Janette K. Klingner, and John J. Hoover

First, who are English learners? English learners (ELs) are students who speak a language other than English as their first language and who are in the process of acquiring English as a second or additional language. They are not yet fully proficient in English. For this reason, we might refer to them as "emerging bilinguals." Some are immigrants; others were born in the United States. Their demographic characteristics vary widely. In this chapter, we begin with a comprehensive overview of the changing demographics associated with English learners (ELs) in today's schools, providing a summary by the US Department of Education, National Center for Education Statistics (NCES) of EL demographics as a backdrop to the discussions that follow in subsequent chapters regarding the linguistic and literacy development of ELs. We then present a brief description of the phenomenon of disproportionate representation, next describe learning disabilities, and finish the chapter with an overview of what we know from research about distinguishing between learning disabilities and language acquisition among ELs.

EL DEMOGRAPHICS

A large and increasing proportion of students in US schools come from a home in which a language other than English is spoken. The United States continues to be the world's leader in immigration and is central to the growth and identity of the United States (Pew Research Center, 2013). Immigrants now compose approximately 13 percent (40 million foreign-born people) of the US population (Congressional Budget Office, 2013, p. 1). In 2014, there were 18.7 million children under the age of eighteen who were immigrants (Child Trends, 2014, para. 1). About 4.40 million students enrolled in public schools were not yet fully proficient in English in the 2012–2013 school year, representing nearly 9.2 percent of the total public school student enrollment (National Center for Education Statistics [NCES], 2015, para. 1). Demographic figures show the EL population has continued to grow over the past decade.

In addition, results from the 2011 American Community Survey (Ryan, 2013) showed that 60.6 million individuals aged five or older spoke a language other than English at home (p. 2). This was a 29 percent increase from the 2000 US Census report. While EL students are spread throughout the United States, their greatest density, or share they represent of total public school enrollment in a state, varies greatly. Western states, such as California (24.5 percent), Texas (15.2 percent), Colorado (13.3 percent), and Washington (10.2 percent), continue to have the largest share of ELs in the country. Meanwhile, eastern and southern states like New York (9 percent), Massachusetts (7 percent), Florida (10 percent), Virginia (8 percent), and North Carolina (7 percent) continue to grow in their EL population (Ruiz Soto, Hooker, & Batalova, 2015, p. 2). While students speak many different languages in public schools, Spanish remains the language most frequently spoken by individuals who speak a language other than English in the United States, representing 71 percent of children (five years and over) with emerging English proficiency (p. 1). However, the percentage of Spanish-speaking students has decreased 8 percent since the first edition of this book was published (i.e., 79 to 71 percent), reflecting an increase in other languages in today's schools. See Table 1.1, compiled from information found in Ruiz Soto et al. (2015, p. 1.) for a list of the most commonly spoken languages other than English in US schools.

Immigrant ELs vary in the extent to which they attended schools in their home countries. Center for Immigration Studies (Camarota, 2012) pointed out that "many immigrants arrive in the United States with relatively few years of schooling" (p. 5). In the United States, Latinos

Table 1.1   Top Ten Languages Spoken by Linguistically Diverse Populations in the United States

Rank Language (estimate)	Language	English Learners (estimate)	% of English Learners (estimate)
1	Spanish	3,598,451	71%
2	Vietnamese	88,906	3%
3	Hmong	70,768	1%
4	Chinese, Cantonese, and Mandarin	46,466	4%
5	Korean	43,969	1%
6	French/Haitian Creole	42,236	2%
7	Arabic	41,279	2%
8	German	37,157	1%
9	Filipino, Tagalog	34,133	1%
10	Yiddish/Jewish	27,029	1%

(e.g., Mexican, Honduran, Guatemalan) represent the largest immigrant group and one of the least educated, which is significant to US schools because children from families with high levels of education tend to have higher academic achievement than those from families with little formal education (Camarota, 2012).

Camarota, 2012 also identified trends in the economic and environmental conditions in which English language learners live. "Among the young children of immigrants (under 18), 59.2 percent live in or near poverty, in contrast to 39.3 percent of the children of natives. As a share of all persons in or near poverty, immigrants, and their young children account for 23.8 percent" (p. 26). In addition, because of poverty, immigrants experience residential segregation by income, which is a strong indicator of quality of education provided to children (Fry & Taylor, 2012). Finally, the one hundred largest school districts had a disproportionate percentage of students eligible for the free and reduced-price lunch program relative to all public school districts. According to NCES (Sable, Plotts, & Mitchell, 2010), among the ninety-nine largest school districts that reported free and reduced-price lunch eligibility, 56 percent of students were eligible, compared to 45 percent of students in all districts. Forty-six of these ninety-nine districts reported 50 percent or more of their students as eligible for the free and reduced-price lunch program.

The increase in the English language learner population continues to stymie practitioners because ELs tend to underachieve in comparison with their White middle-class counterparts on indicators of academic success. For example, according to the National Center for Education Statistics (NCES, 2013), in 2012 only 7 percent of EL fourth graders and 3 percent of EL eighth graders scored at or above proficient on reading assessments, as compared to 37 percent and 35 percent of native English speakers (NCES, 2013). According to NCES (2015), one out of every ten students is a second language learner. Demographers project that by the year 2025, this number will increase to one in every four students. The challenge today is teaching to high standards to students from diverse language, culture, and social class groups (Gay, 2010). Because the number of ELs continues to grow at a rapid rate, it is more important than ever for schools to address misconceptions about how best to meet their needs, including minimizing potential cultural and/or linguistic mismatches between teacher and students.

Teacher Shortages

Culturally and linguistically diverse teachers can have a positive effect on the increasingly diverse student population (Au, 2011; Orosco & O'Connor, 2011). However, supplying enough teachers who are prepared to teach ELs remains a challenge. The benefits of a diverse teaching workforce are numerous including strengths in (a) holding high expectations, (b) ability to increase motivation, and (c) providing positive modeling for English language and other diverse learners, to name a few (Albert Shanker Institute, 2015). The diversity of the teaching workforce has increased from approximately 12 to 17 percent from 1987 to 2012; however, this population of educators continues to be underrepresented in our schools (Albert Shanker Institute, 2015, Publications section, para. 1). The underrepresented minority teaching force, combined with the lack of qualified personnel to meet the needs of the diverse population in our nation's schools, has resulted in a "mismatch" between the teaching force and diverse student populations (de Onís, 2005). For example, "In 2012, 83% percent of full-time public school teachers were White, 7% were Black, 7% were Hispanic, and 1% were Asian (Aud, Hussar, Johnson, Kena, & Roth, 2013)" (Aceves & Orosco, 2014, p. 8), with only about 30 percent of K–12 teachers having training in working with English learners (Ballantyne, Sanderman, & Levy, 2008, p. 9).

Additionally, recent research suggests that a related issue within teacher shortages is found in retention, rather than only in recruitment (Albert Shanker Institute, 2015). Further, issues with recruitment and retention of qualified educators with second language background contribute significantly to persistent educator shortages for ELs.

In regard to the student population in the US public schools, diversity of learners is becoming increasingly culturally and linguistically varied. As discussed, though some progress has been made, teachers and school leaders remain fairly monoracial (US Department of Education, 2013).

Inadequate preparation contributes to the "achievement gap" if teachers enter classrooms with subjective personal and instructional dispositions toward cultural differences (e.g., Orosco & Klingner, 2010). For example, Yoon (2008) found a strong link between teachers' past personal and professional experiences and how these cultural experiences contributed to English learners' positioning of themselves to learn. This positioning was dependent on how well teachers understood ELs' cultural and linguistic identity and how they proactively promoted their learning engagement through interactive teaching experiences. One important conclusion from this research is that teachers who had culturally responsive practice and preparation in schools tended to provide instructional methods that improved English learner engagement and motivation (Yoon, 2008), a type of preparation all educators in today's diverse classrooms should strive to achieve.

Additionally, ELs and their families look to teachers to meet their needs and help them to be successful in our nation's schools, assisting them in the attainment of the "American Dream" (Ladson-Billings, 2009). When there are significant differences between the student's culture and the school's culture, teachers can easily misread students' aptitudes, intent, or abilities because of variations in styles of language use and interactional patterns (Orosco & Hoover, 2009; Orosco & O'Connor, 2014). Second, when such cultural differences exist, teachers may utilize styles of instruction and/or discipline that are at odds with community norms (Harry & Klingner, 2014; Orosco & Klingner, 2010). Added to a lack of cultural awareness, many teachers have received little or no training in English as a second language (ESL), English language acquisition, or bilingual/bicultural education (Herrera, Perez, & Escamilla, 2015), leading to a teaching force that is inadequately prepared to face the growing challenge of educating culturally and linguistically diverse learners. According to the Center for American Progress (Samson & Collins, 2012), teachers were least likely to be very prepared for (a) integrating grade or subject level common standards with ELs' learning needs, (b) addressing the language needs of limited English proficient or culturally diverse students, and (c) addressing the needs of students with disabilities. Since teachers have the main responsibility and play an integral role in the education of ELs, their preparation is crucial to student success.

Students With Limited/Interrupted Formal Education (SLIFEs)

A select subpopulation of English learners (ELs) possesses unique learning experiences reflective of limited or interrupted formal schooling, particularly in their native countries (see WIDA *Focus,* 2015. Reasons for limited or interrupted schooling vary by country due to one or more factors such as poverty, war, natural disasters, isolated geography with limited transportation resources, or supporting family financial needs, to name a few. Whatever the reasons for limited or interrupted schooling, many of these ELs possess limited skills in literacy, functioning below grade level in one or more academic areas (WIDA *Focus*, 2015.) Additionally, cultural differences often indicate variations in the required number of years for schooling or minimum age (i.e., compulsory education may be through Grade 9 in one country while in another a student must remain in school until age 18). Though current statistics are not readily available (WIDA *Focus*, 2015), estimates are that up to 20 percent of secondary ELs are SLIFEs, with many learners missing a minimum of two or more years of school. Montero, Newmaster, & Ledger (2014) report that the dropout rate of refugee learners is 75 percent higher at the secondary level of education. Additionally, according to Calderón (2008), SLIFEs are typically identified in the 4th–12th grades, though missing early elementary school or even preschool instruction in some countries represents limited or interrupted formal schooling.

Students with limited/interrupted formal schooling bring a variety of learning needs to the classroom which directly impact reading and which may be misinterpreted as indicators of a learning disability. As emphasized throughout this book, limited experiential background or exposure to formal schooling and lack of literacy knowledge and skills due to interrupted schooling do not represent reasons for classifying a student an EL with learning disabilities. To best meet the reading needs of this ever-growing population of ELs, educators in both elementary and secondary education should be cognizant of learning characteristics and qualities often seen in SLIFEs, summarized below from material found in Calderón (2008) and the WIDA Consortium (WIDA *Focus*, 2015):

- Newcomers to the district typically enter missing two or more years of schooling.
- Many students may attend US schools, return to their original country for a brief period of time, and subsequently return to US schools.
- Language of instruction may vary and be inconsistent, such as instruction occurring in native language in kindergarten and first grade, English in second grade, and returning to native language instruction in Grade 3.
- Attendance may include two or more schools in relatively brief periods of time (e.g., two schools attended in a six-month time frame).
- Literacy background may be limited and have gaps relative to grade-level peers in US schools.
- Many learners have experienced emotional trauma and therefore have social-emotional developmental needs in addition to literacy.

These and similar educational needs shape the learning of a SLIFE, requiring additional instructional considerations often beyond best practices typically used with ELs who have not experienced limited or interrupted formal schooling. DeCapua and Marshall (2011) concluded from their research that an effective framework for instruction to meet unique needs of a SLIFE requires educators to "accept conditions for learning, combine processes for learning, and focus on academic tasks with familiar language and content" (p. 65). Additionally, instructional recommendations specific to SLIFEs exist and are summarized below from material found in Calderón (2008) and the WIDA Consortium (WIDA *Focus*, 2015):

   a. Address acculturation needs (i.e., adjustment to new and unfamiliar environments).

   b. Focus on social-emotional needs as well as academic literacy.

   c. Provide secondary learners with literacy instruction appropriate for adolescents.

   d. Integrate content and language instruction (i.e., develop and teach toward both language and content objectives).

   e. Address the higher risk of dropping out through culturally and linguistically responsive instruction (i.e., employ literacy best practices appropriate for age and grade level).

   f. Build supportive learning environments to meet immediate needs upon school entry, such as a newcomer center.

   g. Collaborate with colleagues, family members, community organizations, and support staff to best help students during initial time of entry to ease stress and simultaneously address literacy and social-emotional needs.

   h. Provide intensive literacy and language instruction, increase use of sheltered instruction, and adapt required standards to make curriculum more accessible.

Of critical importance is the perspective that it is essential to teach to the whole learner tapping into one's existing funds of knowledge (i.e., skills and knowledge acquired as a result of cultural and home teachings; Moll, Amanti, Neff, & Gonzalez, 1992). Overall, delivery of the best practices discussed in the remaining chapters of this book, along with making instructional adjustments to address the above features unique to students with limited/interrupted formal schooling, creates a rich learning environment that engages students, accesses and builds on prior knowledge, and supports affective development in addition to reading.

ELS AND DISPROPORTIONATE REPRESENTATION

Disproportionate representation has often been defined as an over- or underrepresentation of a particular culturally and linguistically diverse population in a specific disability category (Klingner et al., 2005), and it is often assessed by calculating a group's representation in a specific special education category in comparison with its proportion of the total school-aged population, or in reference to the representation of a comparison group, most often White students (Donovan & Cross, 2002). There is not one agreed-upon best way of determining disproportionate representation, and several procedures and formulas have been proposed and used throughout the history of this problem.[1] Whichever index we use, the disability categories in which we are most likely to see disproportionate representation are intellectual disability, emotional/behavioral disorders, and learning disability (LD). The most common ethnic groups involved in overrepresentation include African American, Chicano/Latino, American Indian, and a few subgroups of Asian American students (see Artiles & Trent, 2000; Donovan & Cross, 2002). Concerns about disproportionate representation focus on the "judgmental" categories of special education, or, in other words, those disabilities usually identified by school personnel rather than a medical professional after the child has started school (Klingner et al., 2005). The school personnel making placement decisions typically exercise wide latitude in deciding who qualifies for special education through a process that is quite subjective (Harry & Klingner, 2014). Notably, overrepresentation does not exist in low-incidence disability categories (such as visual, auditory, or orthopedic impairment; Donovan & Cross, 2002).

When we examine changes in special education identification over the years, one of the most striking findings is the "epidemic" increase in the risk of children of all racial/ethnic groups except Asian/Pacific Islanders for the LD category (Donovan & Cross, 2002, p. 47). Looking at current national averages, Hispanic/Latino students are only slightly overrepresented in programs for students with LD (Klingner et al., 2005). However, placement rates vary widely across states and districts. In some schools, Latino students are actually underrepresented in LD programs based on what would be expected given their percentage in the overall school population. In other schools, they are overrepresented. Artiles, Rueda, Salazar, and Higareda (2005) examined placement patterns in special education programs in eleven urban districts in California with high proportions of ELs and high poverty levels. They found that ELs were not overrepresented in LD in the primary grades, but were overrepresented in Grades 5 and higher. Secondary level ELs were almost twice as likely to be placed in special education as their peers. Furthermore, ELs in English Immersion programs, where there was no primary language support, were almost three times more likely to be identified for special education than EL students in bilingual classrooms. This work suggests that specific patterns become obscured when data are aggregated above district levels (Rueda & Windmueller, 2006). It also suggests the need to broaden examinations of disproportionate representation to include language proficiency in addition to ethnicity.

There are numerous possible reasons for disproportionate representation (Harry & Klingner, 2014). Because ELs tend to underachieve in comparison with their mainstream counterparts, this puts pressure on practitioners to find ways to give the EL student extra assistance to help close the achievement gap. Practitioners may perceive that special education is the only viable option for providing this support and refer the child to special education, or mistakenly assume that the student's struggles are due to an LD rather than a normal consequence of the language acquisition process. These actions can result in the placement of students in special education who do not truly have an LD. On the other hand, some practitioners may be fearful of referring ELs into special education because they believe it is wrong to refer students before they are fully proficient in English, or they might assume that a student's struggles are due to language acquisition when in fact the student does have an LD. When this happens, students who have an LD go without services and continue to struggle with the general education curriculum. These different kinds of inappropriate decisions characterize the complexities of disproportionate representation among ELs.

THE EVOLVING LEARNING DISABILITIES CATEGORY

What are learning disabilities, and how are they best identified for ELs? For nearly five decades, definitions and terminology reflecting perspectives about LD have evolved and been applied in school settings for all learners, including ELs (see Table 1.2).

After more than forty-five years of discussions, revisions, and advocacy, the field of LD continues to struggle to develop an operational (working) definition, especially for culturally and linguistically diverse learners. A brief review of the evolution of the definition and terminology is presented below to frame an understanding of the contemporary views about LD seen in today's schools.

Historical Overview About LD

In the early 1960s, Samuel Kirk (1962) coined the term "learning disability." Bateman (1965) was dissatisfied with Kirk's definition and developed a different one that was the first to refer to an IQ-achievement discrepancy. This was the beginning of forty years of implementation of the IQ discrepancy-based model, which classified students with LD

Table 1.2   Historical Timeline of Key LD Definitions and Initiatives

- *1962 Samuel Kirk:* A learning disability refers to a retardation, disorder, or delayed development in one or more of the processes of speech, language, reading, writing, arithmetic, or other school subject resulting from a psychological handicap caused by a possible cerebral dysfunction and/or emotional or behavioral disturbances. It is not the result of mental retardation, sensory deprivation, or cultural and instructional factors. (Kirk, 1962, p. 263)

- *1965 Barbara Bateman:* Children who have learning disorders are those who manifest an educationally significant discrepancy between their estimated potential and actual level of performance related to basic disorders in the learning process, which may or may not be accompanied by demonstrable central nervous system dysfunction and which are not secondary to generalized mental retardation, educational or cultural deprivation, severe emotional disturbance, or sensory loss. (Bateman, 1965, p. 220)

- *1977 US Department of Education:* The term "specific learning disability" (SLD) means a disorder in one or more of the psychological processes involved in understanding or in using language, spoken or written, which may manifest itself in an imperfect ability to listen, speak, read, write, spell, or do mathematical calculations. The term does not include children who have LD that are primarily the result of visual, hearing, or motor handicaps, or mental retardation, or emotional disturbance, or of environmental, cultural, or economic disadvantage. (US Office of Education, 1977, Federal Register, p. 65083)

- *1981 National Joint Committee on Learning Disabilities:* Learning disabilities is a generic term that refers to a heterogeneous group of disorders manifested by significant difficulties in the acquisition and use of listening, speaking, reading, writing, reasoning, or mathematical abilities. These disorders are intrinsic to the individual and presumed to be due to central nervous system dysfunction. Even though a learning disability may occur concomitantly with other handicapping conditions (e.g., sensory impairment, mental retardation, social and emotional disturbance) or environmental influences (e.g., cultural differences, insufficient/inappropriate instruction, psychogenic factors), it is not the direct result of those conditions or influences. (Hammill, Leigh, McNutt, & Larsen, 1981, p. 336)

- *1997 Individuals with Disabilities Act (IDEA) Amendments:* The term "specific learning disability" means a disorder in one or more of the basic psychological processes involved in understanding or in using language, spoken or written, which disorder may manifest itself in imperfect ability to listen, think, speak, read, write, spell, or do mathematical calculations. *Disorders Included*—Conditions such as perceptual disabilities, brain injury, minimal brain dysfunction, dyslexia, and developmental aphasia, and *Disorders Not Included*—Learning problem that is primarily the result of visual, hearing, or motor disabilities, of mental retardation, of emotional disturbance, or of environmental, cultural, or economic disadvantage. (IDEA Amendments of 1997, Sec. 602(26), p. 13)

- *IDEIA 2004:* The act maintains the SLD definitions found in IDEA 1997 and earlier versions of the law; however, it seeks to update and improve the criteria for SLD identification and eligibility by eliminating the requirement that students must exhibit a severe discrepancy between achievement and intellectual ability in order to be found eligible for services under IDEA (regardless of age). Instead, states may consider how a student responds to research-based interventions when making eligibility determinations, as determined through multi-tiered system of supports (MTSS).

- *MTSS 2010–Present:* This framework incorporates the practice of response to intervention used, in part, to determine a suspected learning disability (Council for Exceptional Children [CEC], 2008; Kovaleski, VanDerHeyden, & Shapiro, 2013), de-emphasizing the IQ-achievement discrepancy method.

based on a significant difference between potential (IQ) and academic performance (actual performance).

At the time, the model was validated by Rutter and Yule's (1975) research, which classified two types of impaired readers based on associations between IQ (potential) and achievement (actual performance). In other words, Rutter and Yule found a cluster of impaired readers at the low end of the scale who seemed to share common characteristics and could be categorized as having reading disabilities because they demonstrated significant discrepancies between expected and observed reading scores. The researchers defined the second type of impaired reader as having "general reading backwardness." These students did not demonstrate a discrepancy between expected and observed reading skills but instead exhibited general learning problems. In subsequent years, researchers determined flaws in Rutter and Yule's research, due to a cluster of impaired readers exhibiting problems resulting from testing procedures (e.g., Stuebing et al., 2002). In fact, students' reading and IQ scores fall along a continuum—there is no cluster at the bottom of the scale.

In 1975, Congress passed public law (PL) 94–142, the Education for All Handicapped Children Act (EAHCA). This is the precursor to the Individuals with Disabilities Education Act (IDEA; 1991, 1997; IDEIA, 2004). However, it was not until 1977 that the US Office of Education put forth a definition of LD, as shown in Table 1.2. This conceptual definition became the most commonly used LD perspective in the United States' public education system. It is important to note that the federal government never explicitly or clearly explained the LD definition or stated how to operationalize it to identify children for special education. Thus, they left state and local educational agencies to figure this out on their own. Rather, the federal government assumed that the definition would provide a theoretical framework for use in identification (Hallahan & Mercer, 2002). Since the inception of EAHCA in 1975, intermittent amendments have passed without any major changes to the LD definition thus continuing the trend of lack of clarification and difficulties reaching consensus in developing LD identification criteria (Gallego, Zamora Durán, & Reyes, 2006).

In 1978, several major LD professional organizations along with the Adults and Children with Learning and Developmental Disabilities Organization (ACLD) formed the National Joint Committee on Learning Disabilities (NJCLD) to attempt to provide a united front in addressing issues pertaining to LD (Hallahan & Mercer, 2002). In 1981, NJCLD put forth its own definition of LD (see Table 1.2). Notably, there was no mention of psychological processes in this definition. The committee omitted this because of negative reactions to the perceptual-motor training programs in the field at that time (Gallego et al., 2006).

Reformation efforts continued through the 1980s and 1990s by various organizations that were unhappy with the federal definition. At the same time, the US Department of Education continued to fund studies to solidify the federal definition and develop effective methods for identification. Despite the NJCLD's strong position and the popularity in some circles of its alternative definition, the federal LD definition remained intact within the reauthorization of the Individuals with Disabilities Education Act of 1997 and 2004.

Contemporary Perspective About LD

As the new millennium began, the IQ-discrepancy criterion was under increased scrutiny. In 2001, the US Office of Special Education Programs (OSEP) sponsored the LD Initiative Summit to discuss various aspects of LD (Gallego et al., 2006). The purpose of this summit was to develop a LD research synthesis that could provide useful information to practitioners when making decisions concerning identifying students with LD. There were eight major points, generated as consensus statements, resulting from this summit (Table 1.3).

As shown in Table 1.3, the results from the summit indicated that the discrepancy-based model was insufficient and ineffective for identifying

Table 1.3   Learning Disability Initiative Summit: Eight Major Consensus Statements

Consensus 1: Concept of specific learning disabilities (SLDs)—Research evidence supports the validity of SLD as an intrinsic disorder of learning and cognition—"LD is not socially constructed."
Consensus 2: Students with SLD—Learners with SLD have the right to receive special education and related services at no cost.
Consensus 3: SLD as lifelong condition—Students' needs with SLD extend beyond the classroom.
Consensus 4: Exact SLD prevalence unknown—Estimates are that 6 percent of students receive instruction and resources that require SLD special education.
Consensus 5: Continued discrepancy between IQ and achievement—There are opposing arguments on this issue. However, the majority opinion supports that a discrepancy is unnecessary and insufficient for identifying LD. The minority opinion supports the discrepancy-based model for identifying LD but believes it is not sufficient to verify underachievement.
Consensus 6: Processing deficits—Some deficits have been linked to SLD.
Consensus 7: Effective interventions—Effective interventions for SLD students are effective with regard to consistency, appropriate intensity, and fidelity.
Consensus 8: Response to intervention (RTI)—Alternative methods must be developed to identify students with SLD. RTI is an alternative model that is the most promising method of alternative identification that can also promote effective school practices and help close the gap between identification and treatment.

students with LD and that further research was needed on the discrepancy-based model in order to verify its validity (Gallego et al., 2006). The position of decreased emphasis on discrepancy, and increased emphasis on response to instruction, is a position that is still held today by many researchers (e.g., Fuchs & Fuchs, 2006; Hoover, 2010; Klingner et al., in press; Kovaleski et al., 2013). Additionally, the "consensus statements" were attempts to put into operation key features that characterize learning disabilities (e.g., effective instruction, response to instruction, evidence of processing issues, etc.). These features are important as they served to frame the contemporary perspective of a learning disability in today's schools.

Specifically, when Congress reauthorized the same LD definition in the Individuals with Disabilities Education Improvement Act in 2004, it also incorporated the summit's recommendations regarding LD identification procedures. By far, the most dramatic change was the elimination of the requirement that a severe discrepancy between intellectual ability and academic achievement be shown in order to qualify as a LD. This clarification and change in practice established the foundation upon which learning disabilities is currently viewed.

As discussed above, the origin of the LD definition lies in the traditional medical model of disabilities. Historically, the field has considered LD a condition needing diagnosis that is centered within the child rather than in the educational environment (Lloyd & Hallahan, 2005). This model is a deficit-based approach (Gallego et al., 2006) that primarily looks for "problems" within the learner with little to no consideration of the quality of instruction. As a result of the 2004 LD Initiative Summit and the revised IDEA, a greater emphasis is now placed on quality of instruction within the contemporary framework known as multi-tiered system of supports (MTSS) (see Chapter 2 for detailed discussion of MTSS). Educators in the field of cultural and linguistic diversity and special education are encouraged by the potential of MTSS effects on the identification of ELs for a learning disability, due to its initial emphasis on ruling out poor or inappropriate instruction as a potential cause for the learners' problems. That is, for ELs, culturally and linguistically responsive reading instruction is required prior to referral to make certain misplacement is reduced.

WHAT WE KNOW FROM RESEARCH ON ELS WITH LD

In a series of large scale studies, Swanson, Orosco, and colleagues investigated ELs who struggle with reading and who may have LD in trying to identify better methods for accurate identification and assessment (e.g., Swanson, Orosco, & Kudo, in press; Swanson, Orosco, & Lussier, 2012; Swanson, Orosco, Lussier, Gerber, & Guzman-Orth, 2011), thus, seeking to improve the LD definition for ELs. In this research, Swanson,

Orosco, et al. wanted to find out what instructional and cognitive components were most effective in accurately identifying EL children with LD. Research indicates that cognitive candidates most often referred to in the literature as potentially at risk for LD exhibit issues related to language development (e.g., phonological processes and vocabulary; see Farnia & Geva, 2011; Lesaux & Geva, 2006, for a review) and working memory (see Swanson, Saéz, Gerber, & Leafstedt, 2004, for an example). In general, the results from Swanson, Orosco, et al. support the notion that native language development (e.g., phonological processing and vocabulary) as well as a general working memory system underlie second language acquisition and LD in children. In addition, their research indicated that cognition is a complicated process influenced by many instructional factors, including but not limited to the sociocultural environment, language proficiency in the first language, attitudes, personality, and perceived status of the native language in comparison with English (e.g., Orosco & R. O'Connor, 2011; Orosco & R. E. O'Connor, 2014). One major theme that emerged from this research was the critical importance of intensive, interactive instruction with ELs that promotes not only English as a second language but also native language development (e.g., Orosco & R. O'Connor, 2011; Orosco & R. E. O'Connor, 2014). This effective instruction focuses on explicit instruction and intervention in teaching core academic elements and oral language development that fosters native and English language academic development (e.g., Orosco, 2014; Orosco, Swanson, O'Connor, & Lussier, 2013).

The Swanson, Orosco, et al. research falls along the line of an early synthesis conducted by Klingner, Artiles, and Barletta (2006) on ELs who struggle with reading and who may have learning disabilities (LDs). In this study, Klingner et al. (2006) found that cultural conflict and affective considerations, such as quality of instructional engagement (e.g., motivation) appear to be of critical importance when considering why students might be struggling, yet practitioners often overlook these factors. Behaviors that appear to indicate LD might be normal for the child's cultural background or be a by-product of the acculturation process. Practitioners involved in referral and placement decision making should consider various characteristics in relation to a child's culture, language, and acculturation. Similarly, they should consider the learning context when considering why a student is not thriving.

Finally, more research is still needed to help us better understand how ELs with and without reading disabilities may differ. By understanding the characteristics of subpopulations of students with different features, the educational community develops more effective identification tools and procedures to address disproportionate representation and more accurately determines which students are most likely to benefit from special education services in reading.

The LD Definition and ELs

As will be discussed in detail in the remaining chapters of this book, characteristics of LD and second language acquisition can appear quite similar. Essential to the education of ELs is the development of language in appropriate learning environments (Lesaux, 2013). The lack of appropriate language development instruction and environments contribute, in part, to practitioners having assessed and diagnosed many ELs as having LD when they may not actually have disabilities (Ortiz et al., 2011). Over the years, a growing number of ELs have met the requirements for LD and have been properly placed for special services. However, for many other ELs, the LD definition, referral, and identification criteria have not adequately taken into account students' linguistic and sociocultural differences, limiting their usefulness and leading to misplacements (Gallego et al., 2006; Ortiz et al., 2011). Though the contemporary emphasis is moving away from IQ-achievement discrepancy through MTSS, many practitioners continue to look for a discrepancy between achievement and intellectual ability in one or more areas related to language processing skills when determining placement into special education. On one side, many practitioners continue to believe that the discrepancy-based model is the foundation of the LD diagnosis, while on the other side, many practitioners favor a more ecologically based identification process that accounts for instructional quality, home-community connections, and contextual considerations (Bronfenbrenner, 1995; Council of Chief State School Officers [CCSSO], 2015; Klingner et al., in press; Orosco, 2010).

Researchers and practitioners continue to question referral, assessment, and identification practices that often do not take into account students' cultural and linguistic backgrounds (Basterra, Trumbull, & Solano-Flores, 2011; Hoover & Klingner, 2011; Ortiz et al., 2011; Hoover & Erickson, 2015). As long as federal regulations do not specify *how* to identify LD in ELs and states must design their own identification criteria, practitioners will struggle with identification and placement procedures. Because LD identification criteria vary widely from state to state, a student may be LD in one state yet not in another. These challenges are compounded when the student is an EL. It is within this backdrop that the remaining chapters are written: *how might we distinguish language acquisition* from language or learning disabilities within the existing parameters of IDEIA 2004 and MTSS for ELs?

Review of Changing Demographics and Educational Features

Though the EL student demographics and associated instructional elements remain consistent since the publication of the first edition of this book, select features stand out and are summarized below to show some of the key changes that have occurred with the EL population and education over the past decade:

a. Though Spanish remains the predominant language other than English in today's schools, the share of Spanish has decreased reflecting continued increases in other second languages that also require attention in the education of ELs who struggle with reading.

b. The practice and framework of response to intervention (RTI) has evolved into the more comprehensive multi-tiered system of supports (MTSS) including emphasis in both academic and affective learning features.

c. Numbers of students with interrupted or limited formal schooling (SLIFE) have increased significantly requiring adjustments to reading instruction to address this contemporary demographic.

d. School systems have continued to de-emphasize identifying LD through consideration of the IQ-achievement discrepancy, placing greater emphasis on effects of multi-tiered support systems.

e. The diversity of teacher demographics is still not commensurate with the changing student demographics.

f. Disproportionate representation of ELs in special education for a reading learning disability continues to exist in select school systems nationwide.

These continuing issues highlight the need for additional emphasis on developing and implementing culturally responsive instruction, referrals, and assessment in the area of reading for ELs, with particular attention to distinguishing between language acquisition and a language or learning disability.

SUMMARY

Practitioners who educate ELs continue to face challenges as the field of LD struggles to (a) establish an acceptable definition; (b) clarify conceptual and operational frameworks for developing adequate referrals, assessments, and interventions, particularly for ELs; and (c) transition from a discrepancy-based identification approach to an MTSS model. Although the research base on ELs who struggle with reading is incomplete, practitioners still have much to draw upon as they continue to strive to make informed decisions about how best to assess and teach ELs. It is through these efforts that ELs who struggle will receive appropriate reading instruction, while inappropriate referrals and placement into special education are reduced.

NOTE

1. The *risk index*, or RI, is calculated by dividing the number of students in a given racial or ethnic category served in a given disability category by the total enrollment for that group in the school population. Thus, a risk index of six for African American students in a given category means that 6 percent of all African Americans were given that label. The *composition index* is calculated by dividing the number of students of a given racial or ethnic group enrolled in a particular disability category by the total number of students (summed across all groups) enrolled in that same disability category. The sum of composition indices for all the groups will total 100 percent. This index does not control for the baseline enrollment of a given group. Finally, the *odds ratio* divides the risk index of one group by the risk index of another (most often White) for comparative purposes. Odds ratios greater than 1.0 indicate greater risk of identification.

2

Multi-Tiered System of Supports (MTSS) and English Learners

John J. Hoover, Laura Méndez Barletta, and Janette K. Klingner

What is a multi-tiered system of supports (MTSS)? MTSS is a structure that has evolved over the past two decades that incorporates the basic tenants of response to intervention (RTI), which has a major focus on academic supports, particularly in reading, and positive behavioral instructional supports (PBIS), which emphasizes affective, social, and behavioral development. MTSS is a systemic, continuous improvement framework designed to provide effective education to all learners, along with early intervention to students who show signs of struggling (Colorado Department of Education [CDE], 2015). MTSS simultaneously considers education at the district, building, and classroom levels to meet both academic and social/behavioral needs of students, grounded in data-based instructional decision making (CCSSO, 2015; Fuchs & Fuchs, 2006). When delivering instruction through an MTSS model, distinguishing between learning differences and disabilities among English learners is essential to provide sufficient opportunities to learn.

In regard to disability identification, MTSS offers, in part, an alternative to the previously used discrepancy-based learning disability identification models that require students to demonstrate a significant gap between potential, as determined with an IQ test, and academic achievement, as measured with an achievement test. Though frequently discussed in the literature as separate aspects of effective education, incorporating important features of RTI and PBIS collectively provides a more holistic and practical structure for educating all learners, including

ELs who struggle with reading. We see potential in the MTSS model as a way to help educators shift from finding a LD or within-child deficits to focusing on providing the best instruction for all.

In this chapter, we provide an overview of MTSS and discuss some of the challenges schools with high percentages of English learners (ELs) face when trying to implement MTSS. This chapter includes two practical application examples describing implementation of MTSS in two school systems. The first is a rural district in which an MTSS model for ELs was developed and implemented in three elementary schools, and the second describes work in an elementary school, the Marble Mountain Elementary School. Both school systems contain high populations of ELs. Marble Mountain School was in the early stages of implementing the original, more academically specific, response to intervention (RTI) model, while the Rural School District model represents one example of the delivery of the more complete MTSS model.

Vignette: Culturally and Linguistically Responsive Multi-Tiered System of Supports

The delivery of an appropriate multi-tiered system of supports (MTSS) for ELs was a stated goal for a medium-sized K–12 educational urban school district. The 50 percent population of diverse learners and 38 percent EL population created significant challenges for the district's school-based MTSS teams. Though the primary first language among ELs was Spanish, the district also contained significant numbers of students whose first language was other than Spanish, most noticeably Russian and Hmong. The MTSS teams decided to initially focus on the content area of reading, as this was the area of greatest need for ELs and other diverse learners in the school district. To reshape and properly structure a multi-tiered system of supports in reading, each school's MTSS team completed the following steps: (a) needs assessment of current instruction provided through different levels or tiers, (b) determination of the quality of core general classroom reading instruction for ELs, (c) establishing a set of guidelines for making certain that cultural and linguistic factors are considered when discussing multi-tiered instruction for ELs, (d) making certain that multiple forms of assessment and data points are used to best understand ELs' reading progress, (e) creating a structure that is sustainable so new teachers to the school are trained and prepared to properly implement the MTSS process, and (f) including all key people in the MTSS process (i.e., classroom teacher, special educator, master or mentor teacher, parents/guardians, principal or designee, student when appropriate). ELs' language proficiency, stage of second language acquisition, experiential background, and preferred ways of learning based on home teachings are incorporated into the MTSS process. Findings from the needs assessments and current instructional situations are documented and discussed, leading to the development of a three-year action plan for systematically implementing the MTSS process school-wide. The action plan includes tasks, responsible persons, timelines, and a process for evaluation of effectiveness in meeting ELs' reading needs through MTSS.

Reflection Items

The above process for structuring an effective MTSS includes many of the most highly recommended qualities to ensure effective teaching and learning for ELs:

1. Why is each step in the above process essential to establish a culturally and linguistically responsive MTSS process?

2. Develop and illustrate a year-long timeline to complete all the steps identified above.

3. Discuss different educator roles in the development of a school-wide MTSS process, making certain each of the above steps is implemented properly.

OVERVIEW OF MTSS

Similar to most educational initiatives and structures, different states and school systems have adopted their own definitions and characterizations of MTSS. Several definitions were found on 2015 state websites:

California: MTSS is an integrated, comprehensive framework that focuses on Common Core State Standards (CCSS), core instruction, differentiated learning, student-centered learning, individualized student needs, and the alignment of systems necessary for all students' academic, behavioral, and social success.

Colorado: MTSS is a whole school, prevention-based framework for improving learning outcomes for every student through a layered continuum of evidence-based practices and systems.

Florida: The MTSS involves the systematic use of multisource assessment data to most efficiently allocate resources in order to improve learning for all students, through integrated academic and behavioral supports.

Kansas: MTSS is a coherent continuum of evidence-based, system-wide practices to support a rapid response to academic and behavioral needs, with frequent data-based monitoring for instructional decision making to empower each student to achieve high standards.

North Carolina: NC MTSS is a multi-tiered framework, which promotes school improvement through engaging, research-based academic and behavioral practices, employing a systems approach using data-driven problem solving to maximize growth for all.

Though some variation exists, MTSS is characterized in similar ways with a focus on academic, social, and behavioral development and growth.

It is important to know how MTSS is defined and interpreted, and it is also productive to know what MTSS is not, which was succinctly addressed by Hanselman (2015) at a No Child Left Behind (NCLB) Conference. She stated that MTSS is not a framework that guides only daily instruction, nor is it a continuum of supports representing a collection of teaching strategies. Rather, it is a framework that includes appropriate instruction and supports that are strength based, student centered, targeted, and layered to address developmentally appropriate academic, social, emotional, and behavioral skills using evidence-based practice, while valuing cultural, linguistic, and ethnic diversity (Hanselman, 2015). Overall, when characterizing MTSS, we are reminded that while MTSS incorporates aspects of RTI and PBIS models, it is the integrated nature of these educational areas that transforms MTSS into a more inclusive and contemporary integrated structure. In regard to reading instruction, Galloway and Lesaux (2014) wrote, "today's reading reform efforts, such as the CCSS, emphasize both preventing reading difficulties and maximizing *all* students' opportunities to learn" (p. 518), a statement most appropriate to the education of ELs struggling with reading.

MTSS and its implementation include several key features illustrated in Figure 2.1 and summarized below. The figure, developed by the authors, illustrates the MTSS components supported by the Colorado Department of Education (CDE, 2015). Other MTSS models may vary in structure as they depict efforts to deliver multi-tiered supports to all learners. This model, however, represents key features found in most MTSS models based on a review of several state and school district websites, and it serves as an important foundation for teaching ELs who struggle with reading.

Within the six-component structure illustrated, MTSS holds promise as a way to improve academic and social/behavioral learning outcomes for culturally and linguistically diverse students and to reduce disproportionate representation in special education (Donovan & Cross, 2002; Hoover & Klingner, 2011). We are particularly encouraged by recommendations to move to a more holistic approach to supporting student learning than has been typical in the past. For example, the National Association of School Psychologists emphasized the importance of a systemic approach, such as what we see in a multi-tiered model, that evaluates a student's response within an ecological context of instruction (Christ, Burns, & Ysseldyke, 2005). Transitioning to an MTSS way of thinking requires a "shift from a within child deficit paradigm to an eco-behavioral perspective; [and] a greater emphasis on instructional intervention and progress monitoring prior to special education referral . . ." (Canter, 2006, para. 7).

The (a) combined emphasis on early intervention in both affective and academic learning, (b) focus on making sure children receive appropriate instruction at the "first tier," or general classroom level, and (c) push to match instruction to a child's needs based on ongoing classroom assessment are all features of MTSS that, when implemented well, should lead to increased opportunities to build reading proficiencies for English learners.

Figure 2.1   MTSS Components: Academic and Social/Behavioral
Development

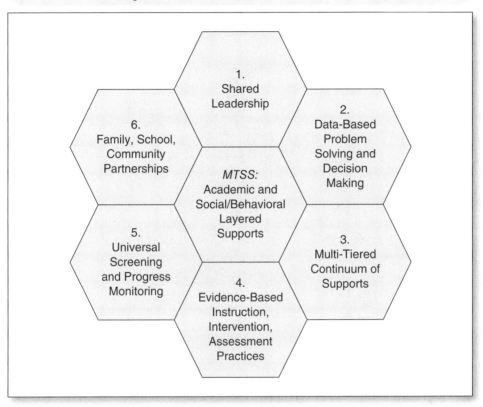

MTSS: A WAY OF THINKING

MTSS is a system of providing leveled support to all students, especially those who show early signs of struggle, through which "general education teachers must provide accessible and differentiated core instruction" (CCSSO, 2015, p. 3). MTSS holds promise as a way to improve learning outcomes for culturally and linguistically diverse students and reduce their misplacement into special education by ensuring that they receive systematic, high-quality, and appropriate instruction, intervention, monitoring, and evaluation (Cramer, 2015; Donovan & Cross, 2002). Each MTSS component illustrated in Figure 2.1 is necessary to distinguish language acquisition from disability. Collectively, the model components, briefly summarized below, provide the foundation for discussions about effective instruction for ELs by addressing positive research findings, while reducing misconceptions as discussed in subsequent book chapters.

1. **Shared Leadership.** Implementation of MTSS requires coordination of resources, training, coaching, and evaluation. To be effective, MTSS

incorporates shared input and decision making among individuals who represent the home-community, district office, school and instructional settings and classrooms (CDE, 2015). Throughout this book, we emphasize and provide examples of ways shared leadership is beneficial to the education of ELs who struggle with reading.

2. **Data-Based Problem Solving and Decision Making.** Achievement and social/behavioral data are used to base important instructional, eligibility, and placement decisions for learners in an MTSS model (CCSSO, 2015; Fuchs & Fuchs, 2006). Additionally, using students' learning rate over time and level of performance grounds ongoing decision making. Learning rate refers to a student's growth in achievement or behavior competencies over time compared to prior levels of performance and peer growth rates. Level of performance refers to a student's relative standing on some dimension of achievement/performance compared to expected performance. Important educational decisions about learning and performance are made regularly using universal screening and progress-monitoring data. Decisions about intensity and likely duration of interventions are based on individual student response to instruction across multiple tiers of intervention (CDE, 2015). Decisions about the necessity for more intense interventions (e.g., eligibility for special education or exit from special education) are based on learning rate and level. The significance of data-based decision making and instructional problem solving cannot be overstated as these are key to distinguishing language acquisition from disability and are examined in greater detail in subsequent chapters.

3. **Multi-Tiered Continuum of Supports.** MTSS addresses academic and social/behavioral needs through Universal (Tier 1) instruction to all learners, Targeted (Tier 2) instruction for those who show signs of struggle, and Intensive (Tier 3) intervention to students demonstrating more significant learning needs. Table 2.1 summarizes details often associated with the common three-tier structure typically found in most MTSS models (Fuchs & Fuchs, 2006; Hoover, 2010; National Association of State Directors of Special Education [NASDSE], 2005).

Students are initially provided evidence-based instruction in Tier 1, and if they do not make adequate progress, or "respond to instruction," supplemental instruction in Tier 2 is provided. That is, students receive instruction that supports specific needs that surface in Tier 1 instruction. For those who continue to experience inadequate progress, Tier 3, or intensive intervention, is provided to meet significant needs, which may include special education in some MTSS models. Estimates in the area of reading are that approximately 80 percent of all learners make adequate progress in Tier 1; 15 to 20 percent may require some supplemental instruction in Tier 2; and 5 percent or less need intensive intervention implemented

Table 2.1   MTSS Three-Tier Instructional Characteristics

MTSS Tiers	Instructional Characteristics
Tier 1	• This first tier provides *high-quality* instruction (that is, research-based instruction) to all students within a general education classroom. • Teachers screen students (for example, in literacy skills) to identify levels of proficiency. • Teachers monitor students' progress using assessments, such as the AIMSWeb, Development Reading Assessment, second edition (DRA2), or Dynamic Indicator of Basic Early Literacy Skills [DIBELS]. • Students who lag behind on critical measures of performance are identified for additional supports at Tier 2.
Tier 2	• Students who are not making adequate progress (as determined by assessments, such as the AIMSWeb, DRA2, or DIBELS) in the first tier receive supplemental instruction. • Tier 2 is geared toward students who did not "respond" to the intervention provided in the general education classroom. • Tier 2 is still part of general education. • The second tier requires a more intensive, small-group reinforcement of the concepts taught in the general education classroom. • When the second tier of intervention does not adequately meet students' needs, they are considered—based on their lack of response—as being candidates for Tier 3 and/or referral to special education. • Students who were not "remediated" in the second tier, that is, students who did not respond to instruction in Tier 1 and 2 combined, receive specialized support in Tier 3.
Tier 3	• Tier 3 is for students who do not respond to the small-group instruction and require specialized, intensive instruction, such as that provided by Title I, district remediation programs, or special education programs (NASDSE, 2005).

in Tier 3 (Hoover, 2013; Yell, 2004). Reference to the different tiers of instruction (as summarized above) is made throughout this book as we examine language acquisition and learning disabilities in reading.

4. **Evidence-Based Instruction, Intervention, Assessment Practices.** MTSS stresses the importance of delivering instruction in each tier grounded in evidence demonstrating effectiveness, and using appropriate assessments to measure progress with that instruction (CCSSO, 2015; Fuchs & Fuchs, 2006). Providing high-quality instruction, intervention, and/or assessment matched to the needs of students is therefore essential in MTSS. The type of instruction and/or intervention selected should have been demonstrated through scientific research and practice to produce high learning rates for students. It is believed that selection and

implementation of high-quality instruction and/or intervention will markedly increase the probability of, but does not guarantee, positive individual response. Embedded in each tier is a set of support structures or activities that help teachers implement research-based curriculum and instructional practices designed to improve student achievement from which lack of progress may indicate a learning disability (NASDSE, 2005). Though monitoring results may inform educators about a *possible* learning disability, evidence-based assessment devices and procedures are used to confirm a disability once language acquisition and learning disability behaviors are distinguished. Several chapters in this book address this particular component in greater detail.

5. **Universal Screening and Progress Monitoring.** Universal screening is an assessment type using quick, low-cost, repeatable data collection procedures to measure academic and behavioral skills of all students (Fuchs & Fuchs, 2006). Universal screening (a) reflects how functional the curriculum and instruction are in the school, (b) determines the extent students are making acceptable progress, and (c) assists to identify students who show signs of struggle. Universal screening is generally administered three times per year to monitor progress and "red flag" struggling learners in a timely manner. Similar to universal screening, progress monitoring is an assessment structure for identifying effectiveness of instruction and identifying learners who show signs of struggle. However, progress monitoring is conducted more frequently (e.g., every two weeks, monthly) to gather academic and behavioral data. Student performance examined frequently over time more quickly informs educators about learners' response to instruction and intervention (Hoover & Klingner, 2011). Screening and monitoring results assume a huge role in efforts to distinguish language acquisition from disability and are examined in greater detail throughout the remaining chapters.

6. **Family, School, Community Partnerships.** The importance of school and district partnering with home and community on academic and social/behavioral progress is well documented in the literature. Herrera, Perez, & Escamilla (2015) wrote that "the family and community in which the CLD [culturally and linguistically diverse] student is being raised define literacy" (p. 7). In an effectively delivered MTSS model, families and community are key participants and partners in school decision making. Regarding the education of ELs, home-community-school connections are critical to reading success. Santiago and Alicea (2015) wrote that an educator's academic preparation should be "complemented with a truer understanding of family as a unit that contributes to the child's holistic literacy and cultural formation" (p. 69).

Given the underlying nature and importance of partnerships, this component assumes an essential role in the education of ELs who struggle with reading and will be referenced at strategic times throughout the remaining chapters as we explore strategies to avoid misinterpreting language acquisition as a learning disability.

In MTSS, ELs who are likely to have reading difficulties are identified and provided instruction and interventions that include the critical elements of reading (e.g., phonemic awareness, phonics, fluency, vocabulary, and comprehension). It is essential that selected methods and instructional practices are researched with and valid for use with ELs. Table 2.2 developed from sources cited in the table, provides a brief overview of instructional methods found effective for teaching reading to ELs. Chapter 5 provides detailed presentation of some of the methods summarized in the table. For additional information the reader is referred to cited sources.

Additionally, an important component of MTSS for reading is the ongoing assessment of a student's proficiency in different academic skills, such as phonemic awareness, rapid letter naming, and comprehension. As discussed, ongoing assessment is significant because information obtained from assessments informs instruction at each tier and also identifies the appropriate level of service for each student in a timely manner (NASDSE, 2005).

Overall, within MTSS, students who make expected gains are said to respond to instruction and are expected to continue to make progress when evidence-based instruction is provided in the general education classroom. Conversely, students who make minimal gains after receiving quality, validated interventions are considered to be inadequately responding to intervention (or to be "nonresponders"). According to researchers (e.g., Al Otaiba et al., 2014; Fuchs, Mock, Morgan, & Young, 2003), these students may need more intensive long-term interventions (Tier 3), and possibly special education services.

The use of MTSS as a means to identifying learning disabilities is a relatively new phenomenon, and supported by the Council for Exceptional Children (CEC, 2008), with the understanding that the evidence about the learner gathered through MTSS represents only part of the material used in the comprehensive evaluation for making eligibility decisions (i.e., other evidence about learner progress is required in addition to MTTS progress data). When used within the context of the broader and more comprehensive evaluation, many proponents of MTSS, including researchers, policy makers, and practitioners, believe that it provides a more valid approach to identifying learning disabilities than previous IQ-achievement discrepancy methods (Fuchs, Mock, Morgan, & Young, 2003; Hoover, 2006, 2012). The premise is that MTSS more accurately identifies students as having LD if their academic performance (i.e., reading) does not adequately respond to an implemented intervention. However, some of the assumptions that underlie MTSS may be faulty when applied to ELs. We discuss these next.

Table 2.2 Select Research-Based Instructional Reading Methods for Use With ELs

Method	Description	Benefits With ELs
Alphabetic Principle Instruction	According to this principle, learning the predictable relationships between sounds and letters allows children to apply these relationships to both familiar and unfamiliar words.	According to research studies in the United States and England (e.g., Gunn, Biglan, Smolkowski, and Ary, 2000; Stuart, 1999), when ELs receive explicit teaching of the alphabetic principle, they outperform their peers in word recognition and comprehension. Similarly, if students first acquire alphabetic principle in their native language, their ability to decode can transfer to later English reading (Durgunoglu, 2002).
Cognitive Academic Language Learning Approach (CALLA)	This instructional model was designed to provide English instruction through the mainstream curriculum (Chamot & O'Malley, 1996). It integrates academic language development, content area instruction, and explicit instruction in learning strategies for both content and language acquisition to support the learners' own prior knowledge and experiences (Hoover, Klingner, Baca, & Patton, 2008). The model has a five-stage cycle of instruction that includes preparation, presentation, practice, evaluation, and expansion (Hoover, Klingner et al., 2008).	The CALLA model was designed to meet the needs of ELs by providing lessons that rely on scaffolding to support students handling challenging material. The goal is for EL students to learn academic content and language, to build their self-efficacy, increase their motivation for learning, and help them become reflective and critical thinkers (CALLA, 2015). Researchers have documented positive effects in the use of CALLA (Chamot, 1995; Galland, 1995).
Cognitive Strategy Instruction (CSI)	CSI emphasizes the development of thinking skills and processes as a means to enhance learning. Strategies consist of "mental routines or procedures for accomplishing cognitive goals such as solving a problem, studying for a test, or understanding what is being read" (Dole, Nokes, & Drits, 2009, p. 348).	Although these strategies are important to the development of academic literacy, very little of this type of instruction is explicitly taught to ELs (Vaughn & Klinger, 2004). Researchers (e.g., Jiménez, García, & Pearson, 1994; Vaughn & Klinger, 2004) have argued that cognitive strategies help ELs develop academic literacy. Along these lines, students from the Pathway Project—an intensive eight-year study that used a cognitive strategies approach to reinforce the reading/writing connection for ELs—averaged over 32% greater success in gain scores on writing assessments over seven years. Pathway students wrote better essays on the posttest and received higher scores than their counterparts in the control classes (Olson & Land, 2007).

Method	Description	Benefits With ELs
Collaborative Strategic Reading (CSR)	CSR was designed to (a) to provide cognitive strategy instruction to help students comprehend texts in the content areas, (b) to assist EL students and students with learning disabilities, and (c) to provide opportunities for students to work in collaborative, peer-mediated environments (Dole et al., 2009). According to Klingner and Vaughn (1998), students learn four cognitive and metacognitive strategies as they read texts, with the purpose of internalizing and routinizing the strategies so that the strategies can be applied to every text they read. Once the strategies have been taught, students work in small groups, and each student has an opportunity to apply/practice one of the strategies to their own texts.	CSR has been found to be beneficial for ELs as well as other average and high-achieving students across a range of grade levels (Hidayah, 2009; Macceca, 2007). According to Wood and Blanton (2009). CSR allows students to read and provides a format for ELs and struggling readers whose voices may not be heard in whole class settings. Similarly, Klingner and Vaughn's (2000) study found that although all students made significant gains on pre-posttest measures after a month of CSR instruction, the students with greater English proficiency did best. Their study suggested that students with low levels of English proficiency may need more support than what CSR provided. Additional studies on CSR have been completed with positive results (Klingner, Vaughn, Boardman, & Swanson, 2012).
Comprehension Strategies Instruction	In order to make sense of texts that are read, readers make connections, ask questions, visualize, infer, determine importance, and synthesize (Kendall & Khuon, 2005).	In small group settings, ELs have more opportunities to interact with both their teacher and peers; it is also much easier for the teacher to check for understanding and personalize instruction to meet the needs of her/his students (Kendall & Khuon, 2005).
Cooperative Learning	Cooperative learning refers to a teaching method that involves having students work in small groups to help one another learn (Slavin, 2008).	According to Colorín Colorado (2007), cooperative learning has been found effective among ELs due to its promoting learning and fostering respect and friendships among diverse groups of students. Furthermore, the method promotes peer interaction, which helps the development of language and the learning of concepts and content. ELs learn to express themselves with greater confidence when working in small teams, acquire new vocabulary, and benefit from observing how their peers learn and solve problems (Colorín Colorado, 2007).

(Continued)

Table 2.2 (Continued)

Method	Description	Benefits With ELs
		In a study conducted by Slavin (1995), Cambodian American students acquired English proficiency during their time in a program based on cooperative learning. Similarly, Calderón, Hertz-Lazarowitz, Ivory, and Slavin (1997) found that students in transitional bilingual programs gained in Spanish and English reading performance as a result of experiencing cooperative learning in second and third grades.
Differentiated Instruction	Differentiated instruction involves all students learning the same thing in different ways. That is, tasks are presented in different ways and at different levels in order for students to approach learning in their own ways (Irujo, 2004). "In a differentiated classroom the teacher uses (1) a variety of ways for students to explore curriculum content, (2) a variety of processes through which students can come to understand or 'own' information and ideas, and (3) a variety of options through which students can demonstrate or exhibit what they have learned" (Tomlinson, 1995, p. 1).	Differentiated instruction takes into account ELs' English language proficiency as well as other factors that can impact learning (Fairbairn & Jones-Vo, 2010). Differentiated instruction is important with ELs because it recognizes that students are different and that teaching needs to be adjusted to these differences. The best way for ELs to learn the same rigorous academic content as native English speakers is through differentiated instruction as it takes into account their English language proficiency, as well as other factors that can impact learning (Fairbairn & Jones-Vo, 2010).
Explicit Instruction	Explicit instruction involves the teacher outlining learning goals (i.e., explaining why the strategy helps comprehension and when to apply the strategy), modeling how to complete a task (i.e., demonstrating how to apply the strategy), guided practice (i.e., guiding students as they learn how/when to apply the strategy), and ability to complete the task independently (i.e., helping students practice the strategy until they can apply it independently) (Tikunoff, 1983).	According to researchers (e.g., Hernandez, 1991; Saunders, O'Brien, Lennon, & McLean, 1998), explicit teaching provides ELs with specific and easy-to-follow procedures as they learn both a new strategy and the language associated with it. Linan-Thompson and Vaughn (2007) indicate that this type of instruction assists EL students in identifying and using the structural and visual cues present in words. Along these lines, Au (1993) argues that ELs decode unknown words by using unique features of words, word patterns, or similarities to other known words.

Method	Description	Benefits With ELs
Fluency Instruction	Fluency is the ability to read words accurately and automatically. It is commonly defined as reading with "speed, accuracy, and proper expression" (National Institute of Child Health and Human Development NICHD, 2000).	According to Ford (2012), instruction in fluency can be particularly beneficial for ELs because activities designed to enhance fluency in reading can also contribute to oral language development in English. Gunn, Smolkowski, Biglan, Black, and Blair (2005) argue that students who are provided explicit and systematic interventions improve their rate and accuracy of reading connected texts. Researchers argue that easy reading material develops fluency and provides practice using good reading strategies (e.g., Allington & Cunningham, 2002).
Guided Reading	Guided reading entails a teacher working with a small group of students who demonstrate similar reading levels. The teacher provides scaffolded reading instruction, which allows her/him to differentiate instruction based on students' needs, interests, and abilities.	Guided reading is beneficial for ELs as it focuses on vocabulary development, allows for individual instruction, and provides verbal interaction between the students and the teacher (Herrell & Jordan, 2008).
Interactive Teaching	Interactive teaching refers to instruction with give and take between learners and teacher (Goldenberg, 2008). During this type of instruction, the teacher actively promotes students' progress by encouraging higher levels of thinking, speaking, and reading (e.g., structured discussions, brainstorming, and editing/discussing writing samples).	Research studies have indicated that an interactive teaching style is effective with ELs (e.g., Curtin, 2005; Hite & Evans, 2006; Thompson, 2004). The reason is due to teachers' awareness of student frustrations and how their students are learning and the use of multiple pathways to determine what students know (Li & Zhang, 2004).
Native Language Literacy Instruction	Oral proficiency and literacy in the first language can be used to facilitate literacy development in English. That is, learning to read in the home language promotes reading achievement in the second language.	According to Ford (2005), there is a strong link between L1 phonological awareness and L2 reading success. Furthermore, efforts to develop literacy skills in L1 will translate into facility with L2 literacy development. Other researchers (e.g., Carlisle, Beeman, Davis, & Spharim, 1999; Proctor, Carlo, August, & Snow, 2005) have found that among ELs, both L1 and L2 vocabulary contribute to achievement in English reading comprehension.

(Continued)

Table 2.2 (Continued)

Method	Description	Benefits With ELs
		Along these lines, in a meta-analysis conducted by the National Literacy Panel, it was concluded that teaching ELs to read in their first language and then in their second language boosts their reading achievement in the second language.
Phonics and Word Recognition Instruction	Phonics is a method for teaching reading and writing by developing a learner's phonemic awareness. Through phonics, learners become aware of sounds (phonemes) of spoken language and the letters and spellings (graphemes) that represent those sounds in written language.	Peregoy and Boyle (2012) argue that English vowel sounds and their spellings present a challenge to many ELs because the one-to-one correspondence between vowel letters and vowel sounds in their first language may not hold true in English. According to the National Council of Teachers of English (NCTE, 2008), reading aloud is a good way to help ELs improve phonemic awareness and phonics knowledge as it allows students to become familiar with the sounds and structure of written language. Furthermore, Slavin and Cheung (2004) argue that research on beginning reading programs for ELs finds consistent positive effects of programs that use systematic phonics (e.g., Success for All and Direct Instruction programs).
Phonological Awareness	Phonological awareness includes a range of understandings related to the sounds of words and word parts including identifying and manipulating words, syllables, onsets, and rimes.	According to research (e.g., Cummins, 1979, 1981; Anthony et al., 2009), children's competence with phonological awareness in one language transfers to their competence in phonological awareness in another language. In addition, abilities are similar across languages. That is, people with poor phonological awareness in a first language will also exhibit that same deficit in their second language.
Reciprocal Teaching	Reciprocal teaching was originally developed as a technique for teaching reading comprehension strategies to struggling native English speakers but later modified as a structure with ELs (Klingner & Vaughn, 1996). It is a multiple-strategy approach that	According to Waxman and Tellez (2002), reciprocal teaching can be beneficial to ELs that experience difficulty with their second language. That is, the teacher can read the text and provide students with the opportunity to learn comprehension strategies without having to wait until they learn to decode. Furthermore, Padron (1992) found that bilingual third, fourth,

Method	Description	Benefits With ELs
	allows teachers to teach students four strategies: ask questions about the text, summarize parts of the text, clarify words and sentences that are not understood, and predict what might occur next in the text. In small groups, students employ these strategies to enhance their understanding of what they've read.	and fifth grade students who participated in reciprocal teaching groups performed better at generating questions and summarizing than those who simply had additional reading instruction.
Sheltered Instruction Observation Protocol (SIOP)	The SIOP model was developed by Jana Echevarria, Mary Ellen Vogt, and Deborah Short. The model consists of eight components (lesson preparation, building background, comprehensible input, strategies, interaction, practice/application, lesson delivery, and review and assessment) that help teachers systematically, consistently, and concurrently teach grade-level academic content and academic language to ELs.	The SIOP model has proven effective in addressing the academic needs of ELs throughout the United States (Echevarria, Vogt, & Short, 2012). Furthermore, it has been found to increase student achievement, improve academic content skills and language skills, deliver results aligned to district objectives, and prepare students to become college and career ready (Pearson, 2015). Through each of the eight components, teachers design and deliver lessons that address the academic and linguistic needs of ELs. The SIOP method adds strategies that enhance academic outcomes for ELs, including presenting language objectives in content lessons, using background knowledge, teaching content-related vocabulary, and focusing on academic literacy practice (Short & Echevarria, 2004). Furthermore, the method encourages teachers to speak more slowly, enunciate clearly, use visuals, scaffold instruction, target vocabulary words and development, connect concepts to students' experiences, promote peer interactions, and adapt materials and supplementary materials for ELs (Moughamian et al., 2009).
Vocabulary Enrichment	This method holds that teaching vocabulary is an important part of reading instruction. With context, students are more likely to learn and retain new words.	According to Watkins and Lindahl (2010), such approach allows ELs to comprehend and demonstrate understanding of vocabulary and improve reading levels.

ASSUMPTIONS UNDERLYING MTSS THAT MAY BE PROBLEMATIC WITH ELS

MTSS is based on certain key principles that can be problematic when applied to ELs and other culturally and linguistically diverse students (Barrera, 2004; Hoover & Klingner, 2011; Klingner & Edwards, 2006). When practitioners understand these assumptions, they are in a better position to make wise choices for children and less likely to draw erroneous conclusions prematurely. They realize that there are many possible reasons an EL might be struggling.

Assumption 1

Evidence-based instruction is good instruction for everyone. English learners who have been taught with generic evidence-based interventions have been provided with sufficient opportunities to learn.

Numerous instructional approaches recommended as evidence-based (or research-based) have not actually been validated or tried out with ELs, or in school contexts similar to those in which many ELs are educated (Klingner & Edwards, 2006). Research can help us make only an educated guess about which practice is most likely to be effective with the majority of students, *not* what practice will work with everyone. In fact, we know that some students learn differently than others—not everyone learns the same. And students have different learning needs. District and school personnel should make every effort to select research-based interventions that actually have been tried and found to be effective, with students similar to those with whom they will be used. For examples of MTSS research conducted with ELs see Haager (2004); Hoover and Soltero-Gonzalez (2014); Linan-Thompson, Cirino, and Vaughn (2007); Linan-Thompson, Vaughn, Prater, and Cirino (2004); and Thorius and Sullivan (2013). In addition, Chapter 5 presents several methods researched with ELs that are appropriate for instruction in reading.

Assumption 2

Learning to read in one's second language is similar to learning to read in one's first language; therefore, instructional approaches that have been found through research to be effective with mainstream English speaking students (and thus deemed "research-based") are appropriate for serving ELs.

Although the developmental processes are similar when learning to read in a first or second language, there also are important differences that must be taken into account when planning for instruction and assessing student progress (see Chapter 4 for a description of these differences; August & Shanahan, 2006; Echevarria et al., 2012; Orosco & O'Connor,

2014). For example, ELs benefit from additional oral language instruction. Districts and schools should provide professional development in teaching reading to ELs, and teachers should do all they can to learn about working with this population of students. It is not enough, for example, to have a master's degree in reading if the graduate program did not include a focus on ELs (Orosco, 2007).

Assumption 3

Students who fail to respond to research-based instruction have some sort of learning problem or internal deficit and perhaps even a learning disability.

There are many reasons a child may not respond to a particular instructional approach (Klingner & Edwards, 2006; Nguyen, 2012). It could be that the method is not an effective one with this child, whereas a different approach and learning experience would yield much better results. Or the level of instruction might not be a good match for the child. The environment might not be conducive to learning. It is important to look in classrooms and observe instruction, materials, content, and the physical environment, as well as make attempts to use different approaches, before determining that a child may have a disability because he/she is not responding to an intervention. It may be more appropriate to provide ELs with extra support at the second tier of an MTSS model while they are acquiring English rather than placing them in special education.

PRACTICAL APPLICATIONS

Practical Application 1: Rural School District Model

Our first practical application example describes aspects of a district-based project implemented during 2012–2015 by two of this book's authors (i.e., Hoover and Klingner). We refer to the project as the Rural School District Model as the setting is a remote rural school district, with approximately 6,000 students of which 37 percent are ELs (Hoover & Soltero-Gonzalez, 2014). The overall goal of the project was to work with the school district to develop and implement an MTSS model, with specific emphasis on literacy instruction for ELs in Grades K–3 in three elementary schools with high populations of ELs. One of the three schools used a dual language model and the other two an ESL model of instruction. The K–3 educators possessed varying amounts of teaching experiences and higher education degrees, with most teaching in the district 3–10 years. The project provided professional development, instructional coaching, classroom observations, materials and resources, and related supports necessary to advance the literacy knowledge and skills of the K–3 educators.

Central to the project work was a university-school district partnership that provided the foundation for the MTSS work. Much went into the partnership and professional development for the MTSS model, leading to a unique two-dimensional framework illustrated in Table 2.3.

The five components in Dimension 1 are research-based derived from over a decade of findings discussed in the literature (e.g., Fuchs & Fuchs, 2006; Hoover & Love, 2011; Klingner & Edwards, 2006; National Center on Response to Intervention [NCRI], n.d.; Orosco & Klingner, 2010). The ten teaching qualities in Dimension 2 are derived from national and state educator preparation accreditation standards (e.g., Council for the Accreditation of Educator Preparation [CAEP], National Council for Accreditation of Teacher Education [NCATE], CEC, Teaching English to Speakers of Other Languages [TESOL] International Association). The underlying premise is that in order to effectively implement an MTSS model (or any educational instructional model) these ten teacher qualities must be present (Hoover & Soltero-Gonzalez, 2014). The effectiveness of the model is limited to the extent that one or more of the teacher qualities is not incorporated into the delivery of MTSS. Nationally, accredited teacher preparation programs must demonstrate, during the accreditation process, how its

Table 2.3   Two-Dimensional Multi-Tiered System of Supports (MTSS) Model

Dimension 1	Dimension 2
Five components frame the Multi-Tiered System of Supports (MTSS) model: (a) Multi-Level Instruction (b) Research-Based Core Literacy Instruction (c) Culturally and Linguistically Responsive Practice (d) Multiple Levels of Assessment and Data Sources (e) Ecological Decision Making	Ten teacher qualities or abilities essential to delivering high-quality instruction were incorporated into the MTSS model: 1. Collaboration 2. Use of Student Data 3. Attention to Cultural Responsiveness 4. Incorporation of Linguistic Supports 5. Parent/Community 6. Outcome Delivery 7. Adherence to Educational Processes 8. Grounding in Research-Based Practice 9. Emphasize Strengths-Based Approach (Differentiations) 10. Attention to Affective Development

teacher candidates possess these ten teaching abilities, and these, in turn, contribute to the implementation of the two-dimensional MTSS model.

Specifically, as can be seen, the two-dimensional model incorporates all six of the recommended components illustrated in Figure 2.1 (p. 29):

1. *Shared Leadership* is evident through the university-school district partnership.

2. *Data-based decision making and problem solving* are included in both dimensions of the model.

3. *Multi-tiered continuum of supports* is one of the five main MTSS model components in the Rural School District Model project.

4. *Evidence-based instruction, intervention, and assessment* are all highly evident in both dimensions of the model, including the quality teaching abilities.

5. *Universal screening and progress monitoring* are incorporated in the multiple sources of assessment and ecological decision-making aspects of the Rural School District MTSS Model project.

6. *Family, school, community partnership* is seen in the university-school district partnership and collaboration and as two of the ten essential teaching qualities in Dimension 2.

Though beyond the scope of this chapter, evaluation of the two-dimensional model includes the gathering of evidence to determine the extent each teaching quality (Dimension 2) is incorporated into the delivery of the five components in Dimension 1. To date, our research findings show that each quality is found in the delivery of each of the Dimension 1 components, providing initial evidence of the fidelity of implementation of the Rural School District MTSS model (Hoover & Soltero-Gonzalez, 2014). Therefore, initial results suggest that this more comprehensive, two-dimensional model for providing quality instruction to ELs is promising, expanding on the six key features framing the MTSS model illustrated in Figure 2.1. Though initial findings are encouraging, several challenges exist that confronted educators during the development and implementation of the Rural School District MTSS model. A few of these challenges are addressed below.

Challenge 1: Competing mandates to deliver district curriculum and methods prevent classroom teachers from implementing the MTSS literacy methods for ELs presented during the professional development.

Schools and school districts have multiple initiatives occurring simultaneously, often leading to confusion and difficulty in implementation. In our project, a key component within the professional development is an *action item* completed by participants detailing how they plan to incorporate their learning into existing instruction. By providing time during each workshop, teachers are able to cooperatively plan the implementation of one key "takeaway" from the workshop, leading to increased success in the classroom. Another effective practice is to guide teachers to not change too much too quickly but rather attempt key changes on a small scale increasing in scope based on initial successes. Additionally, by planning the professional development workshops in partnership with the school and educators, topics will be more relevant to participants leading to increased successful implementation beyond the workshop sessions.

Challenge 2: Professional development incorporated into the delivery of the Rural School District MTSS Model interfered with teacher planning, instruction, and related tasks that affected attention of participants and interest in trying the new ideas in the classroom to improve reading instruction for ELs.

Time has always been one of the most valued and important items in the life of educators. Today, we expect teachers of ELs to do more, with less, in the same amount of time. Recognizing the importance of educator time and the need for focused attention during workshop sessions, the project staff revised the process for delivering workshop sessions. This included (a) holding workshops at times that school professional development was already scheduled, (b) providing teachers a brief amount of time after school prior to beginning the workshop to attend to their most pressing items, and (c) ensuring that the workshops were highly interactive, practical, and relevant. In addition, the workshops included follow-up classroom visits or observations of team meetings to provide additional supports beyond the workshop sessions. Each of these delivery considerations contributed to greater teacher attention, more active workshop participation, a more focused effort to attend to workshop expectations, and increased implementation with fidelity of select workshop topics to best educate ELs in reading.

Challenge 3: Educators interpreting the reading achievement data of ELs focused primarily on the content and skills addressed through the curriculum without attending to the cultural and linguistic responsiveness of the instruction. Lack of consideration of the responsiveness of the instruction limits effectiveness of instructional adjustments for ELs.

ELs require the additional consideration, beyond discussing knowledge and skills, of the cultural and linguistic responsiveness of the instruction. Delivering the proper knowledge and skills in a reading lesson will be only as effective as that delivery reflects the cultural and linguistic needs, teachings, and values ELs bring to the classroom. Unless properly prepared, educators often neglect to consider the cultural and linguistic responsiveness of the instruction when interpreting achievement or social/behavioral data and evidence. To meet this need, a simple checklist was developed and used that contained items to guide team members to specifically consider diversity issues (in addition to knowledge and skills). The checklist used in the Rural MTSS project includes select items from the many guides and forms presented throughout this book. Simply drawing attention to cultural and linguistic considerations through use of an easy-to-use guide is often sufficient to make certain diversity is part of the data interpretation discussions.

Challenge 4: In much of the literature, Tier 1 is usually presented and discussed by itself, while Tiers 2 and 3 are typically paired and discussed together. This presentation format contributes to educators' perception that Tier 2 is more of a "gateway" to Tier 3 rather than a support level to Tier 1. In the Rural School District Model project, linking Tiers 1 and 2 in MTSS decision-making discussions challenged educators to see the Tier 1–2 connection and its significance to reading instruction for ELs.

In today's schools and classrooms, there exist many mandates, expectations, and requirements associated with the teaching of ELs. Students who struggle with Tier 1 instruction should receive needed Tier 2 supports that are clearly designed to support Tier 1 learning. If this is the case, then why do we not discuss the instruction provided in Tier 1 along with the Tier 2 supports thereby linking in a positive and productive way Tiers 1 and 2 instructions? As we continue to discuss Tier 2 as associated with Tier 3 (e.g., Tiers 2 and 3 are frequently discussed in the literature in the same paragraph or section), disconnects between Tiers 1 and 2 may continue to exist. In the Rural School District project, we attempted to guide teachers to think about Tier 2 in more connected ways to Tier 1 by helping them consider improvements to Tier 1 instruction at the same time they were considering needed Tier 2 supports. This process served three important purposes: (a) discussing Tier 3 only when Tiers 1 and 2 collectively are not successful, (b) making adjustments to Tier 1 while providing Tier 2 to improve learners' chances of being successful in Tier 1 during and upon completion of Tier 2 instruction, and (c) teachers beginning to see that many of the same tasks and structures previously implemented in Tier 2 only can now be incorporated into Tier 1 instruction, thereby reducing the future need for some students to require Tier 2 supports (Hoover & Love, 2011).

Practical Application 2: Marble Mountain Elementary School

Marble Mountain Elementary School recently began implementing the RTI aspects of the broader MTSS model. Their student population was 92 percent Latino (of whom 53 percent were considered English learners). North County School District selected Marble Mountain as a pilot school for RTI because of concerns about the high percentages of ELs receiving special education services (31 percent of all ELs) and the school's low performance on high stakes tests. The district carefully collected the available research about RTI and staff felt confident that they were recommending the most effective and feasible RTI model. Three days of professional development were provided to Marble Mountain teachers, support personnel, and administrators on how to implement the various components of RTI. Yet no sooner had the year begun than the practitioners at Marble Mountain began to experience challenges in their RTI implementation. They were especially concerned about using RTI with ELs. Although the educators were aware that second language acquisition, best practices for ELs, and cultural variations need to be considered when assessing student progress and making instructional adjustments, they were not always confident that they had sufficient expertise to carry out these activities. We discuss four of their challenges next.

Challenge 1: According to progress-monitoring data, more than half of the ELs in each first-grade class are not reaching benchmarks even though they are supposedly receiving research-based instruction. It is not feasible to provide Tier 2 instruction to all of these students.

When many or most ELs in the same grade or classroom are not progressing with a particular instructional program, the first step should be to look for ways to make instruction more appropriate for culturally and linguistically diverse students. It is important to (a) examine the program to determine if it has been validated with students like those in the class, (b) determine whether instruction is at an appropriate level for students and the program is well implemented, and (c) establish whether teachers are sufficiently differentiating instruction to meet diverse student needs. Determining how appropriate an instructional program is requires studying the program manual or research reports to find out how the program was developed and tested, and with whom.

For example, what percentage of the students in the original sample (i.e., students who participated in the testing) were English learners? If the answer is *none* or *few*, the instructional program is probably not suitable for these students. If the answer is less than half, do the researchers or program developers report how well the English learners did with the program (separately from other non-EL participants)? This is important to know because researchers can call a practice or program *effective* based on a small majority of the participants achieving better results than when using a comparison program. It is possible, and in fact likely, that some students, including ELs, not in the "small majority" actually did better with the comparison program. However, if this breakdown is not provided then educators may erroneously assume that all learners, including the ELs, demonstrated effectiveness with the tested program.

Determining whether a program is well implemented necessitates observing in classrooms. The program might be an appropriate one, but the teacher may be having trouble applying it with fidelity. Perhaps the teacher is struggling with classroom management and needs assistance in this area before focusing extensively on reading instruction. Or perhaps the teacher has not been trained in how to differentiate instruction. It very well could be that the teacher also requires more professional development in how to teach reading to ELs. In Marble Mountain's case, none of the district-provided RTI professional development included this above training, and most of the teachers lacked sufficient preparation on effective instruction for teaching reading to ELs in their teacher education programs. *In other words, when so many students seem to be struggling in the general classroom, the first step should be to improve the core instruction, since the majority of students in the classroom do not have a learning disability.*

Challenge 2: Teachers and other school personnel are not clear how the RTI process is similar to and different from the prereferral process they had used in previous years. Their RTI meetings look very much like the *child study* team meetings of old.

Teachers' concerns have changed very little over time—they are still frustrated that some students are not learning more quickly and that they are not receiving more needed assistance. However, as discussed in the previous challenge, efforts to assist struggling learners should begin with examining and improving the instruction, as necessary. Unfortunately, discussions at RTI problem-solving meetings still center on possible reasons for a child's struggles from a deficit perspective, in other words, focused on what could be wrong with the child. There still seems to be a push to qualify a student for special education so that he can receive more intensive support. It is natural that it will take time for school personnel to shift their thinking from one of figuring out what is wrong with a student to one of looking more broadly at the instructional context and ways to make it better (i.e., previous challenge), as well as how to provide support for all struggling students in a multileveled instructional system. During this transition period, we advise focusing on ways to improve Tier 1 and Tier 2 instruction and interventions to be more appropriate for ELs, and for all students. Rather than instructing a child through Tier 3, we suggest providing a different form of intervention at Tier 2, perhaps for a longer duration, making sure that educators with expertise in teaching reading to ELs deliver the intervention.

Challenge 3: School personnel were confused about Tier 2 interventions. They wonder (a) whether EL services, such as English language development (ELD) instruction, "count" as a Tier 2 intervention, and (b) whether a special education teacher can provide Tier 2 supports.

Tier 2 interventions are only those small-group interventions that are supplemental to the core curriculum and based on students' needs as assessed by universal screening and progress monitoring. Instructional activities designed to support ELs' English language development (ELD) should be part of Tier 1, similar to other areas such as mathematics and reading instruction. The decision to deliver Tier 2 supports in ELD is also similar to the decision to provide Tier 2 supports in mathematics or reading: only after Tier 1 instruction is determined to be appropriate (i.e., culturally and linguistically responsive), delivered with fidelity, and deemed ineffective based on progress monitoring. Here is a way to think about this:

> We teach all students how to do mathematics in Tier 1. We teach all students how to read in Tier 1. We teach all ELs English language development (ELD) in Tier 1. While we are teaching with fidelity, we are assessing students' progress. When we find that some students are not progressing well in properly delivered Tier 1 mathematics, we should provide them with Tier 2 interventions in mathematics; when some students are not progressing well in learning to read in properly delivered Tier 1 reading instruction, we should provide them with Tier 2 interventions in reading; and when some ELs are not progressing with properly delivered ELD instruction in Tier 1, we should provide them with Tier 2 English language acquisition supports. *Of critical importance is that all three areas of mathematics, reading, and ELD are taught as Tier 1 core instruction, supplemented when adequate progress is not made.*

In regard to the role of special educators, Tier 2 is under the domain of general education, *not* special education. Although the special education teacher might serve as a consultant regarding Tier 2 interventions, and may even occasionally provide Tier 2 interventions, particularly if she is modeling how to teach a particular kind of lesson for her colleagues, this should not be her primary role, and she should not be the school's main Tier 2 intervention provider. A general education reading specialist, mathematics specialist, or English language development specialist would be far more appropriate for providing Tier 2 supports, with special education support as needed.

Challenge 4: The school has limited resources. School personnel are struggling to figure out ways to make RTI feasible. They lack full sets of books in the basal reading series that they are supposed to be using; they are being asked to pay for and implement progress monitoring in addition to the other high stakes testing they have already been administering; they have one reading specialist providing Tier 2 support, but she does not have time to help teachers with their instruction and also provide intensive instruction for all students who need it; they know their teachers need more preparation in how to work with ELs and would like to provide more professional development but cannot afford it.

Schools are part of larger systems. Unless funding structures are changed to provide more support for struggling schools, they are going to find it very hard to implement RTI, or any other reform, for that matter. Marble Mountain's principal has already allocated 15 percent of her special education funding to help pay for the reading specialist's salary, as is allowed by the law. She is reallocating Title 1 funds—that in the past paid for paraprofessionals—to hire two additional intervention specialists as well as to purchase more materials. Although the school cannot afford to bring in an external professional developer, the principal allocated resources to provide a small stipend to the one teacher who has a master's degree in teaching culturally and linguistically diverse students to facilitate a study group that meets one day a week after school to discuss EL reading issues. The principal is now trying to obtain professional development credits for the participating teachers that will contribute to increases on the salary scale. The principal is doing all she can to improve learning opportunities for her school's students, and to make RTI work, but really wishes that she had more guidance in how to do this, along with additional resources to more effectively meet ELs' reading needs.

RESEARCH TO PRACTICE

Researching RTI With ELs Through Project PLUS

Haager (2004) implemented an RTI model of prevention and early intervention for improving early literacy outcomes for ELs who were likely to be identified in later years as having reading-related learning disabilities, calling the program Project PLUS. The researchers provided extensive professional development to school administrators, general education teachers, and special education teachers. They taught teachers how to do progress monitoring using the Dynamic Indicators of Basic Early Literacy Skills (DIBELS; Good & Kaminski, 2002), how to interpret assessment scores, and how to provide intensive support as part of a second tier of reading instruction. In Haager's study, it was the classroom teachers who provided Tier 2 assistance within the context of general education reading instruction. In Haager's model, the third tier was considered special education and was provided by special education personnel (Haager, 2004). Haager implemented the three tiers of the RTI model in Project PLUS as in Table 2.4.

LESSONS LEARNED FROM PRACTICAL EXAMPLES FOR EDUCATING ELS

Both Marble Mountain Elementary and the Rural County School District are not alone in the challenges they face in their attempts to develop and

Table 2.4   Project PLUS

Project PLUS Tiers and Characteristics	
Tiers	**Characteristics**
Tier 1	• Teachers received at least one full week of training in the newly adopted reading program, as well as additional training in English language development methods for English language learners. • Teachers implemented the core program and district-required assessments in reading. Teachers assessed their students in basic early reading skills using the DIBELS assessment system. • At the beginning and middle of each academic year, teachers met in grade-level groups with research personnel to discuss DIBELS results and identify students who might need Tier 2 intervention.
Tier 2	• Teachers were provided with up-front and ongoing professional development from kindergarten through second grade. • Teachers learned how to analyze assessment data to strategically group students according to areas of need (e.g., phonological awareness, decoding, and fluency). • Teachers learned a set of intervention strategies to implement in small groups focusing on the core areas of beginning reading. • Teachers retaught or pretaught aspects of their core program during small-group intervention sessions. • Teachers integrated English language development instruction into their small-group reading intervention instruction for ELs. • Teachers met in grade-level groups to collaboratively plan how to schedule and implement interventions. • Once or twice a month, teachers planned sessions focused solely on intervention and their struggling readers.
Tier 3	• Special education teachers went into general education classrooms to provide services and follow the progress of students who were identified for Tier 2 intervention. • Special education teachers consulted with classroom teachers regarding intervention techniques, which resulted in Tier 2 students receiving intervention from the classroom teacher and special education teacher. • When it was clear that a student was not responding to an intervention and the classroom teacher made a referral, Tier 3 allowed for the special education teacher to be aware of the student's situation thereby allowing for the assessment and eligibility process to run smoothly.

implement effective multi-tiered system of supports (MTSS) for ELs. To help support these and other schools, we developed two tables located at the end of the chapter. The first, Table 2.5, was designed to assist school personnel to think about their readiness to implement MTSS and what factors should be in place. Table 2.6, provides additional decision points about each tier in the MTSS model. Use of these guides provides important information as school districts and individual schools engage in partnerships with universities or other educational organizations that support MTSS development, implementation, and evaluation.

SUMMARY

In this chapter, we discussed the contemporary and widespread practice of MTSS relative to the education of ELs. We provided an overview of the MTSS model, discussed assumptions that can be problematic for ELs, provided an example of a multi-tiered research study, and discussed challenges to MTSS implementation as experienced by educators in two project application examples. In addition, two checklists for practitioners to use to help guide their practice were presented. Our intent in this chapter was to provide a foundation for the chapters in this book that follow. Each subsequent chapter provides more in-depth information about an aspect of differentiating between learning disabilities and language acquisition or learning differences among ELs within an MTSS framework, beginning with discussions of several misconceptions about the education of ELs and reading instruction in Chapter 3.

Table 2.5   MTSS School-Level Assessment of Culturally/Linguistically Responsive Reading Instruction

Instructions: Respond to each question, documenting evidence to clarify school MTSS readiness.	
Current School-Wide Reading Practices	
Questions	
1.	To what extent have core instructional reading programs been validated with similar students, in similar contexts, taking into account cultural and linguistic diversity?
2.	To what extent does the school's reading program differentiate instruction to meet all students' needs?
3.	To what extent do teachers' practices differentiate instruction to meet all students' needs, given their current levels and rates of reading learning as well as their particular cultural and linguistic needs?
4.	To what extent is instruction targeted to and appropriate for the students' level of English proficiency and learning needs?
5.	To what extent are teachers adequately trained in how to implement the comprehensive, supplemental, and intervention reading programs, particularly with culturally and linguistically diverse students?
6.	To what extent do teachers help students make connections to prior knowledge and to their own experiences?
7.	Does the representation of students who have difficulties or are succeeding in reading match the general representation of students in the school; or are some groups over- or underrepresented?

(Continued)

Table 2.5   (Continued)

Current School-Wide Environment
Questions

1.	To what extent do teachers demonstrate caring about all students in ways that reflect understanding of students' cultures and languages?
2.	To what extent are teacher-student relationships positive, and expressed in supportive ways?
3.	To what extent is the learning environment supportive, motivating, and meaningful to students?
4.	To what extent are teachers trained in building on the strengths of all students and families in the school, including those who are culturally and linguistically diverse?
5.	What systems are in place to seek out, welcome, and respond to all families' input on both classroom and school levels in relation to students' reading?
6.	To what extent are the voices of all families in the school heard and considered in a balanced way that is reflective of the student population, rather than some groups being over- or underrepresented?
7.	Does the linguistic capacity of school staff meet the linguistic needs of students and families served by the school?
8.	To what extent does the data management system allow participants to document and analyze both qualitative and quantitative measures of student knowledge and academic progress, in reading as well as other areas?
9.	To what extent are all who are affected by the data management system included in designing a system that addresses their needs, such as core and supplemental teachers, support personnel, paraeducators, administrators, and parents?
10.	To what extent are diverse individuals with expertise in the languages and cultures of the students included in developing the data management system (such as the principal, psychologist, counselor, literacy specialist, special education teacher, EL specialist, social worker, and one or more classroom teachers)?
11.	Are authentic assessments used to measure student knowledge and progress in addition to standardized tests?
12.	Do assessments measure what tasks students with difficulties can perform and in what contexts?
13.	How are multiple kinds of assessment data, including standardized as well as informal and observational data, used to inform ongoing instructional decision making?

Source: Adapted from the Meadows Center (2014) and the University of Texas Center for Reading and Language Arts (2003), both at University of Texas, Austin.

Table 2.6   MTSS Planning Guide for Improving Culturally/Linguistically Responsive Reading Instruction

Instructions: Respond to each question to clarify strategic approaches for improving MTSS.	
School-Wide Plan for Improving Tier 1 Reading Instruction	
Questions	
1.	Are diverse individuals with expertise in the languages and cultures of the students included in developing the school-wide plan (such as the principal, psychologist, counselor, literacy specialist, special education teacher, EL specialist, social worker, and one or more classroom teachers)?
2.	Are representative parents of all students included in developing the plan?
3.	Does Tier I instruction focus on grade-appropriate essential reading components?
4.	Does Tier I instruction focus on the particular linguistic and cultural strengths and needs of students?
5.	Does Tier I instruction differentiate in a way that takes into account all students' levels of reading and rates of progress?
6.	Are most students (including most ELs) experiencing success with Tier 1 instruction?
7.	How is student progress assessed? How often?
8.	Is a system established for Tier I problem solving and decision making that includes diverse individuals with expertise in the languages and cultures of students affected by the plan?
9.	Through what mechanism are teachers provided with professional development in RTI and in how to meet the needs of culturally and linguistically diverse students? Is assessment used to inform professional development needs?
10.	To what extent does the plan for professional development include experts in students' linguistic and cultural backgrounds, community stakeholders such as parents of all students, and teachers' self-assessment of their needs?
School-Wide Plan for Tier 2 Intervention for Struggling Readers	
Questions	
1.	Who will provide Tier 2 intervention (e.g., classroom teacher or specialized reading teacher)?
2.	To what extent will Tier 2 providers have training or expertise in serving culturally and linguistically diverse students?
3.	To what extent will Tier 2 providers have training or expertise in serving struggling readers?
4.	When will Tier 2 intervention be provided (e.g., during learning center time, before or after school)?

(Continued)

Table 2.6   (Continued)

	School-Wide Plan for Tier 2 Intervention for Struggling Readers
Questions	
5.	If time is scheduled before or after school, have transportation and other family needs been considered and accounted for to support student participation?
6.	Where will Tier 2 intervention be delivered (e.g., within the general education classroom, in a resource room)?
7.	To what extent will the learning environment for Tier 2 interventions be supportive, motivating, and meaningful to students?
8.	How will Tier 2 providers help students make connections to prior knowledge and to their own experiences?
9.	Is a system in place for frequently monitoring Tier 2 student progress (e.g., every two weeks)?
10.	Does the system for progress monitoring include multiple kinds of measures (both quantitative and qualitative) that assess what students *can* do as well as their needs?
11.	Are experts on students' linguistic and cultural backgrounds involved in interpreting assessment data and planning instruction?
12.	How will assessment data be used to group and regroup students (small same-ability groups; one-on-one tutoring), to plan targeted instruction, and to make adaptations?
13.	How will parents of all students affected by Tier 2 grouping be included in tracking student progress and changes in interventions?
14.	What criteria are established for entry into and exit from Tier 2?
15.	Will the criteria be implemented and reassessed as needed with the help of experts who are knowledgeable about the cultural and linguistic backgrounds and needs of the students involved?
16.	Is a system established for Tier 2 problem solving and decision making?
17.	Will the system be implemented and reassessed as needed in conjunction with experts who are knowledgeable about the cultural and linguistic backgrounds and needs of the students involved?
	School-Wide Plan for Small Group Tier 3 Intensive Intervention for Struggling Readers With Extreme Reading Difficulties
Questions	
1.	Who will provide Tier 3 intervention (e.g., specialized reading teacher or special education teacher)?
2.	Will Tier 3 providers have training or expertise in serving culturally and linguistically diverse students?

School-Wide Plan for Small Group Tier 3 Intensive Intervention for Struggling Readers With Extreme Reading Difficulties	
Questions	
3.	Will Tier 3 providers have training or expertise in serving students with reading difficulties?
4.	Where will Tier 3 intervention be delivered (e.g., within or outside the general education classroom)?
5.	To what extent will the learning environment for Tier 3 intervention be supportive, motivating, and meaningful to students?
6.	How will Tier 3 providers help students make connections to prior knowledge and to their own experiences?
7.	How much additional instructional time for Tier 3 intervention will be scheduled, and when?
8.	If time is scheduled before or after school, have transportation and other family needs been considered and accounted for to support student participation?
9.	Is the relationship of Tier 3 with 504 and special education services determined? Is a system established for Tier 3 problem solving and decision making?
10.	Will the system for problem solving and decision making be implemented and reassessed as needed in conjunction with experts who are knowledgeable about the cultural and linguistic backgrounds and needs of the students involved?
11.	How will assessment data be used to group and regroup students to plan targeted, more intensive instruction and to make adaptations?
12.	Will experts on students' linguistic and cultural backgrounds be involved in interpreting assessment data and planning instruction?
13.	Will the assessment data include multiple kinds of measures (both quantitative and qualitative) that assess what students *can* do as well as their needs?
14.	How will parents of all students affected by Tier 3 grouping be included in tracking student progress and changes in interventions?
15.	What criteria are established for entry into and exit from Tier 3?
16.	Will the criteria be implemented and reassessed as needed in conjunction with experts who are knowledgeable about the cultural and linguistic backgrounds and needs of the students involved?
17.	Is a system in place for frequently monitoring Tier 3 student progress (e.g., every two weeks)?
18.	Will the system for student monitoring include multiple kinds of measures (both quantitative and qualitative) that assess what students *can* do as well as their needs?

Source: Adapted from the Meadows Center (2014) and the University of Texas Center for Reading and Language Arts (2003), both at University of Texas, Austin.

3

Misconceptions About the Second Language Acquisition Process

Janette K. Klingner, Estella Almanza de Schonewise, Carmen de Onís, and Laura Méndez Barletta

Certainly one of the biggest challenges teachers of English learners (ELs) face is trying to figure out the extent to which a student's struggles can be attributed to the second language acquisition process (Hoover & Klingner, 2011; Ortiz et al., 2011). There still exist a relatively small number of teachers who have obtained advanced degrees in second language acquisition; thus, it is not surprising that they may have many misconceptions about how students acquire a new language. For example, Nguyen (2012) reports "only 29.5% of U.S. teachers with ELLs in their classes are prepared to work with these [EL] students" (p. 131). Though a variety of factors contribute to current misconceptions, a lack of understanding that ELs' level of educational success is very much a negotiation between what they bring to their schooling and what schools offer them is of critical concern (Herrera et al., 2015; Klingner & Eppolito, 2014; Ortiz & Artiles, 2010). Schools that are not prepared for an influx of culturally and linguistically diverse students may not have appropriate materials and programs in place, or enough well-prepared teachers ready to build on students' strengths and meet their needs. Also, teachers' confusions about linguistic and literacy development in a second language tend to contribute to a deficit view of the learning potential of ELs. When ELs do not seem to be progressing quickly enough, teachers may consider the "problem" to be that they do not speak enough English. One frustrated teacher exclaimed, "Why can't these kids just learn to speak English?" (Orosco, 2007, p. 156).

WHAT WE KNOW ABOUT SECOND LANGUAGE ACQUISITION

While language developmental patterns and stages are similar for monolingual and bilingual learners, there is a great deal of natural variation in the language acquisition process (Paradis, Genesse, & Crago, 2011). By gaining a greater understanding of this variability, practitioners are better able to support students' learning and advocate for their students. Our objectives in this chapter are to help teachers understand potential misconceptions about the language acquisition process and learn ways to address these misconceptions so that they can enhance their instruction and reduce inappropriate referrals to special education. To best understand potential misconceptions, it is important to possess a general knowledge of the foundation upon which second language acquisition occurs. Table 3.1, developed from sources cited in the table, illustrates four theories of second language acquisition. Though not all-inclusive, these provide readers with a general overview of select foundations for acquiring a second language based on the research of two of the most influential educators in the field. In addition to brief descriptions of each theory, the table provides Theory in Action examples, based on related research, to assist readers in acquiring an understanding of how different aspects of each theory may be applied in the teaching and learning environment. The reader is referred to the sources cited for more comprehensive coverage of the theories of second language acquisition and associated research.

As highlighted in the table, the acquisition of a second language is a comprehensive and complex process. Numerous insights can be found through review of the extensive research literature about the second language acquisition process completed over the past several decades (August & Shanahan, 2006; Baca & Cervantes, 2004; Collier, 2005; Cummins, 1986, 1989; Figueroa, 1989; Herrera et al., 2015; Klingner & Eppolito, 2014; Ortiz & Maldonado-Colon, 1986; Ortiz et al., 2011; Ruiz, 1989).

In addition to acquiring an understanding of second language acquisition from a theoretical perspective, classroom teachers should familiarize themselves with the different stages and processes a student experiences with learning a second language, along with expected behaviors associated with the different stages. Table 7.1 of this book (pp. 147–148) illustrates ways in which WIDA Can-Do strategies (WIDA, 2014) aligned with second language acquisition stages of development along with select learning behaviors. The reader is referred to this table as it provides assessment and instructional guidance in the education of ELs, regarding second language acquisition.

Table 3.1 Select Theories of Second Language Acquisition

Theory	Description	Theory in Action
Monitor Hypothesis (Krashen, 1982)	The monitor hypothesis forms part of Krashen's monitor model (1982). According to the monitor model, the following five hypotheses account for the acquisition of a second language (the monitor hypothesis being one of the five): • Acquisition-Learning Hypothesis: Acquisition is the product of a subconscious process that requires meaningful interaction in the target language (i.e., natural communication) in which speakers are concentrated on the communicative act. Learning, on the other hand, is the product of formal instruction, and it comprises a conscious process which results in knowledge about the language (e.g., grammar rules). • Natural Order Hypothesis: This hypothesis suggests that the acquisition of grammatical structures follows a predictable natural order. That is, some grammatical structures tend to be acquired early, while others are acquired late. Although the hypothesis applies to both first and second language acquisition, the natural order of a first language is different from the order of acquisition as a second language. • Monitor Hypothesis: According to Krashen (1982), acquisition and learning are two separate ways of gaining knowledge. More specifically, the acquisition system initiates utterances while the learning system acts as a "monitor" or "editor" (i.e., during language	The research studies that follow focus on writing samples produced by English and French foreign language students. Students in the studies were asked to rewrite their essays after receiving feedback by their teacher. The studies meet the conditions for monitor use given that the students in all studies (1) had a significant amount of time to make corrections; (2) had access to their grammar textbook; and (3) all were asked to rewrite their own corrected essay. Fathman and Whalley (1990) conducted an experimental classroom study on the effects of feedback on seventy-two intermediate ESL college students' writing. One group of students received only correction (i.e., underlining grammar errors and not given information on the types of errors nor shown the correct forms), and the other group received both correction and feedback on content. After the corrected versions of the compositions were returned to students, they were given 30 minutes to rewrite. The researchers discovered that students significantly improved their grammar scores on subsequent rewrites when they received grammar feedback that indicated the place but not the type of errors. In other words, indirect feedback was more useful than direct feedback. In Gascoigne's (2004) study of 25 first-year university students in the United States studying French, students were given two days to make corrections to compositions they had written. Correction of grammar errors included

(Continued)

Table 3.1 (Continued)

Theory	Description	Theory in Action
	production) that checks the output of the acquired language and makes alterations or corrections when the following conditions are met: (1) The second language learner knows the rule(s); (2) the second language learner focuses on form or thinks about correction; and (3) the second language learner has sufficient time to apply the rules. According to the monitor hypothesis, there are three types of second language users: monitor overusers, monitor under-users, and optimal monitor users. • Input Hypothesis: The input hypothesis is concerned with language acquisition and not language learning. The hypothesis builds on the natural order hypothesis and describes how second language learners move through the predictable sequence of the acquisition of grammatical structures. It is concerned with how learners move from one level of competence to another. That is, a person acquires (not learns) language by understanding input that is somewhat beyond her/his current level of competence (Krashen & Terrell, 1983). • Affective Filter Hypothesis: This hypothesis suggests that a number of nonlinguistic affective variables (e.g., motivation, self-confidence, and anxiety) influence second language acquisition by facilitating or preventing comprehensible input from reaching the language acquisition device. For example, learners with high motivation, self-confidence, and low levels of anxiety are better equipped for success in second language acquisition. On the other hand, low motivation, low self-esteem, and debilitating anxiety can hinder second language acquisition by	information about the location of the error and a description of the error (at times, the correct form was provided). Gascoigne argues that correction had a "profound effect" on compositions. That is, 88 percent of corrections were successful, 8 percent led to an incorrect change, and only 3 percent were ignored. Results of Chandler's (2003) experimental study of music majors taking advanced ESL classes revealed that students who received correction of grammatical and lexical errors on written assignments were less likely to repeat those same errors in subsequent assignments. Students in the study received four different types of feedback on their writing samples: (1) *correction condition* (i.e., students were provided the correct form); (2) *underline condition* (i.e., only the location of errors was indicated); (3) *describe condition* (i.e., a margin note indicating the kind of error made but without a precise location given); and (4) *underline/describe condition* (i.e., both the kind of error made and its precise location were indicated). Chandler found that both correction and underline conditions were the best methods used. That is, they resulted in the largest increase in accuracy for revisions and subsequent writing. Interestingly, nearly half of the students in the study thought that the underline/describe condition was the easiest way to see what kind of errors they had made as well as the condition that they had learned the most from and was the most helpful in writing correctly in the future. Chandler argues, however, that the latter was not an accurate judgment given that data from the study show that both correction and underline were significantly more effective at reducing error in subsequent writing.

Theory	Description	Theory in Action
Sociocultural Theory (Vygotsky, 1978b, 1981)	preventing information about that language from reaching the language areas of the mind. Vygotsky's theory of human learning describes learning as a social process. That is, social interaction plays a fundamental role in the development of cognition. Vygotsky believed that everything is learned on two levels: "Every function in the child's cultural development appears twice: first, on the social level, and later, on the individual level; first, between people (inter-psychological) and then inside the child (intra-psychological). This applies equally to voluntary attention, to logical memory, and to the formation of concepts. All the higher functions originate as actual relationships between individuals." (Vygotsky, 1978b, p. 57). According to this theory, children learn from their interactions with society and their culture and, as a result, acquire new strategies and knowledge. Furthermore, Vygotsky believed that human action on the social and individual level is mediated by tools and signs: semiotics (i.e., the tools that facilitate the co-construction of knowledge and the means that are internalized to aid problem-solving activity). Semiotic means include "language; various systems of counting; mnemonic techniques; algebraic symbol systems; works of art; writing; schemes, diagrams, maps and mechanical drawings; all sorts of conventional signs and so on" (Vygotsky, 1981, p. 137).	Nicolopoulou and Cole (1993) implemented the Fifth Dimension, an after-school educational computer program for elementary children, at a library and a Boys & Girls Club in order to analyze small-group interactions. The authors argue that the Fifth Dimension encouraged collaborative learning, play, and imagination that influenced children's cognitive development. Furthermore, they argue that the creation and transmission of knowledge can be seen as a product of collective collaborative achievement influenced by environments. In a different study, Ohta (1995) analyzed the ways in which scaffolding occurred between two learners of Japanese (Becky and Mark). Results revealed that both learners (both with different language levels) were able to learn and progress through collaborative meaning-making activities in Japanese and were both learning within their own zone of proximal development. Ohta indicates that both learners were contributing their own strengths to help one another and that such collaborative learner-learner interaction was important in acquiring a second language. Moll and Whitmore's (1993) case study on collaboration in a third-grade bilingual classroom analyzed the interactive and contextual character of cognitive change as students created and participated in a community of learners. The study revealed that students actively and collaboratively created learning situations. According to the authors, students selected groups, reading materials, writing topics, theme topics, and language to use for each. Students also

(Continued)

Table 3.1 (Continued)

Theory	Description	Theory in Action
		generated their own research questions. In short, students had considerable control over their own learning experience. Their study highlights the importance of social relationships and social mediation. Forman and McPhail's (1993) case study of two seventh-grade students (Cindy and Karen) enrolled in the same mathematics course examined the ways in which the girls assisted each other. Their study revealed that although there were initial differences on task goals and definitions, the girls developed a division of labor based on areas of expertise and "watched each other's experiments and used their observations to modify their own task conceptions" (Forman & McPhail, 1993, p. 224). According to the authors, as a result of their collaborative work, both girls provided a zone of proximal development for each other which resulted in growth of higher mental functions.
Sociolinguistic Theory (Vygotsky, 1978b, 1986)	According to Vygotsky (1978b, 1986), the environment to which a child is exposed directly shapes her/his mental development as language is learned and developed through social interactions. Vygotsky believed that children constantly seek to acquire higher mental functions, and in order to reach a higher functioning level, a child needs to acquire a number of skills, techniques, and methods (which he refers to as "cultural tools"). Cultural tools are diverse and range from language, shared activities to rules commonly experienced in children's games. Furthermore, Vygotsky (1978b) indicated that teachers play a central role in scaffolding students' developmental needs which in turn improve their meaning/understanding and linguistic and cognitive development.	Almasi and Gambrell's (1994) study of ninety-seven fourth-grade students and six teachers investigated the sociocognitive conflicts during literature discussions and how the cognitive processes associated with such conflicts were internalized by students. Results of the study found that students learned more through peer-led discussion groups compared to teacher-led groups. During peer-led groups, students were able to express themselves more fully, explore topics of interest to them, entertain multiple interpretations of text, recognize and resolve episodes of conflict, interpret the text's meaning, challenge authors' style, and share opinions. Results also revealed that student-led discussions produced richer and more complex interactions and those students asked more questions compared to teacher-led discussions.

Theory	Description	Theory in Action
		Similarly, Eeds and Wells's (1989) study revealed that fifth- and sixth-grade students constructed meaning when they engaged in student-centered conversations about literature. This was achieved by students discussing key points and negotiating meaning through conversation. Eeds and Wells found that students with different abilities participated in rich and authentic conversation about works of literature and were capable of articulating their construction of simple meaning, sharing personal stories inspired by the reading, predicting, hypothesizing and disconfirming their predictions as they read, and valuing and evaluating the text. Alvermann et al.'s (1996) multi-case study revealed that high school students across five different sites preferred studying and working in small groups with other students who held similar beliefs and that social exchange facilitated learning. The study also found that open-ended tasks resulted in the most discussion, compared with tasks that could be completed alone or shared with only one other student. In addition, the conditions that high school students believed to be conducive to discussions centered more on mutually exploring ideas than on following their teachers' guidelines. Students across the five different sites constructed common expectations for text-based discussions and valued listening to each other as they expressed their opinions and argued about the meaning of what they read. Furthermore, students were able to negotiate roles and responsibilities.

(Continued)

Table 3.1 (Continued)

Theory	Description	Theory in Action
Comprehensible Input Theory (Krashen, 1981)	Comprehensible input is input that is slightly beyond the current level of competence of the language learner. According to this theory, learners require comprehensible input in order to move from their current level of acquisition (i) to the next level (1). Krashen refers to this concept as $i+1$, where i symbolizes the learner's present stage of acquisition and the 1 symbolizes the more advanced input that will need to be provided in order for the learner to progress beyond the present stage. Krashen's theory complements Vygotsky's (1978b,) zone of proximal development (ZPD), which is "the distance between the actual developmental level as determined by independent problem solving and the level of potential development as determined through problem solving under adult guidance or in collaboration with more capable peers" (p. 86). According to Vygotsky, concepts that a child is currently developing (such as a new language) are located within the ZPD.	Swain (1986) compared sixth-grade-immersion students to their francophone counterparts and found that native speakers performed significantly better on grammar tasks despite minimal differences in sociolinguistic tasks (i.e., immersion students tended to perform as well as the native speakers). The authors also found that francophone students' performance on grammar led them to outperform immersion students on tasks where grammar was a factor (e.g., in cases that would require students to use the conditional). Based on these findings, Swain emphasized the importance of comprehensible input for immersion students' acquisition of the language. In other words, the significant input allowed students to comprehend by allowing them to focus on meaning without attending explicitly to form. In a study conducted by Rodrigo, Krashen, & Gribbons (2004), fourth semester university students of Spanish as a foreign language participated in two kinds of comprehensible input-based approaches: (1) an extensive reading class that focused on meaningful reading combined with assigned and self-selected reading and (2) a reading-discussion class that consisted of assigned reading, debates, and discussions. Direct teaching of grammar or error correction was used in neither approach. Results of the study indicated that students in both classes outperformed students that were taught in traditional classrooms on both a checklist vocabulary test and a grammar test. More specifically, both comprehensible input groups did noticeably better than the controls in four

Theory	Description	Theory in Action
		out of six comparisons (they tended to do better in another, and there was no difference on the other). Findings of the study support the efficacy of comprehensible input approaches as well as the hypothesis that they are more effective than traditional methodology.

In a similar study, Isik (2000) investigated the combined effects of different amounts of comprehension-based and form-focused instruction on skill-based proficiency and knowledge of grammatical structures of beginner-level English foreign language students (EFLs). One experimental and one control group of Turkish EFL students (from two different schools), enrolled in different programs of instruction participated in the study. The experimental group was enrolled in a program of comprehension-based instruction supported by form-focused instruction and the control group was enrolled in a form-focused program of instruction. Throughout the study, different instruments were used to see the effects of instruction with respect to reading, listening, writing skills, and knowledge of grammatical structures. Results of the study indicated that the experimental group (i.e., the program of comprehension-based EFL instruction supported by form-focused instruction) was more effective than the control group (i.e., the form-focused program of instruction) in helping beginner-level students develop their listening, reading, and writing skills as well as their knowledge of grammatical structures. |

SECOND LANGUAGE ACQUISITION MISCONCEPTIONS

Our goal is to draw from this literature to offer educators positive and constructive solutions to the challenges they face in their schools and classrooms with students who are in the process of becoming bilingual and bi-literate. We list misconceptions and corresponding realities in Table 3.2 and then elaborate about each misconception in the remainder of the chapter.

Misconception 1

Bilingualism means equal proficiency in both languages.

Bilingualism is a unique characteristic shared by many ELs with and without special needs and one that continues to be misunderstood by the education community at large. ELs in our public school system include children who are foreign born as well as those native to the United States, and they reside in both urban and rural geographic areas (Herrera et al., 2015). The language proficiencies that ELs bring to their schooling are different from those of monolingual English speakers. ELs' linguistic proficiencies are the *sum* of their proficiencies in their different languages. Variation also exists in the linguistic proficiencies among ELs. ELs vary in how proficient they are in their home language as well as in English.

Language acquisition is dependent on the cultural and linguistic environments of students, developing in domains to which an individual is most exposed reflecting meaningful contexts, intensity, and usage (Cha & Goldenberg, 2015; Paradis et al., 2011; Valdés & Figueroa, 1994). As discussed previously, some immigrant children arrive as newborns or before formal schooling age. Other immigrants arrive at school age, some with and some without formal schooling in their native country. Other ELs are born in the United States of recent immigrant parents, representing a first, second, or third generation. It is important to acknowledge that EL backgrounds vary, and consequently, a variety of linguistic proficiencies in native languages and English are represented within this broad group.

ELs by definition are speakers of a language other than English who are in the process of acquiring English proficiency. Many ELs enter schooling as emergent bilinguals in both languages, with some degree of proficiency in two languages. These students are referred to as *simultaneous* bilinguals, where exposure to two languages occurs early in life. Students who enter school as monolingual in their native language are referred to as *sequential* bilinguals. When sequential bilinguals enter public school, they quickly begin to negotiate two languages. Both routes involve the process of bilingualism (Escamilla & Escamilla, 2003; McLaughlin, 1984).

In simple terms, *bilingualism* can be defined as knowing two languages rather than one (American Speech-Language-Hearing Association

Table 3.2   Misconceptions and Realities

Misconception	Reality
1. *Bilingualism means equal proficiency in both languages.*	Bilingualism rarely means equal proficiency in both languages—ELs' backgrounds and linguistic proficiencies in the native language and English vary.
2. *Semilingualism is a valid concept, and non-non classifications are useful categories.*	Semilingualism and non-non categories are the results of tests that do not measure the full range and depth of students' language proficiencies.
3. *Native language assessments present a clear picture of linguistic proficiency.*	Commonly used native language proficiency assessments provide a limited view of ELs' oral language proficiency.
4. *Literacy instructional frameworks developed for monolingual students are appropriate for developing ELs' literacy skills in their native or second languages.*	Literacy instruction in a second language differs in key ways from native language instruction; a different framework is needed.
5. *The more time students spend receiving English instruction, the faster they will learn it.*	Students who receive some native language instruction achieve at higher levels in English than students who do not receive any native language instruction.
6. *All ELs learn English in the same way at about the same rate.*	The length of time it takes students to acquire English varies a great deal, from four to seven years or more. There are many different variables that affect the language acquisition process.
7. *English language learners acquire English in the same way they acquire their first language, through exposure and interactions with others.*	Exposure to English and interactions with others are important, but they are not enough to provide the support ELs' need to be able to fully participate in classroom learning and achieve to their potential; explicit instruction at an appropriate level helps.
8. *Errors are problematic and should be avoided.*	Errors are a positive sign that the student is making progress and are a necessary aspect of second language acquisition. Errors provide clues about a student's interlanguage.
9. *The majority of ELs in the United States are sequential bilinguals.*	Most ELs, particularly long-term ELs, are simultaneous (not sequential) bilinguals.

[ASHA], 2004). Valdés and Figueroa (1994) noted that a common misconception ascribes bilingualism "only [to] those able to function as native speakers of each of their two languages" (p. 7). However, they disagree with this view, and they point out that very few individuals actually achieve a state of bilingualism in which both languages reach native-like proficiency levels. In reality, bilingualism rarely means equal proficiency in both languages (Cha & Goldenberg, 2015). These authors also discuss the concept that variability of contexts in which children are immersed influences children's exposure to language, and as a consequence, the development of linguistic proficiency in each language. Homes and schools are rarely balanced environments. Language and knowledge are gained in different domains, for different functions, not necessarily in the same domains or functions in both languages (Escamilla & Escamilla, 2003; Valdés & Figueroa, 1994). In other words, a student may know science terms better in English than Vietnamese because he has been taught in English in school, but he/she may know more everyday language in Vietnamese.

MacSwan and Rolstad (2010) emphasize that diverse communities possess languages with unique varieties and conventions which must be valued by educators. Previously, Valdés and Figueroa (1994) emphasized the complex and multifaceted nature of bilingualism, advocating for a broader definition that places an emphasis on "more than one language" and "competence and ability" to function in more than one language. A contemporary perspective requires the educational community to more readily adopt the position that values *native* language abilities, or bilingualism, that ELs bring to their schooling.

Implications for Practice

1. ELs include students with a wide range of proficiencies in their native language and English.

2. Bilingual students may be stronger in some areas in their native language and stronger in other areas in English.

3. Students who begin school proficient in a language other than English are potential bilinguals.

Misconception 2

Semilingualism is a valid concept and non-non classifications are useful categories.

Bilingual development differs from monolingual development with the process of becoming bilingual being highly complex for ELs with and without a learning disability. However, assessment tools used with ELs typically utilize monolingual, not bilingual, speakers as a point of reference (Basterra, Trumbull, & Solano-Flores, 2011), with results often leading to the erroneous conclusion that ELs possess "low" level language. MacSwan (2004) points to flaws in theories and assessment practices that characterize minority students as "non" speakers in their native language and English. Yet assessments rarely capture this bilingual complexity (Mahoney & MacSwan, 2005). In order to identify anomalies in the language acquisition process (i.e., determine which students may have a true language delay), accurate "norms" of bilingual development need to be developed and understood. One of these norms includes how we characterize and classify students who are bilingual. The next section provides a brief historical perspective about how educators and society typically characterize and classify students who are bilingual, leading to a significant misconception witnessed in today's school and classroom environments.

"Semilingualism" is identified as a type of bilingualism characterized by "low level [ability] in both languages" in the threshold hypothesis (Cummins, 1979, p. 230). Cummins (1981) replaced semilingualism with the term "limited bilingualism." However, theoretically the two terms refer to the same notion (MacSwan, 2000) since in practice bilinguals with low levels of language development are typically placed in programs designed for limited bilingualism. This is in contrast to more advanced levels of bilingualism, which refers to native-like ability in one language and high levels in both languages. Negative cognitive effects are associated with *limited* bilingualism (semilingualism), neutral cognitive effects with *dominant* bilingualism, and positive cognitive effects with *additive* bilingualism.

At a fundamental level, MacSwan and Rolstad (2010) and MacSwan (2000) refute semilingualism. They assert that language minority students come to school with language variation that in and of itself is rich, complex, and fully evolved, challenging the characterization of the language variation by masses of language minority students in both their native language and English brought to public schools at a low level. MacSwan cites studies by linguists, who universally find that children by the age of five or six have acquired the language of their community (Chomsky, 1965; Gleitman & Landau, 1994; Pinker, 1994). The reason ELs often appear limited is that language assessments do not adequately measure the full range of students' linguistic skills (Note: Chapter 6 examines assessment of ELs in greater detail).

Additionally, when we categorize children as "limited English proficient" (LEP), we evoke particularly negative connotations for them. The term LEP was coined by Congress in section 9101 of the Elementary and Secondary Education Act of 1965 and continues to be used for legislative purposes. While this term serves the purpose of identifying students who are in need of educational assistance based on their linguistic status and appropriating funding for such programs, unfortunately, it also establishes a "limited" mind-set toward ELs in the United States, which permeates our society. Concerns about the negativity of the LEP label have long been iterated by many in the educational community (Crawford, 1999; Klingner & Eppolito, 2014; MacSwan, 2004; Ovando, Collier, &

Combs, 2003). Labels such as *potentially English proficient, linguistically and culturally diverse, English learners,* or *emerging bilinguals* represent a more positive perspective and view of individuals who speak a native language other than English.

MacSwan (2004) also addresses the pervasive deficit view of language minority students in the educational field (e.g., MacSwan & Rolstad, 2003; MacSwan, Rolstad, & Glass, 2002) and challenges the widely accepted view of many English learners as "non-nons" which refers to classifying children as limited in both English and native languages. MacSwan refers to the 6,800 children classified by the Los Angeles Unified School District as non-nons, as reported by *The Los Angeles Times* (1996) as a case in point. MacSwan (2000) argues that "it is unnecessary and insufficient" to characterize the language many English learners bring to school as low level and lacking, for academic and social-political reasons (p. 15). MacSwan attributes this non-non "crisis" to the widely accepted construct of "semilingualism," arguing that the acceptance of this condition, so frequently ascribed to language minority students in the United States, propagates a widespread deficit orientation, ultimately setting in place a self-fulfilling prophecy for their academic failure. MacSwan (2000) asserts, "If teachers believe that some children have low language ability in both languages, then this belief may have a strong negative effect on their expectations for these children and the curricular content and teaching practices students receive" (p. 6). The overarching message for educators is that the language of minority students, in their native language and English, may vary from monolingual norms; however, their language is still fully viable and evolved.

Implications for Practice

1. The vast majority of children begin school having acquired the morphological and syntactic rules of their language.

2. Current language assessment measures rarely capture the full range of skills that bilingual children bring to the classroom. This inadequate understanding of bilingual children's skills and abilities can contribute to low expectations for ELs.

3. Classifying students as low-lows or non-nons is not useful because it does not guide teachers as to what students know or need to learn; rather, it encourages teachers to have low expectations for these students.

Misconception 3

Native language proficiency assessments commonly administered to ELs to determine their native language proficiency present a clear picture of linguistic proficiency.

Native language testing of ELs is problematic because it is used to legitimize a deficit orientation toward ELs by falsely identifying them as nonspeakers at a high rate (Bailey & Carroll, 2015; MacSwan, 2004; MacSwan et al., 2002; Mahoney & MacSwan, 2005). MacSwan and colleagues point out that there are numerous flaws in the test construction and validity of the commonly administered native language assessments used to justify semilingualism and non-non labels. They concur with Valdés and Figueroa (1994) who articulated the need to critically examine the practice of native language testing, given that bilingual students do not fit monolingual norms due to the nature of bilingualism.

One problem with some native language tests used in the United States is that although they are intended to assess children's oral language ability, they also tap into other literacy skills (Basterra, 2011; MacSwan & Rolstad, 2010). To avoid labeling nonliterates as semilingual or alingual, we should carefully distinguish between *oral* language, an integral part of every person's identity, and *written* language, used by some but not all individuals and human societies. Some test makers include items on their oral language instruments that assess aspects of language use that are specific to academic culture—and, in some cases, items or subparts that are not specifically related to language ability at all. Doing so in the context of oral native language assessment, and characterizing the results as an index of native language ability, leads to false impressions about students' potential (MacSwan & Rolstad, 2003). Abandoning the routine practice of testing language minority students' oral native language is a recommendation put forth by some researchers (e.g., MacSwan, 2004; MacSwan & Rolstad, 2010; MacSwan et al., 2002), suggesting that decisions of program placement and identification for language services are more effectively accomplished through home language surveys, brief parent interviews, and a second language assessment.

Implications for Practice

1. The routine practice of administering formal assessments of students' native language proficiency should be reconsidered.

2. Widely used native language proficiency assessment instruments may yield invalid results that could lead to inappropriate educational services.

3. Other forms of authentic assessment should be used to determine language proficiency levels of ELs, including natural language samples.

Misconception 4

Literacy instructional frameworks that were developed for monolingual students are appropriate for developing bilinguals' literacy skills in their native or second languages.

While there are some aspects of "good teaching" in general that transfer to good teaching for ELs, effective instructors also know that there are important differences between native English learners and bilingual learners, and they capitalize on these to enhance student learning (Goldenberg, 2013; Herrera et al., 2015). For example, benchmarks differ for younger as opposed to older English learners because primary and secondary level students tend to develop bilingualism differently. That is, high school students may need to build vocabulary yet are already more likely than primary students to understand many components of grammar, based on prior native language instruction about grammar that transfers to their second language (Jiménez, 1997). In addition, within groups of bilinguals, some may simultaneously develop oral and written language, while others may develop one mode of language, such as writing, faster than another, such as speaking.

An additional difference between teaching ELs and native English speakers is that ELs have learned some principles of language that will transfer to English. Yet students may not automatically recognize these. Studies demonstrate that linguistic elements that do transfer from students' native languages to English should be explicitly taught to help students understand the connections between their native language(s) and English (August & Shanahan, 2006). Teachers would be wise to find out which linguistic elements do not transfer, so they can target instruction to meet the needs of their particular students. These linguistic elements will vary depending on which native languages students speak and how similar or dissimilar they are to English. Some schools serve speakers of many languages, and it may be difficult to teach to all of the similarities and differences between all the languages and English. However, schools with diverse language populations should invest in educating teachers about similarities and differences between the most prevalent native language(s) and English to best provide culturally and linguistically responsive instruction and assessment.

One example of a general education best practice that may not always be "best" for ELs is the process approach to writing instruction, delivered without necessary modifications. For example, Ferris and Hedgcock (1998) noted that second language learners may have different understandings of how to paraphrase or include citations to others' work, and they may have had limited experience with peer reviewing, revising, and teachers' indirect forms of feedback, such as the use of questions or suggestions rather than directives (e.g., "Have you considered saying this a different way?" rather than "Say this in a different way."). Therefore, ELs may initially benefit from more direct instruction in order for process approaches to serve them adequately (Harper & de Jong, 2004), being gradually released (Fisher & Frey, 2008) to more paired and independent literacy tasks.

Another practice that is commonly part of writing instruction that may work with native and fluent English speakers, but not necessarily with

ELs, is to ask students to notice what sounds "right" or "best." ELs in the early stages of English development may struggle with these terms due to the fact that they have not acquired sufficient English to develop intuitions about aspects of English writing such as best or right. Overall, teachers who are well-informed about second language acquisition stages of development and associated learning behaviors (e.g., WIDA Can-Do strategies) are best equipped to provide effective differentiated and scaffolded classroom instruction to meet the language needs of ELs in literacy. Select aspects useful to be aware of include "cross-linguistic differences at the phrase, sentence, and discourse levels (e.g., basic differences in word order at the phrase or sentence level, or differences in purpose and position of a topic sentence at the paragraph level)" (Harper & de Jong, 2004, p. 157). See Chapter 4 for additional information about ways reading instruction should differ for ELs.

Implications for Practice

1. Ongoing professional development can help teachers better understand the ways instruction for ELs should differ from general education best practice.

2. Many of the perceived writing "problems" of ELs are typical of second language learners and should be expected; these are not signs of low levels of development in both languages or of a learning disability.

3. Focusing on students' strengths, rather than only on errors, provides a different view of what learners know and are capable of doing.

4. ELs benefit from explicit instruction in ways English is similar to and different from their first language.

Misconception 5

The more time students spend receiving English instruction, the faster they will learn it.

This is only common sense, right? After all, we know that time on task increases opportunities to learn and generally enhances academic outcomes. But, counterintuitive though it may be, research shows that a strong foundation in one's native language is more conducive to English acquisition than submersion or immersion in an English-only environment (August & Hakuta, 1997; Cha & Goldenberg, 2015). In fact, in their review of research on teaching ELs to read, August and Shanahan found that some native language instruction led to greater gains in English than no native language instruction (August & Shanahan, 2006). Four previous reviews noted the same thing (Greene, 1997; Rolstad, Mahoney, & Glass, 2005; Slavin & Cheung, 2005; Willig, 1985). In other words, students who are taught using at least some of their native language perform significantly better on standardized tests in English reading than similar students taught only in English. For example, Goldenberg (2006) found that use of primary language during instruction contributes to student achievement in English. Misperceptions about the emphasis on use of English are further highlighted when we consider the importance of teachers supporting use of first language, efforts to support first language at home, and effective interpretations of time on task for ELs.

Use of First Language. When teachers support students' use of their first language, they can rest assured that they are helping them and not doing them a disservice (Goldenberg, 2013; Goldenberg, Hicks, & Lit, 2013). Strategic use of the first language, when it is possible, (a) helps ELs learn grade-level content while they are acquiring English, (b) builds a solid foundation that can serve as a bridge to English, and (c) helps build a bond between the home and the school. Skills developed in the first language transfer to English, particularly when the teacher helps students make connections across languages.

Home Language Support. Similarly, parents and other caregivers should be encouraged to speak to their children in their home language and engage with them in literacy-related activities in their first language, even when their children are being instructed in English in school (Wong Fillmore, 2000).

Time on Task. One reason that time on task in English by itself is not sufficient for helping students acquire English proficiency, and learn to read, is that instruction must be comprehensible and at an appropriate level to be effective (Hererera et al., 2015). It is essential to teach concepts and language simultaneously, providing scaffolding or support of some kind to help the child make sense of learning input (e.g., through gestures, visuals, or simplified language). Teacher directed time on tasks is essential for ELs in reading instruction, with the gradual release toward independent time on task expectations.

Implications for Practice

1. Native language instruction helps students learn English and is more effective than immersion in English only.

2. Skills developed in students' native language transfer to English, particularly when teachers help students make connections across languages.

3. Students acquire English when they receive comprehensible input and are provided explicit instruction with gradual release.

Misconception 6

All ELs learn English in the same way at about the same rate.

Effective teachers know that not all students learn in the same way (Herrera et al., 2015), so it would seem obvious that ELs would differ in how they learn English as a second language. However, many people seem to believe that language learning is a universal process, similar for everyone. Yet if we think about it, we all know individuals who seem to learn a new language effortlessly, almost by osmosis, and others who really struggle to speak an additional language, despite years of trying. In their summary of the research on ELs, August and Hakuta (1997) noted, "The most striking fact about second language learning, especially as compared with first language learning, is the variability in outcomes" (p. 37).

There are many reasons the language acquisition process can vary so much. These reasons include the tremendous variability in students' background experiences, the extent to which students have a strong foundation in their first language, how much schooling they have already had, how effective their early literacy instruction has been, and how many opportunities are afforded to them to use their target language in meaningful ways (Cummins, 1986; Klingner & Eppolito, 2014; Portes & Rumbaut, 2001; Valdés, 2001). The child's experiences in the home culture affect values, patterns of language use, and interpersonal styles.

Perhaps one of the most overlooked factors that affect language acquisition is the role of the status of the first language in comparison with that of the majority language along with the attitudes of the society toward the child's first language (Cummins, 2000; Paradis et al., 2011). If students feel that their teachers and the general public devalue their language and culture, they may be less motivated to learn the dominant language of the society. Also, social class differences and cultural differences can contribute to students' sense of safety at and around school, their identity as an English learner, and thereby their learning of academic English. Children are more likely to be responsive to a teacher who is sensitive to and appreciative of their culture and language.

It takes several years for students to acquire full proficiency in English, longer than many teachers realize. Cummins estimated that it takes five to seven years for students to be able to learn cognitively demanding academic material in their second language (1984). How long it takes seems to vary depending on the nature of the instruction students receive. Garcia (2004), referring to Thomas and Collier's 1997 research, noted the following:

- Typical bilingually schooled students achieving on-grade level in native language (L1) will require 4–7 years to make it to the fiftieth normal curve equivalent (NCE) in English (L2).
- Typical "advantaged" immigrant learners, who possess 2–5 years of on-grade level schooling in their home country in the native

language, require approximately 5–7 years to reach the fiftieth NCE in English, when educated in all English in US schools.

- Typical young immigrant students taught in English only in US schools require up to seven and perhaps ten years to achieve at the fiftieth NCE.

Additionally, many of these students will not achieve at the fiftieth NCE unless provided educational supports for native academic language and cognitive development in the home (Garcia, 2004; Thomas & Collier, 1997).

It is important for teachers to keep this in mind because many students appear to be fully proficient in English before they are able to engage with highly demanding, abstract tasks in English. When students struggle, teachers and others may become concerned and suspect that the students have learning disabilities. Or teachers may misinterpret students' behaviors as a lack of motivation. One teacher shared, "I find that these students tend to not understand what I say during instruction. It seems like they are not listening" (Orosco, 2007, p. 157). Yet the most likely explanation for their slow progress is that they are not as fully proficient in English as was thought.

Implications for Practice

1. The length of time it takes ELs to acquire English varies a great deal.

2. Teachers who are aware of students' sociocultural backgrounds can more easily create safe and welcoming environments that affirm students as participants in class and encourage learning.

3. The language acquisition process takes several years; there are no shortcuts.

4. Even when ELs appear to be quite proficient in English, they may not yet have acquired full proficiency.

5. The reason for an English learner's struggles when learning to read is much more likely to be the language acquisition process than a learning disability.

Misconception 7

English learners acquire English in the same way they acquire their first language, through exposure and interactions with others.

This misconception is similar to the previous one. Many well-meaning teachers believe that children acquire a second language in much the same way they learn their first language—through exposure and interactions with others in the target language, without the need for direct or explicit instruction (Goldenberg, 2008, 2013). Although important, these conditions by themselves are not sufficient for most ELs. And although it is true that the developmental process of learning a second language is similar to that of learning one's first language, there also are important differences that limit the extent to which simple exposure to a new language is effective. For one, children acquiring their first language have many years to do so before they start school. They do not feel the pressure of needing to understand in order to be able to comprehend grade-level curriculum and apply language in complex, often abstract, ways (Swain, 1995). ELs benefit from conscious attention to their language learning needs, including the grammatical, morphological, and phonological aspects of language (Harper & de Jong, 2004). They need explicit instruction that helps them notice the relationships between the forms and functions of language, and between their first and second languages (Herrera et al., 2015). Also, teachers must understand that although ELs may be limited in their ability to express themselves in English, they are *not* limited in their ability to think.

One version of this misconception is the belief that all ELs develop oral proficiency before they become literate. Yet some students, particularly older ELs who are already literate in their first language, may actually become proficient with written language before oral language. Interactions with print help them in much the same way oral interactions can help others (Harper & de Jong, 2004; Xu, 2014). Previously, it was thought that students should not begin literacy instruction in English until they had developed sufficient oral proficiency in English. And while it certainly is true that students must develop oral proficiency in order to become fully literate, in a recent review of the research on teaching reading to ELs, Slavin and Cheung (2005) noted that the most effective programs for helping students develop their oral as well as written skills in English are programs in which students learn to read in both languages at much the same time, though at different times during the day (e.g., dual language program). The reason for this is that skills developed in one language transfer to another, particularly when teachers provide explicit instruction, interactions, and opportunities to practice skills in meaningful ways in both languages. Additionally, it is essential to maintain rigor in challenging curriculum, assisting learners to access content while learning English (Herrera et al., 2015; Wong Fillmore, 2014).

Implications for Practice

1. The language acquisition trajectories of EL students are likely to be different from those of monolingual students.

2. Exposure to English and interactions with others are important, but these are not enough to provide the support ELs need to be able to fully participate in classroom learning and achieve to their potential.

3. ELs benefit from explicit instruction as well as varied opportunities for meaningful practice.

4. Although ELs may be limited in their ability to express themselves in English, this does not mean they are limited in their ability to think.

Misconception 8

Errors are problematic and should be avoided.

Many teachers frequently interpret ELs' errors in the target language as a sign that they may have a learning disability or a developmental delay (Harper & de Jong, 2004; Ortiz & Artiles, 2010; Paradis et al., 2011). Yet it is natural for students to make errors while they are learning. In fact, errors are a sign of progress and an indication that students are feeling comfortable enough to take risks. Teachers should keep in mind that ELs' mistakes often demonstrate the ways in which students are drawing on their native language to help them learn a second language. The process of acquiring a new language incorporates a stage in which the learner uses an "interlanguage" (Saville-Troike, 2006), which includes features of both languages (Selinker, Swain, & Dumas, 1975). This developmental process is obviously different from language development in monolingual English children who do not develop an interlanguage. Errors such as confusion with verb tenses, plurals, possessives, subject/verb agreement, word order, and the use of articles are common (Ferris, 2002; Harper & de Jong, 2004). For example, *"la niña rubia tiene seis años"* in Spanish means "the blonde girl is six years old" in English. However, a literal translation of each word would read, "the girl blonde has six years." A Spanish speaking child who mistakenly says "the girl blonde" rather than "the blonde girl" or "she has six years" rather than "she is six years old" would be transferring knowledge of Spanish to English. This is a normal aspect of second language acquisition, not an indication the child has a language disorder or disability. The kinds of interlanguage errors a child makes vary depending on the characteristics of the first language. In other words, a child who speaks Japanese as his first language will make different errors than a child who speaks Hungarian.

Teachers who are experienced in learning a second language and who know more about the structure of English and other language systems are more likely to understand how students' errors reflect their attempts to make meaning based on their understandings of both their native and target languages. ELs benefit when teachers accurately interpret errors as clues about language development, rather than indicators of a disability. Also, teachers should keep in mind that because of some errors' usefulness in students' interlanguages, some mistakes are more or less amenable to correction at different times in students' trajectory of developing proficiency in the target language (Harper & de Jong, 2004). Additionally, many bilingual individuals engage in *code-switching*, which is the practice of combining two languages in one phrase or sentence, or going back and forth between two languages (Herrera et al., 2015). This is also a normal phenomenon and should not be considered an error or sign of confusion (Genesee & Nicoladis, 2006; Herrera et al., 2015). In fact, code-switching can indicate mastery of two languages rather than that the speaker has limited proficiency in either language. Code-switching is also quite common as a sophisticated use of language for social purposes.

Implications for Practice

1. Errors can be useful clues to understanding the interlanguages that students are developing and can be a sign of progress.

2. Errors such as confusion with verb tenses, plurals, possessives, word order, subject/verb agreement, and the use of articles are common among ELs and should not be interpreted as signifying that a student has a disability.

3. It is natural that some errors are more amenable to correction than others given their usefulness as part of students' interlanguage.

4. Code-switching is common among bilingual individuals around the world and should not be considered a sign of confusion.

Misconception 9

The majority of ELs in the United States are sequential bilinguals.

The reality is that a high percentage of ELs who enter school do so as "simultaneous" rather than "sequential" bilinguals (Capp et al., 2005; Escamilla & Hopewell, 2010; Garcia, 2009). *Sequential* bilingualism is defined as acquiring the second language after learning the first language. *Simultaneous* bilingualism is defined as the learning of two languages (from birth) at the same time, stressing the importance of each language facilitating the proficiency of both languages (Richard-Amato, 2010; Zepeda & Rodriguez, 2015). ELs born in the United States are likely to be exposed to both English and their native language, and as such, represent a high number of simultaneous bilinguals. As a result, there is a need to acknowledge that many ELs come to school having developed their home language concurrently with English (i.e., simultaneous bilingualism). The significance of recognizing this misconception is seen in the instructional framework associated with each type of bilingualism. The sequential bilingual perspective provides English language development in a sequential way, in which mastery of the native language occurs prior to mastery of English as a second language. However, given the high numbers of simultaneous bilinguals, the suggested instructional framework should reflect and align with emerging bilingual profiles, in which both languages develop simultaneously. As such, the instructional literacy framework consistent with teaching English as a foreign language or sequential (second) language should be avoided in the education of ELs. Educator emphasis on a sequential perspective for students who require a simultaneous perspective contributes to misinterpretation of ELs' progress in literacy, which impacts one's ability to accurately distinguish language acquisition from learning disabilities.

Implications for Practice

1. Simultaneous bilinguals bring language proficiencies in both English and the home language.

2. ELs' emerging bilingualism needs to be acknowledged and built upon to develop effective literacy instruction.

3. Maintaining an instructional emphasis toward sequential bilingualism perpetuates misidentification for disability due to misinterpretation of ELs' progress in literacy.

SUMMARY

ELs' academic outcomes are greatly influenced by the interactions between what students bring to school and what schooling offers them. We stress the need for well-prepared teachers who understand the language acquisition process to serve as advocates for students (Herrera et al., 2015). In this chapter, we have discussed nine common misconceptions that limit the extent to which ELs receive appropriate instruction and possibly lead to inappropriate referrals to special education.

Various researchers (e.g., Goldenberg, 2013; Harper & de Jong, 2004; Herrera et al., 2015) recommend that, in addition to providing exposure to a language-rich environment and creating opportunities to interact with native speakers of the target language, teachers must

- ensure that ELs have the language skills to perform a task, and if not, teach these skills through explicit modeling and scaffolding;
- understand the complex contribution of individual learner variables to the second language acquisition process;
- consider a wide range of factors when trying to understand the behaviors of ELs (e.g., personality, motivation, attitude, educational background, literacy level in the first language, age, and previous opportunities to learn);

- examine the linguistic and cultural assumptions underlying their instructional choices (e.g., simultaneous vs. sequential bilinguals);
- learn about ways other cultures structure their children's educational experiences;
- recognize similarities and differences between first and second language learning and understand the implications for their own instructional practices;
- understand the role that language plays in learning and acknowledge that language development must be integrated as a goal of instruction when teaching ELs;
- consider all possible alternative explanations to a student's struggles, including the possibility that instruction might not be appropriate, before thinking that the child might have a learning disability.

4

Helping Classroom Reading Teachers Distinguish Between Language Acquisition and Learning Disabilities

Janette K. Klingner
and Diana Geisler

The reading challenges experienced by some ELs can give teachers the false impression that they reflect a learning disability or lack intelligence when in fact they are simply experiencing normal effects of the language acquisition process. According to Hamayan, Marler, Sanchez-Lopez, and Damico (2013), oftentimes "teachers are likely to choose special education as the source of support for ELLs" (p. 1), leading to misplacements and overrepresentation, particularly for reading. The focus of this chapter is on helping classroom teachers distinguish between second language acquisition and learning disabilities (LD) among ELs by explaining some of the challenges ELs face when learning to read in English.

Vignette: The Changing School Environment

Carole teaches first grade at King Elementary School. She has been teaching there for two decades and over the years has seen the community change from mostly White middle class to predominately Latino working class. Many parents are immigrants and work at the new meat-packing plant nearby. Almost two-thirds of Carole's students speak some Spanish in their homes, and about 40 percent are considered less than fully proficient in English or, in other words, to be ELs. King Elementary provides *pull out* ESL services for their ELs, for about one hour a day. Carole earned a master's degree in elementary education during her early years in the classroom, and over the years, she has been considered an effective teacher by her principal, other teachers, and parents. She is a confident, experienced teacher. Recently, she attended district-sponsored professional development workshops on Reading First Program and the five "big ideas" of reading emphasized in the National Reading Panel report (2000).

Like many schools around the country, her district is pushing the use of evidence-based practices. Carole has seen the reading pendulum swing from a focus on whole language to an emphasis on explicit instruction in phonics. She considers herself to be in favor of a balanced approach—something in the middle. She has not taken any coursework or received any professional development in teaching ELs how to read. She, like those who determine the curriculum in her district, believes that the evidence-based reading practices promoted by the National Reading Panel are appropriate for all students. After all, how much can teaching letter sounds and names vary? She wonders, "Isn't good teaching just good teaching?" Yet Carole's students are now struggling, and she is not sure why. She believes that, in part, the reason is that her current students are not as prepared for school as were her previous students. Factors related to poverty create additional challenges for them. She sees that not being fully proficient in English creates barriers, and she gets quite frustrated that, despite her best attempts to meet their needs, many of her students simply cannot seem to learn to read. She suspects that a disproportionate number of them might have LD.

Reflective Items

1. What are some issues experienced by Carole you most identify with in your classroom or school?

2. What might be suggested that Carole initially undertake to address her concerns?

3. Why isn't "good teaching" for all sufficient for instructing culturally and linguistically diverse learners in the process of acquiring English as a second language?

Similar to Carole, many teachers nationwide often misunderstand ELs' lack of progress (Hamayan et al., 2013; Orosco, 2007). A common scenario is that a principal or someone in the school district such as the language arts director mandates or recommends using a particular instructional practice, emphasizing that it is research based.[1] The principal might stress that the practice has been *proven* to work. The teacher assumes that because she is using an evidence-based practice, students' struggles must be because something is lacking in the students, not the program. Yet what works with some students may not work with all students. Most commercially produced curricula in the United States are created to meet the needs of middle-class, native English speakers. They are designed based on assumptions about the cultural and linguistic knowledge this demographic of student brings to the instructional situation. English learners differ from their mainstream counterparts in significant ways, affecting how successful an instructional practice may be in the classroom (August & Shanahan, 2006; Herrera et al., 2015).

STANDARDS-BASED EDUCATION AND READING

Nested within the overarching five big ideas of reading (i.e., *phonological awareness, alphabetic principle, fluency, vocabulary,* and *reading comprehension*) discussed in this chapter is the instructional and assessment emphasis on standards-based teaching and learning (e.g., Common Core State Standards; Standards for the English Language Arts; English as a Second Language; TESOL Standards, etc.). Specifically, a reading standard represents the initial point for instructional planning, providing educators information about content and the sequence of what is to be taught through reading lessons and units of study. Though standards-based education is not without its critics, it provides educators a design to follow to support student successes in achieving reading benchmarks.

In regard to the use of standards when instructing ELs, Herrera, Perez, and Escamilla (2015) emphasize their importance in framing instruction to master literacy while promoting high expectations for success. Additionally, though adopted in forty-five states (Klassen & Maune, 2015), the Common Core State Standards (CCSS) "presents an even greater challenge for ELLs than for their peers" (p. 79). As emphasized in the remainder of this chapter and throughout the book, the learning process for ELs may vary significantly based on language background, requiring classroom teachers to adjust reading instruction to meet challenges associated with the delivery of common core state standards. An understanding of the main ideas about reading discussed below will guide classroom teachers to properly adjust instruction associated with standards, thereby providing ELs increased sufficient learning opportunities with reading development. Thus, our hope is that if teachers can better understand the reasons for ELs' reading struggles, they will be less likely to judge them as deficient.

THE "FIVE BIG IDEAS" OF READING

Although there certainly are many similarities in the best instructional practices for ELs and students who speak English as their first language (Klingner et al., in press), there also are key differences. Previously, to review the research on teaching reading to ELs, the National Literacy Panel on Language Minority Children and Youth was convened (August & Shanahan, 2006). The panel found that the same five components identified by the National Reading Panel (2000) are also important for ELs, including several ways to adjust instruction for ELs' benefit. In other words, one size does not fit all. Our goal in this chapter is to point out key differences in instruction in each of these big idea areas, with a focus on those aspects of instruction that can be particularly challenging for ELs and can lead to false impressions about why they are struggling. It is these problematic areas that can confuse teachers and contribute to the over-referral of culturally and linguistically diverse students to special education. Specific evidence-based methods and practical suggestions for teaching reading to ELs to appropriately address the challenges are presented in subsequent chapters. Table 4.1 provides a summary of the core reading components and associated potential challenges for ELs.

Phonological Awareness

Phonological awareness is the ability to identify and manipulate the parts of spoken language (Herrera et al., 2015). Phonemic awareness is a subcategory of phonological awareness and is the ability to identify and manipulate the phonemes or sounds in spoken words. Numerous research studies indicate that phonological awareness is predictive of later reading ability (National Reading Panel, 2000); however, this needs to be taught in context, not isolation, to be of value to ELs (Cloud, Genesee, & Hamayan,

Table 4.1   Possible Problematic Aspects of Instruction for ELs in the "Five Big Ideas" of Reading

Reading Component	Potential Challenges for ELs
Phonological Awareness	• The following typically occurs when the student's first language, or L1, does not include some English phonemes: ○ The student is not accustomed to hearing these sounds. ○ It can be quite difficult to distinguish between sounds. ○ Pronouncing new sounds can be difficult. ○ Phonological tasks in general become more challenging.

Reading Component	Potential Challenges for ELs
Alphabetic Principle	• Some orthographies are very different than English; even when the orthography of the student's L1 is similar to English, such as with Spanish, differences can be quite confusing: o Letters might look the same but represent different sounds. o Unfamiliar English sounds and their various spellings can make decoding and spelling difficult. o Not knowing the meanings of words limits an EL reader's ability to use context clues. o Learning letters and sounds can seem very abstract. • ELs typically have fewer opportunities to read aloud in English and receive feedback than their English speaking peers do.
Fluency	• ELs may read more slowly, with less understanding. • ELs can have an accent and still read fluently. • Students may become good word-callers but not understand what they are reading.
Vocabulary	• ELs can be confused by common words, such as o prepositions (e.g., *on*, *above*), o pronouns (e.g., *she*, *they*), o cohesion markers (e.g., *therefore*, *however*), o words with multiple meanings (e.g., *bat*, *light*), o figurative language, such as similes (e.g., swims like a fish) or metaphors (e.g., his stomach was a bottomless pit), o idioms (e.g., to know something inside out) • False cognates can perplex students (e.g., *fast* in German means "almost"; *embarasada* in Spanish means "pregnant").
Reading Comprehension	• Many factors affect comprehension, such as o oral language proficiency o word recognition skills o fluency o vocabulary knowledge o the ability to use comprehension strategies o variations in text structure o interest o cultural differences • To determine what students comprehend, teachers should o provide them with alternative ways to show understanding (e.g., in their native language, using diagrams), o focus more on content than grammatical errors or accents.

2009). With ELs, phonological awareness in English or Spanish seems to predict English reading achievement (Chiappe, Siegel, & Gottardo, 2002; Lindsey, Manis, & Bailey, 2003). In fact, Spanish phonological awareness might be a better predictor of English word reading than English or Spanish oral proficiency or English word recognition (Durgunoglu, Nagy, & Hancin-Bhatt, 1993).

For ELs learning to read in English, phonological awareness can be especially challenging when the student's native language does not include some English phonemes (Antunez, 2002). For example, most dialects in Spanish do not include "sh" or the short vowel sound for "i." When this happens, the student is not accustomed to hearing these sounds, and it can be quite difficult to distinguish them from other sounds. Pronouncing the new sounds can also be tricky for the student, as phonological tasks in general become more challenging. If teachers are not aware of these challenges, they might assume that the child has a deficit in auditory discrimination and/or in phonological awareness. Since these can be early signs of a learning disability, the potential for misunderstanding is great and teachers need to remember that some confusion about and difficulty with sounds is a natural by-product of learning a second language (Hamayan et al., 2013). Teachers can help ELs with phonological awareness by finding out which phonemes do not exist in the student's native language and helping the student discriminate the sounds. Teachers can also help by not prematurely drawing the conclusion that the student has a disability.

Alphabetic Principle

The alphabetic principle is the understanding of sound-symbol correspondence, or in other words, which letters make which sounds, thereby, increasing their phonological skills (Herrera et al., 2015). It also involves combining sounds into words. For ELs, learning the alphabetic principle in English can be challenging if they have not already developed this literacy skill in their first language and/or have not acquired sufficient oral English proficiency to make sense of the words they are reading. The process can be quite abstract and meaningless for them. Many ELs become good *word-callers*—that is, they become good at sounding out words without knowing their meaning (August & Shanahan, 2006). In fact, they sometimes do better than their English-only peers on subtests requiring students to read nonsense words. After all, for some ELs most everything they are reading may seem like nonsense. Commins (2012) stresses the importance of using text to represent authentic reading in meaningful ways.

When students are already literate in their first language, learning to read in English is easier. This is particularly true when the orthographic systems of the two languages are similar, as with Spanish or French, and much more challenging when they are not, as with Chinese or Korean. Yet even when the orthographies have much in common, as with English and

Spanish, differences can be quite confusing. For example, the sounds represented by the letters *b, c, d, f, l, m, n, p, q, s,* and *t* are alike enough that they transfer to English (Antunez, 2002). Vowels, however, look the same in Spanish and English but represent different sounds. Thus, when a child pronounces a vowel sound as he would in Spanish, the word sounds incorrect (e.g., saying "beet" instead of "bit"). Unfamiliar English sounds and their various spellings can make decoding as well as spelling difficult. Another challenge is that not knowing the meanings of words limits the EL reader's ability to use context clues to help her figure out how to read words (August & Shanahan, 2006).

It is easier for us to learn and remember new information when we can plug in or connect to existing schema. *Schema* refers to the way our brains organize and store concepts we already know (Herrera et al., 2015). For example, try this exercise as a test of this idea:

Have someone name ten random words that have no apparent connection to one another. See how many you can remember. Then ask the person to name ten words that are clearly related, such as different rooms in a house. Again, try to remember them. Which task was easier? Which way did you remember more words? Most likely, you remembered more words the second way because it is easier to remember information we can readily connect. If you were trying to remember rooms in a house, most likely you visualized a house and perhaps even pictured yourself walking through different rooms.

What does this have to do with ELs learning phonics? Often students are asked to learn sounds in quite abstract ways, perhaps quite unintentionally. For example, *zoo-phonics* is a common way to teach letter names and sounds to kindergartners by well-meaning teachers who assume they are helping students connect with their prior knowledge. Yet "Queenie Quail," "Umber Umbrella Bird," and "Nigel Nightowl" can seem quite meaningless to children who have not been exposed to these names or animals prior to starting school. ELs are being asked not only to learn new letter names and sounds but also to acquire new concepts and vocabulary. If the teacher does not help students make these connections and allow them more time for this additional learning, what might she assume when they struggle? Many teachers erroneously conclude that their ELs must have LD or "can't learn to read" (Orosco, 2007). ELs benefit from explicit instruction that is comprehensible and at their level (August & Shanahan, 2006).

Fluency

Fluency is the ability to read quickly and accurately, with expression. Fluency requires both word recognition and comprehension (Herrera et al., 2015). One challenge ELs face is that they typically are afforded fewer opportunities to read aloud in English and receive feedback than do their English speaking peers (August & Shanahan, 2006). It is not uncommon for them to read more slowly than their fluent English classmates and with less understanding. One way to help build fluency is to make sure students understand text and can decode all words before they read it. For example, provide ELs opportunities to hear a more expert reader model fluent and expressive reading, such as through echo reading or partner reading (Hamayan et al., 2013). Struggling EL readers might also listen to and follow along with books on tape or on CDs (Hiebert, Pearson, Taylor, Richardson, & Paris, 1998; Peregoy & Boyle, 2012). Antunez (2002) reminds us that fluency should not be confused with having an accent. Many ELs and fully proficient English as a second language speakers read English with an accent, but they can still read fluently. When ELs read more slowly and lack expression, teachers should recognize that this is quite common for ELs and does not indicate a learning disability. At the same time, teachers should provide them with additional opportunities to practice oral reading.

Vocabulary

Zacarian (2013) wrote that when educating ELs, "providing students with multiple active practice and exposure opportunities to use vocabulary to the point of mastery should be fundamental to our work" (p. 108). ELs by definition are in the process of acquiring English and do not have English vocabularies as extensive as those of their fully English proficient peers. They might, however, have extensive vocabularies in their native language. How to assist ELs increase their vocabularies is one of the greatest challenges their teachers face (Antunez, 2002). Vocabulary development is an essential aspect of reading fluency and comprehension. However, it is not uncommon for ELs to be able to decode words without understanding what they mean (i.e., word calling) (Lesaux & Geva, 2006). Many teachers understand that students benefit from explicit instruction and from preteaching of key vocabulary terms they will encounter in text (e.g., content vocabulary in science, such as *ecosystem* or *photosynthesis*). Yet they might not consider that their ELs also need help with more common words that can be confusing, such as prepositions (e.g., *on, in, above*), pronouns (e.g., such as *she* in the sentences, "Maria was not feeling well. She hoped she would be able to leave early."), and cohesion markers (e.g., *therefore, however*). Words with multiple meanings (e.g., *bat, light*), figurative language, such as similes (e.g., as quick as a cricket, swims like a fish) or metaphors (e.g., his stomach was a bottomless pit), and idioms (e.g., a piece of cake, or to know something inside out) can be especially challenging for ELs.

Many words in English have cognates in other languages (Herrera et al., 2015), that is, words that are the same or similar, such as *bandage*, which is the same in French and English, or *animal,* which is the same in Spanish and English). Knowing this can be quite helpful for ELs who are already literate in their first language, especially when the teacher points them out. Yet false cognates can be quite confusing for students (e.g., *fast* in German means "almost" rather than "rapid"; *embarasada* in Spanish means "pregnant").

Teachers need to keep in mind that there is a difference between words for which the student understands the underlying concept and knows the word in her native language, and words for which the meaning is unknown in both the student's first language as well as in English (August & Shanahan, 2006). When the student already understands the concept behind a new word in English, simply providing the native language label most likely will facilitate understanding. Yet when the concept is new, the teacher should provide ELs more extensive instruction in what that concept means (Commins, 2012; Herrera et al., 2015; Richard-Amato, 2010) and not assume that EL students' understandings of words are the same as those of their fully English proficient peers.

Just because students are in the process of developing their English vocabularies, this does not mean they might have LD or lack intelligence. As a group, ELs are every bit as intelligent as their fully English proficient peers. Yet it seems to be human nature to assume otherwise. Astute teachers are aware of this and make sure they do all they can to help their students develop their vocabularies, while at the same time being careful not to judge their students as somehow less capable.

Reading Comprehension

Reading comprehension is the ultimate goal of reading (Snow, 2002), and one of the most important academic skills taught in school (Polloway, Patton, & Serena, in press) After all, knowing how to decode words has little value if comprehension is missing. Reading comprehension is a complex process of constructing meaning by coordinating a number of processes, including decoding, word reading, and fluency along with the integration of background knowledge and previous experiences (Snow, 2002). Many factors can influence the reading comprehension of ELs, such as oral language proficiency, academic and cognitive skills, word recognition skills, fluency, vocabulary knowledge, abilities in both languages, interest, and the ability to use comprehension strategies (Herrera et al., 2015). Variations in text structure (i.e., the way narrative and expository texts are organized) can be perplexing for ELs and affect their comprehension. Dissimilarities in cultural understandings also make a difference (August & Shanahan, 2006). For example, the typical wedding ceremony is quite different across cultures. Thus, a student who is reading about a wedding in the United States but whose background knowledge is about weddings in India will have different expectations for what will happen in the text and may become confused.

There are many promising practices teachers can use to help ELs understand what they read and develop reading comprehension skills (August & Shanahan, 2006; Herrera et al., 2015; Peregoy & Boyle, 2012), several of which are addressed in Chapter 5. Unfortunately, however, teachers typically spend little time actually teaching reading comprehension strategies to their students (Klingner, Urbach, Golos, Brownell, & Menon, 2010). Rather, they are more likely to ask students comprehension questions about text they have listened to or read. Even though all students are part of the comprehension activity, when called upon, only a few students may raise their hands to answer. The teacher is likely to call one student who responds, evaluate the student's response, and then move on (Cazden, 2001), making the oftentimes erroneous assumption that all learners comprehend the reading material without checking directly with the other students.

Conversely, teachers might think that their ELs understand very little when in fact they comprehend a fair amount. ELs may understand more than they can demonstrate orally or in writing in English (Herrera et al., 2015). Teachers might also draw the wrong conclusions about ELs' comprehension if they pay more attention to students' grammatical errors, their accents when speaking, or the mechanics of their writing than they do to the substance of their responses. When the goal is to determine the extent to which students understand the material they are learning, the teacher's focus should be on the content rather than the form of students' answers.

Two More "Big Ideas"

In addition to the five big ideas discussed above, the National Literacy Panel on Language Minority Children and Youth (August & Shanahan, 2006), and other researchers (Commins, 2012; Herrera et al., 2015) noted that oral language development should be considered an essential component of effective instruction for ELs. Motivation is another factor that is critical for all students (Hamayan et al., 2013), and perhaps especially important for culturally and linguistically diverse students who are more likely to underachieve in schools across the United States (Lee, 2002). We describe these next.

ORAL LANGUAGE

For ELs, the challenge in teaching reading goes beyond providing explicit instruction in reading and writing, as it also includes how to develop oral English proficiency (Klingner et al., in press). Oral language proficiency affects literacy acquisition (August & Shanahan, 2006), being closely related in at least three ways, (a) both are primary language systems that develop naturally within the proper learning context, (b) development of both often occurs within predicable stages, and (c) literacy development is reinforced by oral language (Hamayan et al., 2013). When students' oral language improves, so does their reading fluency and comprehension. Generic literacy programs are inadequate for ELs because they guide teachers to explicitly teach only reading and writing skills, assuming that the prerequisite oral language skills are sufficiently under control (Gentile, 2004). Such programs neglect much needed explicit teaching for oral language development. To more successfully facilitate literacy acquisition of ELs, Gentile recommends that literacy programs emphasize explicit teaching of both talk and text. *Oracy* is Gentile's term for literacy instruction that includes explicit teaching for literacy and oral language acquisition, as well as a focus on the child's culture and an emphasis on the importance of child-teacher interactions, as represented by Figure 4.1.

The less-than-full English oral proficiency of students who are becoming bilingual plays out in different ways. As already discussed, students may be unfamiliar with key vocabulary words. They likely are confused by English grammatical structures. They may need to strengthen their narration and retelling skills. They might not respond well to large group instruction or might refrain from contributing during whole class

Figure 4.1 Adaptation of Gentile's Oracy Model

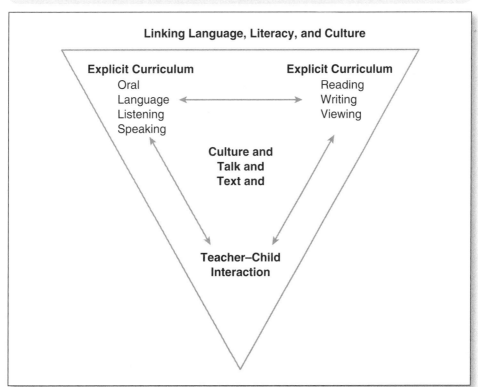

activities. They may have little understanding of the connections between oral and written language (Gentile, 2004).

Therefore, it is important for teachers not to assume their ELs have sufficient oral language proficiency to benefit from instruction (Commins, 2012; Hamayan et al., 2013; Herrera et al., 2015). Previously, Harry and Klingner (2005) observed literacy instruction in classrooms with ELs at beginning levels of English proficiency and noted that some teachers almost exclusively provided verbal explanations without the visual cues or other scaffolding that might have helped their instruction be more comprehensible to students. It was obvious to the observers that many students did not understand, yet teachers were likely to scold students for "not listening" or "not paying attention." One such teacher referred several of her students to the school's Child Study Team (i.e., special education pre-referral team) because she suspected they had LD, intellectual disability, or an emotional/behavioral disorder.

Teachers should observe their struggling learners closely to determine ELs' oral language needs. "Observing student attitudes and performance during instruction and assessment is key to knowing the type of assessment that yields best results in depicting student knowledge" (Basterra, 2011, p. 82). Additionally, Frances, Rivera, Lesaux, Kieffer, and Rivera (2006) emphasized the importance of more structured "talk" in classrooms to informally assess ELs' oral language development in different instructional contexts. Zacarian (2013) also wrote that the learning of literacy is "a developmental process that is dependent on a variety of elements including . . . prior learning experiences and proficiency in oral language" (p. 73). A period of daily oracy instruction would be a logical, appropriate prereferral intervention for emergent readers struggling with literacy and language acquisition. In her research with ELs, Haager (2004) found that teachers who emphasized oral academic language development achieved greater gains in students' reading scores than teachers who did not. This finding is supported through the work of other researchers such as Herrera, Perez, and Escamilla (2015) and Commins (2012).

MOTIVATION

There is no doubt that the extent to which students are motivated affects their learning. "If students are motivated to learn the content in a given subject, their achievement in that subject is most likely high" (Hamayan et al., 2013, p. 114). Actions taken by teachers at the beginning of a lesson directly affect learner motivation (Brophy, 2010; Burden & Byrd, 2012). Snow, Burns, and Griffin (1998) stressed the significance of motivation in their precursor to the National Reading Panel report (2000) titled "Preventing Reading Difficulties in Young Children." They wrote that "motivation is crucial" (p. 3 of Executive Summary) and noted that one of the principle reasons students struggle to learn to read is a loss of motivation. Frustration can lead to a lack of motivation, as can tasks that seem meaningless or disconnected from the realities of everyday life. Certainly, many ELs are faced with learning situations like this on a daily basis. Rueda, MacGillivray, Monzó, and Arzubiaga (2001) emphasized the role of context and sociocultural factors in influencing reading engagement and motivation for ELs. They noted that motivation is not only something the student brings to the learning situation but also is an aspect of the task and a part of the learning environment. When ELs seem to lack motivation, before teachers conclude that they do not want to learn, are lazy, or do not care, they should first look at factors such as whether the assignment is meaningful, relevant, and at an appropriate instructional level, and whether the students understand what is being asked of them and have all of the tools they need to accomplish the task.

What does a motivating program look like? Careful thought is given to the nature of the texts and activities used for instructing ELs. The texts should be both interesting and at an appropriate level to nourish children's developing literacy and language skills. The topics, the relevancy, and the language all affect how children interact with the texts and how well they learn from them. Students bring linguistic and cultural resources to school that can be used to construct a relevant and engaging curriculum. Reading, writing, listening, and speaking should build upon these "funds of knowledge" (Moll & Greenberg, 1990). Instruction should account for the impact of culture and experience on cognition, literacy learning, behavior, oral language development, and motivation. In a subsequent section of this chapter, we offer a synopsis of the Early Authors Program (Bernhard et al., 2006) as an example of a successful research-based literacy program that capitalizes on students' strengths and interests.

RESEARCH TO PRACTICE

Research on Reading Achievement for English Learners

Haager (2004) and [National Center for Culturally Responsive Educational Systems (NCCRESt) Conference] colleagues examined the critical features of beginning reading instruction that lead to improved reading achievement among English learners receiving instruction in English. Their research studies took place in urban schools with high percentages of ELs. The researchers observed reading instruction to determine which aspects of first-grade literacy instruction were seen most often in classrooms with higher academic outcomes for ELs. They conducted pre- and posttesting of students in key areas of beginning reading instruction and compared these test scores with their ratings of teachers in several domains on an observation instrument.

(Continued)

(Continued)

Haager (2004) and conference colleagues found that it is very important to integrate English language development with basic reading instruction. Effective teachers integrate vocabulary and language development into their core reading instruction when teaching ELs (e.g., teacher-planned, specific vocabulary-building activities). Furthermore, Haager suggests that during reading intervention, instruction should integrate English language development and reinforce vocabulary taught in the core reading lessons. Haager (2004) indicates that in order to make significant reading gains with ELs, teachers need to

1. use effective instructional techniques in general;

2. adjust their instruction for individuals having difficulty;

3. engage their students in interactive and engaging oral language, vocabulary, and comprehension development;

4. provide high-quality explicit instruction in phonemic awareness and decoding.

DECISION POINTS WHEN
STUDENTS STRUGGLE WITH READING

What should teachers do when their ELs are struggling? What if some students really do have LD? How can teachers tell which students should receive additional interventions or who to refer for an evaluation for possible placement in special education? A useful rule of thumb is to look at how many ELs are struggling. As previously discussed, if the majority of ELs are making little progress, the teacher should focus on improving instruction. If most ELs are doing well and only a few are struggling, the teacher should look more closely at what is going on with those individual students and consider that they may need additional support.

First let us focus on classrooms where the majority of ELs are struggling. How should classroom teachers adjust instruction when their ELs are making little progress? Effective teachers of ELs must become keen observers of children and should have a wide repertoire of instructional practices at their fingertips in order to match instruction to a particular child's needs (Commins, 2012; Herrera et al., 2015). Instructional approaches that demand one particular pathway are inappropriate for ELs because they lack the flexibility needed to meet the widely varying needs of the EL population. This is problematic because when reading instruction is scripted or a method insists on a predetermined sequence of what is to be learned and how it is to be learned, the responsibility to adjust falls on the *child* to match the curriculum. The child who cannot meet the program where it begins and stay in step soon falls behind. In such programs, teachers have little flexibility to adapt the program to meet children's individual differences. Thus, the first question the teacher should ask when ELs are struggling is,

1. Is my instruction culturally, linguistically, and pedagogically appropriate to meet students' needs? If the answer appears to be *no*, then the next question should be,

2. How can I adjust instruction to be more appropriate?

RESEARCH TO PRACTICE

The Early Authors Program (EAP)

The Early Authors Program is a language intervention program for bilingual preschoolers with the main goal of promoting early bilingual literacy. The program combines teaching, home language, cognitive engagement, and personal investment in the teaching and learning process (Bernhard, Cummins, Campoy, & Ada, 2004). It was first implemented in Miami-Dade County, Florida, with 1,179 children of families receiving subsidized day care in thirty-two early childhood centers. Children participated in bilingual literacy activities that involved writing and illustrating their own dual-language books in which the children themselves were the protagonists. They produced 3,286 books. Essential features of the program include

- home-school joint productive activities,
- bilingual literacy activities involving children and their families writing and illustrating dual-language books with children as the protagonists (authoring, reading, storytelling),
- children taught to recite culturally relevant rhymes and poems in their home languages,
- high value placed on home language maintenance and English acquisition,
- cognitive engagement and identity investment in the learning process,
- professional development for teachers including on-site coaching of teachers by literacy specialists,
- teachers taught to relate letter teaching to names of children, their friends, and family members,
- monthly workshops for parents,
- bookmaking materials provided (i.e., computers, digital cameras, color printers, laminators).

(Continued)

(Continued)

In their investigation of the effectiveness of EAP, Bernhard et al. (2006) found that EAP children gained in language and cognitive skills, as measured by standardized instruments. The three- and four-year-old EAP children's gain in language development (both expressive and receptive) was about ten months compared to the control children's gain of about three months. In other words, participation in the EAP intervention prevented the children from continuing to fall farther behind their national peers. Also, the affective and cognitive engagement of the children was markedly high. The book writing work was social and interactive, and the affective climate was warm and intimate. The work was personally meaningful and relevant to the children and their families thus affirming the children's identities. Bernhard et al. (2004) emphasized that affect matters; in other words, learning is influenced by emotion (Wolfe & Brandt, 1998).

EAP also had a positive effect on the literacy environment of the classrooms. The number of literacy-related activities in which the teachers engaged increased significantly. Teachers liked the EAP program and believed it was sustainable. They reported positive effects on children's identity and self-esteem and that the project was a success for all involved: the children, their parents, and the teachers themselves.

Optimal literacy instruction for ELs accounts for the influence of culture and experience on cognition and learning, behavior and communication, and language development and motivation. Some LD diagnoses of ELs are made not because the students have internal deficits of some kind but rather because they have not received an adequate opportunity to learn (Harry & Klingner, 2005; Ortiz et al., 2011). Another way to think about this is that the children are in "disabling contexts," not that they have disabilities. Many ELs are provided with too few and insufficient opportunities to develop their language and literacy skills. Klingner, Soltero-Gonzalez, and Lesaux (2010) stressed the importance of providing culturally and linguistically responsive challenging literacy instruction. Prior to referring a young EL for evaluation of a reading disability or for more intensive interventions as part of MTSS, teachers should consider the types of language and literacy instruction to which the child has had access. The following table provides ten select questions, derived from content found in several sources, including Herrera, Perez, and Escamilla (2015), Commins (2012), and Zacarian (2013), to guide teachers as they self-reflect on instructional practices for language and literacy learning for ELs.

Positive responses to these questions suggest that most ELs in the class are progressing, with additional support provided to those few students who continue to struggle (e.g., scaffolding, explicit instruction, personalize learning). Researchers now suggest examining both students' rate of progress in comparison with that of similar peers and also whether students are reaching learning goals, or benchmarks (Compton, Fuchs, Fuchs, & Bryant, 2006) to best understand instructional needs and associated decision making.

Table 4.2   Self-Reflecting Instructional Decision-Making Questions

Question 1: What evidence suggests that I have developed a strong, positive relationship with the child and his or her family?

Response:

Question 2: How is instruction personalized, valuing the child's linguistic and cultural background? In what ways does my instruction connect classroom learning to the child's daily experiences?

Response:

Question 3: In what ways does my instruction give sufficient attention to affect, interest, and motivation?

Response:

Question 4: How does my instruction pay sufficient attention to the development of oral language?

Response:

Question 5: How have I accommodated aspects of reading that can be confusing for ELs?

Response:

Question 6: In what ways is my instruction adjusted for sounds and letters that are different in the child's first language from English so that I can clarify misunderstandings and provide additional practice?

Response:

Question 7: Which instructional adjustments are made to provide students with additional support when they do not seem to understand (e.g., explicit instruction at their level, more opportunities for meaningful practice, etc.)?

Response:

Question 8: Are the books I use at levels students can read and understand?

Response:

(Continued)

Table 4.2   (Continued)

Question 9: What strategies are used to preteach key vocabulary to ensure use of multimedia, real items, appealing photos, charts, and other visuals to help make instruction comprehensible?

Response:

Question 10: What evidence demonstrates that I maintain a focus on the content of students' responses, over form, when checking for comprehension, providing multiple and varied ways of demonstrating learning?

Response:

SUMMARY AND A CAVEAT

The point of this chapter has been to help teachers understand the struggles faced by their ELs while learning to read so that they do not misjudge them and inappropriately refer them to special education. However, we must offer a caveat. Some ELs truly do have LD and would benefit from the extra support they would receive in special education. We do not want our advice to be construed as suggesting teachers should wait until ELs are fully proficient in English before considering whether they might have LD.

In some schools, the tendency has been to take a wait-and-see approach and delay addressing the possibility that ELs are experiencing reading difficulties due to language or learning disabilities (Frances et al., 2006). Because the characteristics associated with language acquisition can mirror those of LD, school personnel have wanted to avoid the possibility of incorrectly placing a child in special education. Certainly we share the concerns behind this approach; however, just as it is a problem to identify a child as having a disability who does not have one, it is also a problem to hold off on providing interventions to ELs who really need them. For this reason, we suggest following the guidelines outlined in this chapter so that reading instruction for all ELs improves and fewer inappropriate referrals are made. Once we have done that, we can feel more confident that the few students who are still experiencing difficulties will benefit from explicit, intensive interventions (e.g., Tier 3; special education) delivered above and beyond what they are receiving in their core Tier 1 and supplemental Tier 2 general education.

NOTE

1. *Evidence-based* and *research-based* are often used interchangeably to refer to an instructional practice that has been the focus of experimental or quasi-experimental research studies and determined to be more effective than a comparison approach.

5

Select Reading Methods for Teaching English Learners

Amy L. Boelé

As discussed in previous chapters, language supports are essential for literacy learning, especially for English learners (Klingner et al., in press). Without appropriate supports, ELs are more likely to be referred for and misplaced into special education (Artiles, Kozleski, Trent, Osher, & Ortiz, 2010; Hamayan et al., 2013; Hoover, 2012; Hoover & Klingner, 2011; Linan-Thompson, 2010; Samson & Lesaux, 2009). When instructional reading methods value language as a resource, students are provided opportunities to engage with spoken and written language in ways that enhance their literacy learning in both languages. This, in turn, supports the instructional efforts in distinguishing language acquisition from language disorder or disability.

Vignette: Examining Effective Reading Curriculum for ELs

Two teams of teachers, one in third grade and one in tenth grade, engaged in a process to self-examine the reading/language arts instruction and curricula they currently delivered to ELs in their elementary and secondary schools. Each team included three classroom teachers. Selection of effective reading and language arts methods for instructing ELs requires consideration of several important factors by the classroom teachers. Each team considered the following in the self-assessment:

(Continued)

(Continued)

- Academic language and English language proficiency level required for successful use of the reading/language arts curricular materials
- Various components of reading instruction incorporated into the instruction, especially vocabulary, fluency, oral language, and comprehension
- Cultural relevance of the reading material used with the students
- Connections between the teaching of discrete skills (e.g., phonics) and comprehension
- Emphasis placed on both language development objectives and content objectives
- Process of connecting basic writing abilities in the development of reading
- Procedures and devices used to measure and monitor learners' reading progress
- Connections made between the school and home environments to support reading

Upon completion of the self-study, instructional recommendations were made about the teachers' existing curricula to ensure a cultural and linguistic responsive reading or language arts program.

Reflection Items

1. To what extent is each of the above items incorporated in your school's elementary reading or secondary language arts curriculum and instruction?

2. Elementary Educators: Summarize items above that require additional implementation in your school; provide examples of best practice reflecting items currently being implemented. Secondary Educators: Select three of the above items and discuss unique challenges encountered to best implement in your secondary school; generate strategies to address the identified challenges.

3. What recommendations would you suggest to other school staffs to best facilitate self-examination of their reading/language arts curriculum and instruction for ELs?

The purpose of this chapter is to present six reading methods that provide ELs with integrated literacy skill development while valuing language usage, such as that described in the vignette. Presentation of each method includes a brief overview, steps or procedures for implementation, skills emphasized, and considerations for use with ELs, based on material found in the different citations for each method. These methods are not all-inclusive and others exist; however, these represent select approaches researched with and found effective in the teaching of reading to ELs. Methods are not presented in order of importance, as each is effective in teaching ELs. The reader is referred to the different sources cited for additional information about each evidence-based reading practice as well as other methods for inclusion in the teaching of reading to struggling ELs. Also, some methods are described on the Intervention Central website (at http://www.interventioncentral.org) and may be consulted for additional insights into implementation.

METHOD 1: LANGUAGE EXPERIENCE APPROACH (LEA)

The language experience approach is a method developed decades ago (Allen, 1979; Thorn, 1969; Waterman, 1969), yet it is still a highly effective practice that capitalizes on ELs' own language and experiences. For example, Herrera, Perez, and Escamilla (2015) described the strengths of using the LEA with bilingual learners, highlighting its ability to enhance the overall learning experience in meaningful ways. The LEA is implemented individually or in pairs, small groups, or whole class format. Each structure has its own strengths, and I will present the method using a paired format (*Note:* The same procedures are used should the LEA be used in one of the other formats). Through the LEA, students discuss a shared experience, and the teacher writes down their account of the experience. This written version becomes the text that teachers can use with students to develop various facets of literacy.

Steps/Procedures

1. Along with the teacher, a pair of students describes an experience they collectively had. It could be a field trip, a school event, or observation of an unusual object, as long as the experience was shared among all of the members. During this process, students use oral language to discuss their reactions and observations of the experience. This affords students opportunities to listen as their partner and teacher use language to describe something familiar and to develop oracy skills as they tell their own account.

2. As the pairs of students dictate the experience, the teacher writes verbatim their account on chart paper by eliciting statements from the students. When students see their words written on the chart paper, they are able to connect the spoken language to the written words. This becomes their text that is used for fluency, vocabulary, and comprehension development.

3. The teacher then reads the text, modeling fluency for the students. Students, in turn, read the text aloud in unison with the teacher, and in pairs, they reread it together multiple times until they are familiar with it.

4. The teacher then uses the account as a resource for developing specific literacy skills.

Vocabulary from the text can be starting places for teaching various word recognition approaches, such as the alphabetic principle, phonics, sight words, or morphological awareness, making certain to also emphasize comprehension.

Skills Emphasized

This method frames discrete skills as embedded within a larger context of literacy and communication. Not only does it integrate the dimensions of language: reading, writing, listening, and speaking, but it situates as well the act of literacy within students' social world and allows them to co-construct the meaning of their experiences. Teachers should be intentional about structuring the literacy skills taught within this approach so that the instruction is meaningful, connected, and focused on areas of need.

Considerations for Use With English Learners

The language experience approach is appropriate for ELs because it incorporates the four dimensions of language: listening, speaking, reading, and writing. Each dimension interacts with the others to build overall language and literacy.

Students are supported in their language development in an authentic context and with direct connections between experiences and the language used to describe those experiences. In using this method, English learners also have an opportunity to establish cross-cultural texts (Landis, Umolu, & Mancha, 2010), which provides additional context and relevance.

METHOD 2: REPEATED READINGS

The strategy of repeated readings of familiar text proved effective with ELs for increasing reading fluency. "Through repeated readings, (ELs) increase their reading rate and accuracy, and when teachers preteach and use the words from the text throughout the lesson, (Els) develop greater comprehension" (Herrera et al., 2015, p. 184). Additionally, as fluency requires practice, repeated readings are helpful for developing speed and accuracy (Vaughn & Bos, 2012). Reading repeatedly may include reading a connected text in multiple iterations or using word walls, flash cards, and reader's theater.

Steps/Procedures

1. Demonstrate to the students how to use the repeated reading procedure.

2. Pair the EL with a more proficient reader.

3. Choose a short, interesting, and culturally responsive passage that students can read relatively easily, followed by discussion of the story, plot, and characters.

4. Preteach vocabulary and provide students the opportunity to hear the passage, whether read by a teacher, peer, or a recording.

5. Instruct each student in the pair to read the passage 3–5 times.

6. Develop a monitoring system for the students to keep track of their reading and accuracy rate, by figuring out how many correct words per minute they read. The teacher frequently should monitor each student's progress. If the readings by the students are recorded, these may be used to assess and monitor progress over time.

7. Incorporate comprehension questions and activities to ensure that students are actively constructing meaning as they read, not just attending to their oral production.

Skills Emphasized

Though the previously described procedure is presented as a paired activity, students can also work in small groups. With partners, one student reads the passage aloud to serve as a model; then, the less fluent reader practices the passage with help from the peer as needed. In small groups, the teacher reads portions of the passage as a model; then the students echo read in unison. Last, the teacher and students read the whole text together. Afterward, students can practice reading the passage individually. This approach is most effective for students whose reading difficulties are rooted in decoding processes, high-frequency words, and word patterns (Herrera et al., 2015). Thus, the reading skills emphasized include vocabulary, fluency, and comprehension.

Considerations for Use With English Learners

Repeated readings have been used successfully with English learners for a variety of reasons. First, it allows them to hear the teacher model fluency while reading. Second, by practicing reading the text aloud themselves, ELs can then attend to the meaning of the text. This procedure moves students beyond word-by-word reading to attending to connected text that is composed into meaningful phrases. Finally, when the vocabulary of the text is generally familiar with some new concepts that are shared across multiple passages, students read the words in multiple contexts, enhancing their understanding of the meaning.

METHOD 3: RECIPROCAL TEACHING

"Reciprocal teaching is an instructional practice identified as a way of improving reading comprehension through explicit teaching of skills needed for metacognition" (McAllum, 2014, p. 26). With reciprocal teaching (Palincsar & Brown, 1984), students use four reading comprehension strategies: summarizing, questioning, clarifying, and predicting. It has been used with elementary and secondary students alike and is designed to support students' comprehension abilities (McAllum, 2014). With teacher direction, students work in collaborative groups and discuss the meaning of the text, facilitated by the four strategies. It is built upon the sociocultural principle of the zone of proximal development, in which learning occurs when it is mediated by the presence of experts, with the students gradually gaining independent expertise (Vygotsky, 1978a).

Steps/Procedures

The teacher initially models the four reading comprehension strategies, providing guidance and feedback as students begin to use the strategies with their peers. Addressing some of the challenges discussed in the previous chapter, reciprocal teaching engages students to draw upon their background knowledge, monitor comprehension, infer meaning, draw conclusions, and evaluate the accuracy of their work.

These are emphasized as students take turns as the dialogue leader, guiding the discussions (Burden & Byrd, 2012). Further, this approach is built upon the principle that mature readers (a) consider how the content of the text fits within their existing understandings of the topics, (b) make and test generalizations, and (c) apply correction strategies when comprehension breaks down (Palincsar & Brown, 1984).

The strategies of focus are summarizing, questioning, clarifying, and predicting (McAllum, 2014). Within all four strategies, students are activating their prior knowledge.

Summarizing: Through summarization, readers attend to the most important ideas. Teachers can then evaluate the extent to which students have understood the text.

Questioning: In generating questions, students also are required to attend to major content. They are asked to formulate teacher-like questions that capture the main ideas.

Clarifying: Clarifying requires students to actively monitor their comprehension and critically evaluate the extent to which they understand the reading material.

Predicting: This feature within the process requires learners to predict what they believe they will learn when they read the material.

Importantly, they base their predictions on clues from text features (e.g., title, headings) and/or from what they have already read about the topic.

Skills Emphasized

As ELs engage in reciprocal teaching activities, they are developing crucial skills required to improve comprehension by adhering to the four comprehension strategies (McAllum, 2014). It is important to provide opportunities for readers of all abilities and levels to participate in the discussion and use of the strategies. Extensive teacher modeling of the strategies is essential. Further, students will need many opportunities to practice the strategies, with increasingly less teacher direction to best comprehend reading material. As students acquire expertise in use of the strategies, the teacher acts as merely a facilitator and supporter, while the students initiate strategy application and use.

Considerations for Use With English Learners

Various authors have discussed the cultural and linguistic effectiveness of reciprocal teaching (Alton-Lee, Westera, & Pulegatoa-Diggins, 2012; Colombo, 2012; Hoover, 2013; McAllum, 2014; Palincsar & David, 1991; Rosenshine & Meister, 1994). Its components of applying background knowledge, paying explicit attention to strategies for comprehension, and using context for engaging in authentic dialogue with peers about text support reading and language development for English learners.

METHOD 4: COLLABORATIVE STRATEGIC READING (CSR)

Adapted from reciprocal teaching, collaborative strategic reading (CSR; Klingner et al., 2012) is a multicomponent strategy model in which students work collaboratively to comprehend text. Key to students' collaborative efforts are various "expert" roles that each member of the group fulfills to guide the others through the strategies. Built upon principles from cognitive psychology (Flavell, 1979) and sociocultural theory (Vygotsky, 1978a), CSR makes dialogue an important component for the process of co-constructing meaning from text.

Strategies are used before, during, and after reading texts so as to support content learning. They include preview, click and clunk, get the gist, and wrap up (see Table 5.1).

Preview: During preview, the teacher tells the students the topic and asks them to think about what they already know, *activating* their background knowledge. The teacher then *builds* students' background knowledge, providing them with definitions and associated images of important terms. She/he then directs the students to look at the title, headings, pictures, captions, and other text features in order to first activate their background knowledge of the topic and second leads them toward a prediction of what they will learn.

Click and Clunk: When students use the click and clunk strategy, they identify unknown words, or clunks. These are words that they cannot define, rather than proper nouns or words they cannot pronounce. Students then apply fix-up strategies in order to figure out the meaning of the clunks, whether using contextual clues or examining the word's morphological structure or by thinking of cognates.

Gist: The gist strategy involves generating a main idea statement about sections of text, with each text passage typically divided into three sections. To frame the gist for each section, students engage in three tasks: (a) identify the most important who or what, (b) identify the most essential part about the most important who or what, and (c) generate a statement that is approximately ten words, or slightly more, combining material from the first two tasks.

Review: After reading the text, the students review, which includes both question generation and writing an overall review statement. When generating questions, students write questions based on the question-answer relationships three-part framework as discussed by Raphael (1986):

1. Right There question—to which the answer can be found explicitly in the text.

2. Think and Search question—requires a synthesis of information from at least two different parts of the text in order to answer.

3. Author and You question—response requires use of information from the text and the reader's own ideas.

Teachers introduce the strategies in phases as illustrated in Table 5.1, which was developed from several sources, including Boelé, Boardman, and Klingner (2013), Klingner et al. (2012), and Scornavacco et al. (2015).

In the first phase (prior to reading), strategies are taught explicitly to a group of students. In the second phase (during reading), students begin to apply the strategies to text in collaborative groups with direct guidance from the teacher, and in the third phase (after reading), students work collaboratively to use the strategies to work toward comprehension of text. The expert roles include leader, clunk expert, gist expert, and question expert.

Table 5.1   Essential Features of Collaborative Strategic Reading (CSR)

The three phases of reading (prior, during, after) include specific tasks completed by learners:

Phase CSR Strategy Skill Sets

Prior to Reading: Preview, brainstorm, build background, predict

During Reading: Click and clunk, identify clunks; employ fix-up strategies (e.g., reread sentence with clunk and those prior to and after the clunk; look for prefixes, suffixes, root words, and cognates)

Get Gist: Identify most important who or what and locate information about the who or what

Generate Gist statement (Note: Repeat during reading strategies three times per text)

After Reading: Wrap up; generate question for each type:

1. Right There

2. Think and Search

3. Author and You; review material by identifying the most important information

Steps/Procedures

When planning a CSR lesson, a few steps are necessary for the teacher:

1. Select an appropriate text, which is usually informational and related to a content area under study. The text should be conducive to learning and applying the strategies. For example, when learning the get-the-gist strategy, texts should not include sections that are essentially lists of disparate facts.

2. Divide the text into three distinct sections.

3. Identify two or three key words to preteach during preview. Find images (e.g., pictures, films, realia, etc.) that support students' understanding of the words.

4. Identify potential clunks and the fix-up strategies that student might use to understand the meaning.

5. Write a gist for each of the three text/passage sections.

6. Write possible questions and a review statement.

7. Organize students into heterogeneous groups and assign each to an expert role.

Skills Emphasized

Through CSR, students engage in a comprehension method that facilitates skill development in preview, brainstorming, and building background knowledge along with problem solving, question generation, and written expression. It is important for teachers to lay a foundation for managing collaborative groups. This may include applying rules for group work (e.g., talk only to members of your group.). In addition to strategy-focused lessons during the initial phase, students can benefit from role-focused lessons to help them understand how to implement the roles in their groups. Cue cards are available for students to use as they engage in the roles. Relatedly, all students should have opportunities to play each of the expert roles. For example, the leader role should not exclusively be assigned to the "good" readers.

Considerations for Use With English Learners

Studies have found CSR to be effective for English learners because of student access to rich opportunities with language (Scornavacco et al., 2015) and of the ways in which students help their peers (Klingner & Vaughn, 2000). Overall, CSR supports ELs in a variety of ways. It provides students with opportunities to access and build their prior knowledge with linguistic, conceptual, and visual supports. Teachers provide comprehensible input with respect to building background knowledge and teaching vocabulary. Within structured language supports for discussion, students have access to academic language and higher-level thinking in an authentic context. Students are taught important reading strategies that can capitalize on their linguistic resources, such as using cognates, and they receive immediate feedback in a low-risk setting.

RESEARCH TO PRACTICE

Colorado CSR

In 2010, researchers collaborated with a large urban school district to use CSR as a major improvement strategy to accelerate reading comprehension district-wide. The ultimate goal of the initiative has been to integrate CSR in all middle-school language arts, science, and social studies classrooms across the district. Over five years, 520 teachers and 8,000 students in twenty-one schools in one large urban school district have implemented CSR. During this time, 1,200 underrepresented families participated through its connected parent engagement component. Schools were supported with coaching, professional development, teacher leaders, and CSR instructional materials. Key highlights of results from four cohorts are detailed below.

Boardman, Moore, and Scornavacco (2015) found that students receiving CSR instruction in Cohort 1 scored higher on the Gates MacGinitie standardized reading comprehension assessment (GMRT) than their peers in control classrooms ($g = .18$, $p < .05$). For this study, twenty-eight sections of social studies/science section pairs were randomly assigned either to CSR or a comparison condition (n = 1,074 students and 19 teachers). This finding is consistent with previous CSR research that used an experimental design to evaluate student outcomes (Vaughn et al., 2011). In analyses conducted on Cohorts 2 and 3, CSR students in five schools made gains similar to students in comparison classes on various reading performance tests (Blackorby et al., 2014a, 2014b). For Cohort 4, random assignment occurred at the teacher level and the study took place in eleven middle schools with 4,383 students and seventy-three teachers that had not previously participated in the initiative. Higher state assessment writing ($g = .19$, $p < .05$) and GMRT reading comprehension ($g = .29$, $p < .05$) scores were found among sixth graders receiving CSR compared to sixth graders in the comparison condition. When combining data across three years, students in CSR received significantly higher state assessment writing scores than students who did not receive CSR ($g = .07$, $p < .05$). In addition, when looking at 659 students in three middle schools who received CSR for two years, results indicated that students who received CSR instruction gained more than one school-year's growth in reading comprehension in each year during the intervention time period, as measured by the GMRT standardized reading assessment ($F(2,9894.6) = 119.2$, $p < .01$; Buckley, Klingner, & Boardman, 2014).

Examining the role of fidelity, or the extent to which teachers implemented CSR as intended, Buckley and Moore (2015) found that higher fidelity to the CSR model is associated with higher reading achievement ($\beta = 0.05$, SE $= 0.02$, p $< .001$). The greatest relative gains were obtained by students who started the intervention with lower scores and for students with disabilities.

Qualitative analyses indicated an increase in collaborative discussions between English language learners (ELs) and their non-EL peers. Case studies were conducted with three teachers, twelve EL students, and thirty-six non-EL students to examine the participation and engagement of ELs in CSR classrooms. Discourse analysis of talk during collaborative groups revealed that students who were exposed to high-quality CSR with teacher-student interactions that focused on academic content and promoting collaboration among group members participated in discussions in similar ways and amounts to non-EL peers (Eppolito, Boardman, Jensen, & Wang, 2014). Guided by these teachers, all students participated in higher-quality discussions than in classrooms without these features.

In terms of sustaining CSR over time, findings from a cross case analysis of interview and survey data of twenty-five principals, district leaders, project members, and teacher leaders from seven middle schools suggest that school leaders are integral to sustaining CSR. School-specific patterns and variations in the perceptions and enactment of stakeholders' roles were related to teacher implementation

(Continued)

(Continued)

of CSR, including the integration into school structures and priorities (Scornavacco, Boardman, & Klingner, 2014). The success of CSR is generated from the commitment of teachers using the strategies and the school administrators who support CSR. Below are some comments made by educators in this CSR project:

CSR Strategies

"I just think they're great strategies to teach the kids, and I think we'd be doing a disservice not to teach them the strategies of how to comprehend or dig deeper, get a bigger picture, make real-world connections with the text. So I really support the CSR strategies within the classroom" (Jane, 7th grade teacher).

Collaborative Grouping

"One thing I really like is that each child is working. It's not just one person that's doing [the] job. And so I really like that each of them is working on it and that the expert is just facilitating the conversation about it" (Margaret, 8th grade teacher).

High-Quality Implementation

"I am amazed by the consistent implementation of key academic language used by our students. It is because of CSR that our students are making that jump to the next level" (Alan, middle school assistant principal).

METHOD 5: INSTRUCTIONAL CONVERSATIONS (IC)

Instructional conversations (IC) was originally developed as a framework for dialogic talk for ELs and students with disabilities (Echevarria, 1995; Goldenberg, 1992–1993; Roskos, Boehlen, & Walker, 2000; Saunders & Goldenberg, 1999; Saunders, Patthey-Chavez, & Goldenberg, 1997; Tharp & Gallimore, 1988; What Works Clearinghouse [WWC], 2006). IC is built on a sociocultural framework that views the teacher's role as a facilitator of student movement through the zone of proximal development (Echevarria, 1995; Roskos et al., 2000). Instructional conversations include extended discussions between and among students and the teacher, in which statements are analyzed, clarified, and expanded upon to engage learners and discuss reading material (Goldenberg, 1992–1993). The IC approach has been compared to traditional basal approaches, and it has been found to yield higher levels of discourse and greater participation.

Steps/Procedures

1. The teacher ensures that the social and physical organization of the classroom is conducive to conversation among various groups of students.

2. When planning lessons, the teacher generates clear academic language and content objectives, toward which the dialogue is guided. He/she shares these objectives with the students.

3. When facilitating the discussion, the teacher is intentional about doing the following:

    a. Ensures that students are talking at a higher rate/more frequently than the teacher and that there is an equitable balance across the students, while still allowing for self-initiated speaking turns

    b. Uses a thematic focus, of text or of concepts

    c. Activates background knowledge

    d. Provides direct teaching with exploration

    e. Asks few known answer questions

    f. Promotes more complex language (e.g., "Tell me more," "What do you mean by that?")

    g. Elicits justification for statements (e.g., "How do you know that?")

    h. Encourages students to respond to each other to build a connected discourse

    i. Restates students' words. When teachers restate students' ideas by using expanded, or different, language, they should be careful to check with the student to determine if they are correctly conveying his or her ideas

    j. Clarifies when necessary

4. Teachers and students evaluate whether or not their conversation met the academic language and content objectives presented at the outset.

Skills Emphasized

IC assists ELs to develop skills associated with intentional dialogue, supporting and defending ideas, and evaluating other perspectives. The teacher's questions within the instructional conversations method are intended to elicit extensions of student thought and bases for students' statements or positions; few questions should seek responses that allow for only a single correct answer (Echevarria, 1995; Roskos et al., 2000). Questioning practices that align with the parameters of instructional conversations are more likely to lead to richer opportunities for students to display deeper levels of thought and interaction with text.

Considerations for Use With English Learners

The What Works Clearinghouse (WWC, 2006) rated IC as an intervention that showed statistically significant positive effects for ELs. Previously, Echevarria (1995) studied the effect of instructional conversations on language and concept development of Hispanic students with learning disabilities. Even when the rules of discourse were not explicitly stated, students were able to take on roles consistent with the framework. Importantly, Echevarria concluded that "students with learning disabilities [will use] higher levels of discourse when given the opportunity to do so" (p. 551). This approach is beneficial for English learners because it challenges them to engage in higher-level thinking, and it supports their language development as they are asked to elaborate or provide justification to their ideas. Further, questions in an IC approach will activate and build upon students' background knowledge, clarify student ideas, connect the discourse, and encourage language production.

METHOD 6: CLASSWIDE PEER TUTORING

Classwide peer tutoring (CWPT) was developed in the 1980s through the University of Kansas Juniper Children's Project. It is a research-based method (Smith, Polloway, Patton, & Dowdy, 2012) that employs a peer-mediated approach in which pairs of students work together in a game-like context to develop reading skills. Pairs of students take turns in the roles of student and tutor, with the tutor posing to the student questions related to concepts initially taught by the teacher. CWPT was designed to be integrated into use with most existing reading curricula, and it was found to have potentially positive effects on general reading achievement (WWC, 2007).

Steps/Procedures

1. Students are taught the process of working in pairs. The teacher focuses on the importance of collaboration, fairness, encouragement, and positive corrective feedback. She/he may use role play to reinforce the procedures.

2. Assign pairs and teams: To organize the pairs of students at the beginning of the week, the teacher creates a list of the students in the class, ordering them by skill proficiency. Then, the teacher

divides the list in half and pairs the top student of the top half with the top student of the bottom half, the second student of the top half with the second student of the bottom half, and so on. The teacher creates teams for a class competition.

3. Students engage in the peer tutoring process. The tutor asks questions, and the student responds. The tutor evaluates the response, provides feedback, and awards points accordingly.

4. Points from each pair are tallied daily, and the team with the most points is announced to the class.

5. At the end of the week, the students are tested on the content from that week.

Skills Emphasized

Although CWPT was initially developed for beginning reading skills, it can be implemented in other content areas. It is typically used for practice with discrete skills that can be memorized.

Considerations for Use With English Learners

CWPT was originally designed and implemented with elementary-grade-level English learners (Greenwood, Arreaga-Mayer, Utley, Gavin, & Terry, 2001). It provides ELs with authentic interaction with peers in a fun and engaging context. Students experience contexts in which they can practice and develop language and reading skills. Hoover (2013) and Gersten and Jimenez (1994) discussed a variety of features within CWPT that reflect effective reading instruction for ELs including respect for diversity, scaffolding, challenging curricula, cooperative learning, and other related ESL strategies. Additionally, Greenwood, Terry, Utley, Montagna, and Walker (1993) found a statistically significant difference in the reading performance of students who engaged in CWPT, as compared to a control group, further suggesting effectiveness as an acceptable reading method for use with ELs.

SUMMARY

Methods for teaching English learners to read require multiple components. First and foremost, they need to be delivered in a culturally and linguistically responsive supportive environment (Klingner, Boelé, Linan-Thompson, & Rodriguez, 2014). Additionally, ELs benefit from the opportunity to use language in authentic contexts, integrating the four language domains: listening, speaking, reading, and writing. Similarly, instruction should make as many cross language connections within and across the domains as possible (Escamilla, Ruiz-Figueroa, Hopewell, Butvilofsky, & Sparrow, 2010). English learners should be challenged to engage with complex ideas in texts, using higher levels of thinking, avoiding use of reading texts written only at lower levels of complexity. Educators support students' understanding in a variety of ways, including building upon background knowledge, providing explicit instruction, supporting understanding of content through nonlinguistic means, making the content relevant, and intentionally providing students opportunities to participate in dialogue at challenging levels. Finally, most of the methods described here are intentionally designed for peer interaction, which is essential for effectively educating ELs. As reading is a social activity, engagement with peers is critical when developing reading abilities of English learners.

6

Special Education Assessment of ELs

John J. Hoover and
Laura Méndez Barletta

A variety of assessment devices and practices (i.e., multiple assessments) are undertaken to best meet the needs of ELs who show initial signs of struggling with learning (Basterra et al., 2011). However, Ortiz et al. (2011) found that "data from three interrelated studies of English Language Learners who were identified as having reading-related learning disabilities suggest that the majority of participants were misclassified" (p. 316). Issues resulting from using only one or two norm-referenced testing scores of ELs indicate the importance of multiple forms of assessment, including authentic assessment.

The focus of this chapter is assessment-related issues and practices that most contribute to appropriate (and inappropriate) assessment of ELs. Though the primary emphasis is on linguistic features, cultural aspects of assessment are also important. In this chapter, we address issues associated with assessment devices and practices, followed by decision-making implications discussed in the next chapter. The linguistic issues that shape selection of appropriate assessment devices and practices are primarily emphasized in this chapter, with more focused attention on the role of cultural teachings and values presented in Chapter 7. Collectively, Chapters 6 and 7 provide a solid foundation for assisting educators to (a) deliver culturally and linguistically responsive assessment and (b) interpret appropriately the assessment results through effective decision-making practices and considerations. Specific chapter topics include an overview of appropriate referrals of ELs for special education, EL linguistic testing issues, and two highly appropriate assessment practices (i.e., Curriculum-Based Measurement [CBM],

Dynamic Assessment). We begin with our vignette describing an assessment situation that highlights some of the chapter features addressed.

Vignette: Culturally and Linguistically Responsive Assessment Procedures

An elementary school located in a rural county community has an overrepresentation of ELs in special education, and the principal wishes to establish an assessment process that is more culturally and linguistically responsive to the diverse needs of the student population. Findings from an initial examination of the existing assessment procedures and devices suggest that the process itself is contributing to the misidentification of ELs for learning disabilities, particularly in the area of reading. The EL student population brings a variety of cultural and linguistic qualities and strengths to the teaching and learning environment, and the principal is concerned that the school staff lacks sufficient training and skill sets necessary to best understand its school's diversity to select unbiased and culturally and linguistically responsive assessment devices and practices. Subsequently, through self-assessment, the school educators determined that a need exists for becoming more skilled with applying several important assessment features to best establish and sustain a culturally and linguistically responsive assessment process:

- Second language acquisition stages of development and the role of using both native and English languages in the assessment of reading strengths and needs
- Interrelationship among culture, language, reading achievement, and suspected learning disability characteristics
- Reality that the assessment devices being used with their bilingual learners were developed primarily with mono-speaking English students thereby creating linguistic assessment challenges for ELs
- Influence of home teachings and values on ELs' preferred approaches to learning and instructional methods
- Role and impact of limited proficiency in both first and second languages on reading development and assessment
- Effects on reading of limited or interrupted formal educational experiences in US schools
- Significance of using multiple assessments and data sources (i.e., classroom-based authentic and diagnostic) to best identify ELs' reading skills and learning conditions under which reading skills are best acquired

The above items represent some of the key elements needed for delivering a culturally and linguistically responsive assessment for ELs.

Reflective Items

1. To what extent do the above items shape your school's assessment process? Which items require further development to improve the process?

2. Design a professional development plan for helping your school staff acquire and incorporate each of the above elements into the school-wide assessment process.

3. Self-assess current knowledge of each of the above items and develop a personal action plan to increase your own knowledge and skills in the lowest-rated items.

As previously discussed in Chapter 2, students who do not demonstrate adequate progress toward curricular benchmarks through the use of evidence-based interventions in MTSS may eventually be referred for special education evaluation and possible placement. In addition to various cultural and linguistic considerations discussed in the previous chapters and the above vignette, to reduce measurement error and increase assessment validity, other factors must also be addressed in the formal assessment of ELs suspected of having a disability. An underlying assumption when assessing ELs is that every effort is made to ensure that learning characteristics and behaviors are assessed, observed, and interpreted appropriately to avoid inappropriate referrals and misplacement into special education (Hoover & Klingner, 2011; Ortiz et al., 2011). These efforts, along with addressing the items in the vignette, are essential in the assessment process for ELs to avoid misinterpreting language acquisition as learning disabilities (LD). Therefore, student assessment assumes a central role in the education of ELs in MTSS to meet a variety of purposes:

- Aiding educators in monitoring students' academic language development (in their first and/or second language)
- Helping teachers monitor instructional quality and associated progress of ELs' day-to-day academic and social-emotional learning
- Determining the best instructional situation, such as bilingual education, ESL instruction, Tier 2 instruction, or program for students with gifts and talents, to name a few
- Informing the referral and placement of students for possible special education

Different states and school districts use (or should use) various methods to assess ELs. That is, effective assessment draws upon multiple methods such as home language surveys, observations, interviews, grades, work samples, curriculum-based measurements (CBMs), and formal diagnostic testing to monitor and provide students intensive intervention (i.e., Tier 3) or special education services. Aceves and Orosco (2014) discussed the assessment of diverse learners stating that "teachers should select informal measures and assessment procedures and formal (i.e., standardized) assessments that consider students' linguistic and cultural identities" (p. 19). It is important to note that when ELs are tested to determine academic achievement, the tests tend to be administered in English. Frequently, ELs do not fully understand test instructions or the tests themselves (Abedi, 2011; Basterra et al., 2011; Zehler, Hopstock, Fleishman, & Greniuk, 1994). When an achievement test is administered in a language a child does not fully understand, the test becomes a language test rather than a test of knowledge of subject area content or skill. It is also important to remember that proper assessment for special education begins with a proper referral. Drawing on four decades of research, educators are provided guidance for ensuring that a special education referral of an EL, specifically for learning disabilities in reading, is culturally and linguistically responsive.

WHAT CONSTITUTES AN APPROPRIATE EL REFERRAL?

An appropriate referral for an EL is grounded in a culturally and linguistically responsive multi-tiered instructional process (Hoover, 2012; National Center on Response to Intervention [NCRI], n.d.), creating unique challenges for all educators. These authors also wrote that proper referrals guide educators in the assessment process by helping reduce bias, poor validity, and misplacement in special education by making certain that ELs who are placed with a disability are properly identified, based on true disability rather than cultural and/or linguistic learning differences (Garcia & Ortiz, 2006; Ortiz et al., 2011). A proper referral is critical in that "most students referred for consideration of special education are eventually placed in special education programs" (Hosp & Reschy, 2003, p. 70).

Prior to referral of an English learner, educators are required to ensure the delivery of instruction designed to improve the acquisition of a second language in Tier 1 general education, with supports from English language development (ELD) instruction. Contrary to the perception of some educators, English language development instruction is delivered as core Tier 1 instruction (i.e., not Tier 2 or 3), and it should not be confused with specially designed instruction (i.e., special education). That is, providing ELs appropriate opportunities to learn through delivery of culturally and linguistically responsive instruction, including English language development, is a requirement prior to referral for special education eligibility assessment.

Also, a University of Texas Meadows Center document (Meadows Center, 2014) provides examples of second language learner behaviors that may be confused with a language or learning disability. Similar behaviors include articulation and pronunciation errors, poor comprehension, difficulty following directions, anxious behaviors, or poor oral language abilities, to name a few. As emphasized in previous chapters and expanded on in this and Chapter 7, educators who are knowledgeable of stages and behaviors in second language acquisition are best positioned to reduce misinterpretations of language development as reading types of learning disabilities. This, in turn, reduces inappropriate referrals of ELs for unneeded special education.

RESEARCH TO PRACTICE

Culturally and Linguistically Responsive Referral Project

Hoover and Erickson (2015) completed a project designed to improve and strengthen a rural county school district's referral process for ELs. The district had 37 percent ELs who were overrepresented in special education. Prior to the referral project, many of the research-based items recommended for inclusion in a referral for ELs were not typically addressed. The project was designed to gather research about the best practice necessary in the referral process for ELs by identifying essential cultural and linguistic features to consider prior to referral. The project was developed and implemented through a university–school district partnership and included literature reviews, expert review and analysis, focus group input, and year-long piloting. The primary project outcome was the piloted ten-item culturally and linguistically responsive referral guide as illustrated below. Provided are the referral features and the rationale for inclusion in the referral process and guide (Hoover & Erickson, 2015):

Checklist of EL Referral Items and Rationale

____ *Referral Feature 1*: Minimum of eight achievement data points gathered and charted.

Rationale: A proper EL referral is grounded in appropriate progress monitoring with results accurately illustrated.

____ *Referral Feature 2*: Consideration of referral body of evidence with true peers.

Rationale: Examination of why the struggling EL is being referred over other struggling ELs from the same classroom or small-group learning environment is essential to make certain that learning is compared with true peers, while avoiding comparison with non-ELs (i.e., true peers are ELs with similar English language proficiency, experiential background, time in school or program, etc.).

____ *Referral Feature 3*: English language development (ELD) is prioritized and emphasized in each instructional MTSS level.

Rationale: ELs in different stages of acquiring English (i.e., WIDA ACCESS levels 1–6) require development and use of English in both a defined ELD setting and the general classroom (i.e., ELD in both types of settings is the preferred structure).

(Continued)

(Continued)

____ *Referral Feature* 4: If bilingual or emerging bilingual, both native and English, languages are used and encouraged in the education of ELs.

Rationale: For students who are bilingual and/or acquiring English, the benefits in the use of both native and English languages are well documented in the literature and should form the foundation for effective MTSS instructional levels.

____ *Referral Feature 5*: Proper EL referral requires evidence of high-quality culturally and linguistically responsive Tier 1 instruction.

Rationale: Reducing unnecessary EL referrals begins with effective Tier 1 core instruction.

____ *Referral Feature 6*: High-quality, culturally/linguistically responsive Tier 2 supplemental instruction is delivered and documented prior to referral.

Rationale: A proper EL referral requires culturally and linguistically responsive supplemental instruction provided as Tier 2 in which selected interventions are research-based for use with ELs.

____ *Referral Feature 7*: Body of evidence includes relevant work samples.

Rationale: Performance-based work samples are essential to an appropriate EL referral to reduce bias often associated with progress monitoring and other assessments designed primarily for non-ELs.

____ *Referral Feature 8*: Referral body of evidence includes material gathered from multiple sources.

Rationale: The complexities and potential misuses of assessment information are offset through collection of referral evidence gathered from several sources thereby reducing the tendency to rely solely on one or two pieces of information.

____ *Referral Feature 9*: Indicators of a learning disability (LD) are observed and recorded.

Rationale: Evidence of behaviors typically associated with the disability for which the EL is being referred (e.g., learning disability) should be observable and documented relative to true peers.

____ *Referral Feature 10*: Potential learning problems are evident in both languages/cultures, if the EL is bilingual or an emerging bilingual.

Rationale: Learning behaviors typically associated with a learning disability (e.g., processing, short-term memory, significant social deficits, etc.) should be exhibited in both languages/cultures to be considered evidence of that disability.

As shown, the project researchers identified, reviewed, and piloted a guide that contains several important features essential to making an appropriate EL referral. The extent to which one or more of these features is absent or not evident raises a "red flag" concerning the appropriateness of the referral. When the guide was applied to previously referred ELs, one important finding was that many of the items were not found to exist in the referral body of evidence. District adoption of the referral guide and process followed the development and piloting thereby improving the referral process for ELs in one rural county school district. The overall conclusion based on this research is that each of the ten referral items requires some level of confirmation in order to make a proper EL referral and ensure subsequent proper assessment.

EL TEST ISSUES AND SPECIAL EDUCATION ELIGIBILITY

Once referred properly, additional concerns surface regarding a culturally and linguistically responsive assessment for special education eligibility. Specifically, the "process for determining whether students' difficulties are due to the normal process of English language acquisition or limited opportunity for acculturative knowledge acquisition rather than a disability is neither well understood nor applied by school personnel" (Rinaldi, Ortiz, & Gamm, n.d.). In support, other researchers have expressed concerns over the validity of assessments and classification procedures for ELs that affect both instruction and assessment decisions (Basterra et al., 2011), particularly for special education (Hoover & Klingner, 2011). However, EL students with lower levels of English proficiency may experience a more critical problem. These students may be misidentified as students with LD, since deficiencies in English may be misinterpreted as a sign of LD or reading disabilities (Abedi, 2004a, 2011; Ortiz et al., 2011). The following challenges contribute to the problematic nature of EL testing:

- Academic language factors affect testing performance of ELs, which in turn, influences educator perceptions about ELs and suspected LD.
- Similarities between language background characteristics and the level of English proficiency may make EL students with lower levels of English particularly vulnerable for misclassification in learning and/or reading disabilities.
- Misrepresentation is significant for ELs, and educators must better understand the role of language in assessments conducted in English to ensure reliable and valid testing results.

Overall, educators conducting a formal assessment of an EL for special education within the MTSS process must keep in mind the following general testing characteristics:

1. ELs generally perform lower than non-ELs on content-based assessments (i.e., math, science, social sciences), even though they might not actually know less.

2. Low English language proficiency affects instruction and assessment results.

3. Language background variables may confound ELs' content-based assessment outcomes.

4. Assessments for EL students have lower validity and reliability, particularly for those at the lower end of the English proficiency spectrum (Abedi, 2004a)—that is, WIDA ACCESS 1–6.

5. Academic language factors may be a source of measurement error, affecting validity and reliability (Basterra et al., 2011).

Therefore, given the influences that language has on testing, educators conducting formal assessment of ELs for possible special education must consider three key language features to ensure valid results:

- linguistic features
- dialect and register
- linguistic misalignment

Second language learners (particularly those at the lower level of English proficiency distribution) may have more difficulty with test items due to unfamiliarity with select words and/or complex linguistic structures.

LINGUISTIC FEATURES

A variety of linguistic features can impact assessment results for ELs (Basterra et al., 2011). When considering the needs of ELs, reliable and valid assessment results are critical to making sound educational decisions. Assessment is *reliable* if it produces consistent results. A *valid* assessment occurs when the assessment measures what it purports to measure (Best & Kahn, 2006; Cohen & Spenciner, 2015). Various linguistic features may impact formal assessment results, especially comprehension, and must be considered in the special education assessment process as illustrated in Table 6.1. ELs' lack of familiarity with these linguistic features will usually generate unreliable and invalid test results.

Table 6.1   Linguistic Features in the Assessment of ELs

Feature	Instructional Example	Assessment Considerations for ELs
Word frequency/ familiarity	Words most frequently used in reading/spoken language	Words high on a general frequency list for English are likely to be familiar to most readers because they are encountered often. Readers who encounter familiar words are more likely to interpret them quickly and correctly, having a positive impact on comprehension and test results.
Word length	Use of single syllable to multisyllable words	Words tend to be longer as their frequency of use decreases. In one study, language minority students performed better on math test items with shorter word lengths than items with longer word lengths.
Sentence length	Use of two–three word sentences through lengthy multi-word sentences	The length of a sentence serves as an index for its complexity and can be used to predict comprehension difficulty.
Active/ passive voice	Use of active (e.g., Juan hit the ball) versus passive (e.g., The ball was hit by Juan) structure	Passive constructions can be especially challenging to nonnative English speakers.
Long noun phrases	Sentences that contain several interconnected phrases requiring learners to comprehend more complex ideas	Noun phrases with several modifiers provide a potential source of difficulty in test items. Romance languages (e.g., Spanish, French, Italian, Portuguese) make less use of compounding than English.
Long question phrases	Questions that contain longer phrases and numerous words	Longer question phrases occur less frequently than short question phrases. Low-frequency expressions (long question phrases) are often harder to read/understand.
Comparative structures	Comparing/Contrasting ideas	Comparative constructions often represent potential sources of difficulty for nonnative speakers as well as for speakers of nonmainstream dialects.
Prepositional phrases	Phrases within a sentence that begin with a preposition	Students may experience difficulty with prepositions. English and Spanish may differ in their use of prepositions.

(Continued)

Table 6.1   (Continued)

Feature	Instructional Example	Assessment Considerations for ELs
Sentence and discourse structure	Complexities of words/phrases used in a sentence or group of sentences	Although sentences may have a similar number of words, one may be more difficult to understand due to syntax complexities or discourse relationships among sentences.
Subordinate clause	Clauses in sentences designed to show relationships and connect ideas that do not stand alone	For many students, subordinate clauses may increase the complexity of the sentence generating confusion or lack of understanding.
Relative clauses	Clauses that characterize (e.g., The dog, who loves bones, barked for a treat.)	Relative clauses are less frequent in spoken English than in written English, and some students may have limited exposure to them and their usage in writing/reading.
Concrete versus abstract/impersonal presentations	Use of concrete examples or statements, avoiding the use of vague abstractions	Students tend to perform better when content is presented in concrete rather than abstract terms.
Negation	Use of negatives in sentences (e.g., no, not, none, never)	Sentences that contain negations are more difficult to understand than affirmative sentences. In Spanish, double negative constructions retain a negative meaning, rather than the affirmative meaning as in English.

Sources: Developed from material found in Abedi (2011, 2004b); Abedi et al. (1997); Adams (1990); Basterra et al. (2011); Celce-Murcia and Larsen-Freeman (1983); Cummins et al. (1988); Freeman (1978); Hunt (1965); Mestre (1988); Orr (1987); Slobin (1968).

LINGUISTIC MISALIGNMENT: ASSESSMENT IMPLICATIONS FOR EDUCATORS

Abedi (2011) best sums up the issues illustrated in the above table: "Low performance of ELL students on content-based assessments may be due to a lack of understanding of the language of the test rather than a lack of content knowledge" (p. 50). Though in-depth understanding of these and similar linguistic features is typically beyond the training of most educators, a working knowledge serves a most critical need by having educators compare the linguistic features found in the questions on the selected test to the linguistic features most associated with the EL's stage of second language acquisition and home language. To the extent that the learner possesses linguistic qualities, similar to the test items, is the extent to which the test might be considered valid. Conversely, significant misalignment between linguistic features known by the EL and those used in test items indicates lack of validity in using that particular test with the student. Item analysis looking for evidence of the linguistic features in failed test items serves to inform testers of the language validity of the test used with the EL (i.e., Is the test primarily an English test or does learner possess sufficient English to take the test?). The phenomenon of linguistic *misalignment* between linguistic features that a testing device requires and what the EL possesses is discussed further in a subsequent section of this chapter. The guide presented in Table 6.3 specifically addresses the above linguistic features.

DIALECT AND REGISTER

Dialect and register are as important as overall language abilities in affecting the validity of measures of academic achievement for ELs (Solano-Flores, 2004; Trumbull & Solano-Flores, 2011). Since dialect and register cannot be disassociated from language, testing policies and practices for ELs must consider these varieties of language in order to make more substantial progress toward the use of valid and fair measures to assess ELs' academic achievement.

Dialect and Language

Dialect is a variation of a language used by a subset of a larger population who shares a common language (Trumbull & Solano-Flores, 2011). Dialects are different ways of expressing the same idea as they reflect the social structure (e.g., class, gender, and origin). Every language has different dialects or varieties. Every version of a language is a dialect. In other words, standard English is a dialect. Linguists define dialect as a variety of a language that is distinguished from other varieties of the same language through use of pronunciation, grammar, vocabulary, discourse conventions, and other linguistic features (Solano-Flores, 2004). Dialects pertain to the linguistic and cultural characteristics of the students who belong to the same broad linguistic group. Dialects are governed by defined systems whose deviations from other dialects of the same language are systematic rather than random (Crystal, 1997). For example, a soft drink may be referred to as *soda, pop, soft drink,* or the brand name of the product. In another example, an automobile may be referred to as *wheels, car,* or *auto* by different people living in different parts of the country.

Influence of Dialect in the Assessment of ELs

- Although the term *dialect* often refers to the language used by people from a particular geographic or social group or to mean a substandard variety of a language, *everyone* speaks a dialect (Basterra et al., 2011; Preston, 2003).

- Standard English is one of many recognized English dialects (i.e., variations within the English language occur based on factors such as region of the country or socioeconomic status; Wardhaugh, 2002).
- The origins of variations in dialects stem, in part, from contact with other languages or from specific features of a language shared by its speakers (Wolfram, 2000).
- Linguists note that several nonstandard English dialects are "as complex and as regularly patterned as other varieties of English, which are considered more standard" (Farr & Ball, 1999, p. 206).
- The dialect associated with a form of spoken English by African Americans, African American Vernacular English (AAVE), contains language structures similar in complexity to standard English dialect.

Register and Language

Register refers to a variation of a language determined by situation or context (Trumbull & Solano-Flores, 2011). Registers are ways of saying different things; they reflect social processes. A register is the words and patterns of usage that the members of a particular culture or group typically associate with a specific context. It is language used for a specific purpose. For example, baseball players share a common set of terms and way of talking, or register, about their sport. A *bag, plate,* and *strike* mean something different when talking about a baseball game than when discussing shopping, doing the dishes, or boycotting work. A situation, and its associated register, may vary in degree of specificity. The register is recognized as a specific selection of words, structures, and even body language; however, a register is defined in terms of meanings (Halliday, 1978; Trumbull & Solano-Flores, 2011). As related to student assessment, registers have to do with academic language and the contexts in which students receive instruction or are tested through the use of language.

Influence of Register in the Assessment of ELs

- ELs' responses to assessment items vary across items and languages (Solano-Flores, 2004).
- ELs' linguistic proficiencies vary tremendously across language domains (i.e., writing, reading, listening, speaking) and contexts (e.g., at home, at school, with friends, with relatives).
- ELs' linguistic proficiencies are shaped by schooling (e.g., bilingual or full immersion programs) and the way in which language instruction is implemented (e.g., by emphasizing reading or writing in one language or the other) (Genesee, 1994; Herrera et al., 2015; Valdés & Figueroa, 1994).

- Students might perform better in their first language than in English for some test items but better in English than in their first language for other items (Basterra et al., 2011).

Therefore, when assessing ELs, practitioners should determine

1. English language proficiency,

2. native language proficiency,

3. content area strengths/weaknesses in *each* language,

4. the student's experiential background,

5. ways in which language instruction has been implemented with the student.

Assessment Implications for Educators

In regard to dialect, when assessing ELs, practitioners must (a) know that whenever ELs are tested (in any language) *some* dialect of that language is being tested (most often the standard form of the language); (b) consider the student's pronunciation, grammar, and vocabulary features, which may differ from those of other students who speak the same language but a different dialect; (c) identify the linguistic and cultural characteristics of the learner; (d) remember that the dialect of the language in which students are tested is a powerful influence that shapes student testing performance; and (e) understand that knowing more about a student's dialect is crucial to obtaining valid academic achievement test results (Basterra et al., 2011; Solano-Flores, 2004).

In regard to register, when assessing ELs, practitioners should consider the extent to which the learner is familiar with these terms:

1. *Semantics* (e.g., "root" has different meanings in colloquial language and in mathematics), word frequency (e.g., "ion" is mostly restricted to the content of science)

2. *Idiomatic expressions* (e.g., the option "None of the above" is a phrase used almost exclusively in multiple choice tests)

3. *Notation* (e.g., "A divided by B is represented as A/B")

4. *Conventions* (e.g., uppercase letters are used to denote variables); syntactical structures (e.g., the structure of multiple choice items in which an incomplete sentence—the stem—is followed by several phrases—the options)

5. *Ways of building arguments* (e.g., "Let A be an integer number")

LINGUISTIC MISALIGNMENT: ASSESSMENT IMPLICATIONS FOR EDUCATORS

Linguistic misalignment is defined as the mismatch between the features of the dialect and the register used in a test, and the features of the dialect and the register used by students (Solano-Flores, 2004). An example of this type of misalignment may be found in a word or a syntactical structure on a test that is uncommon in the dialect and register used by the student being assessed. It is important for practitioners to keep in mind that while one or two misalignments will not necessarily affect student performance, multiple misalignment instances in the same test can have significant detrimental effects on test results for ELs (Solano-Flores, 2004). Two dimensions of linguistic misalignment are evident:

> *Frequency* refers to the number of instances of misalignment (e.g., an unfamiliar idiomatic expression, a word of low frequency in the student's dialect, a slight variation in a notation convention), which can range from none to many.

> *Criticality* refers to the importance of instances of misalignment, which can range from trivial to significant (Solano-Flores, 2004).

Test items are likely to be *linguistically sound* when there are few or mild instances of linguistic misalignment. Items are likely to be linguistically challenging when there are many unimportant instances of linguistic misalignment—each of which would not affect the student's performance by itself—or when there are few but severe instances of linguistic misalignment (Solano-Flores, 2004).

Test items can also be thought of as unintended samples of dialect and register. When either too many mild or too few but severe instances of linguistic misalignment occur, the likelihood increases that an item affects performance due to language. However, given its significance, linguistic misalignment is extremely difficult to predict with judgmental methods. Table 6.2 provides a survey for educators to use as an initial guide to determine the appropriateness of an assessment device based on language, dialect, and register factors discussed in this chapter.

As shown, a variety of factors are included, and the more of these that exist as *yes*, the more confident the tester may be in recognizing the need to accommodate language, dialect, and register in the assessment process for ELs. In addition, one strategy for addressing linguistic misalignment consists of ensuring that the number of items included in a test is large enough to ensure that language will not be a source of measurement error in spite of the fact that some of the linguistic features of the test represent instances of misalignment (Solano-Flores, 2004).

Table 6.2   Survey for Determining Linguistic Appropriateness of Assessment Device

Linguistic Feature	Response	
	Yes	No
Test language is similar to instructional language	Y	N
Test norms reflect a variety of dialects within the language spoken by the test taker	Y	N
The standard dialect used in the test is determined to be the most socially acceptable dialect in the language of the test (e.g., Spanish; Haitian-Creole)	Y	N
The dialect of the language found in the test is compatible with the dialect used by the test taker	Y	N
Test avoids the use of colloquial terms with unusual meanings	Y	N
Word meanings found on a test are similar to their use in colloquial language	Y	N
Test taker understands meaning of expressions typically found only in tests (e.g., "none of the above")	Y	N
Test questions are not in conflict with previous school experiences of test taker (e.g., understands the difference between a comma and a decimal point)	Y	N
The number of test items with unfamiliar expressions is low	Y	N
Summary of Scoring: Number Identified as _____ Y (Yes) _____ N (No)		

Source: Developed from material found in Solano-Flores (2004).

In summary, many concerns over the reliability and validity of assessments for ELs are due, in part, to students' lack of familiarity with the linguistic features embedded in English tests. One reason it is so challenging to assess ELs accurately is that the field has not yet developed a precise test of language proficiency (Herrera et al., 2015; Langdon, 1989; Ortiz, 1997). A related challenge is that the accuracy of the information about an EL's language background obtained from a Home Language Survey may be suspect, since inconsistent information may be provided by the parents for a variety of reasons, including concerns over equity of opportunity for their children, citizenship issues and immigration status, and the literacy of the parent (Abedi, 2004b, 2011).

EXPERIENTIAL BACKGROUND WITH LINGUISTIC FEATURES

Assessment tools that have complex linguistic structures may provide inaccurate results for ELs (Abedi, 2004a). Table 6.3 provides a survey for educators to use to rate ELs' experiential backgrounds with linguistic features found in assessment devices.

Table 6.3   Rating ELs' Experiential Background With Assessment Linguistic Features

Linguistic Feature	None	Little	Some	Extensive
Word frequency/familiarity	1	2	3	4
(English words high on a general frequency list)				
Word length	1	2	3	4
(Longer versus shorter word lengths)				
Sentence length	1	2	3	4
(Longer versus shorter sentences)				
Active/Passive voice constructions	1	2	3	4
(Exposure to passive voice)				
Long noun phrases	1	2	3	4
(Noun phrases with several modifiers)				
Long question phrases	1	2	3	4
(Longer rather than shorter question phrases)				
Prepositional phrases	1	2	3	4
(Interpretation of prepositions)				
Sentence and discourse structure	1	2	3	4
(Syntactic structure or discourse relationships among sentences)				
Subordinate clause	1	2	3	4
(Clause in a sentence that cannot stand alone)				
Relative clauses	1	2	3	4
(A dependent clause introduced by a relative pronoun)				

Linguistic Feature	None	Little	Some	Extensive
Concrete versus abstract/impersonal presentations	1	2	3	4
(Abstract versus concrete and expository versus narrative)				
Negation	1	2	3	4
(Sentences containing negations, e.g., no, not, none, never)				
Comparative Structures	1	2	3	4
Comparing/Contrasting Ideas				

Sources: Developed from material found in Abedi (2011, 2004b); Abedi et al. (1997); Adams (1990); Basterra et al. (2011); Celce-Murcia and Larsen-Freeman (1983); Cummins et al. (1988); Freeman (1978); Hunt (1965); Mestre (1988); Orr (1987); Slobin (1968).

The reliability of the commonly used standardized assessments in content-based areas may be negatively affected by the complex linguistic structure of test items, such as those presented in the above guide. Decisions based on the results of formal special education assessments, including those made within MTSS, may be problematic for EL students and other subgroups of students who may have limited English language proficiency, lacking familiarity with these linguistic features. As a result, assessment of ELs for special education must include the use of authentic assessment to best understand their linguistic features and educational needs.

AUTHENTIC ASSESSMENT

Authentic assessment reflects real-world experiences and learning providing a more educationally relevant context for measuring student knowledge and skills (Cohen & Spenciner, 2015). In regard to diverse learners, some special educators are often not well informed when assessing students who primarily speak a language other than English or whose ethnic and linguistic backgrounds differ significantly from mainstream English speakers (Barrera, 2004). As discussed, second language learners may display learning characteristics very similar to their peers with LD. Like students with LD, they might exhibit severe discrepancies, or gaps, between actual and expected achievement based on age or grade, often representing severe underachievement. Because ELs are likely to come from diverse cultural and linguistic backgrounds or lack exposure to schooling, their learning difficulties can be mistaken for deeper cognitive deficits. As a result, educators should use a variety of assessment tools to best measure EL performance (Basterra, 2011). A variety of authentic assessment practices are appropriate for helping to differentiate between language acquisition and learning disability, and these practices are often preferable to traditional approaches (Hoover & Klingner, 2011). The current emphasis on MTSS also provides a structure for facilitating the use of authentic assessments within a structure designed to provide prevention and intervention services to students. Two relevant authentic approaches particularly useful when assessing ELs within the overall structure of MTSS include curriculum-based measurement (CBM) and dynamic assessment (DA). These two types of assessments are considered critical to effective assessment of ELs (Barrera, 2004; Hoover & Klingner, 2011).

Curriculum-Based Measurement (CBM)

CBM is a standardized process initially developed in the 1980s and used for gathering student progress data (Deno, 2005). Through implementation of CBMs, teachers use classroom-based tasks sensitive to direct assessment to determine student progress and growth in reliable and valid ways (Burns & Gibbons, 2008; Fuchs & Fuchs, 2006; Hoover, 2013). In CBM, specific basic skills tasks have been validated with other measures of achievement. To use in the classroom, a teacher examines student abilities in the area being assessed, using tasks and content the student has encountered in the instruction (Barrera, 2004). Specific qualities of CBM include (a) frequent progress monitoring, (b) easily delivered process, (c) sensitivity to growth following short instructional periods of time (e.g., 1–2 weeks, monthly), (d) use of data scores gathered in a timely manner, and (e) grounding for informing effective instruction (Fuchs & Fuchs, 2006; Hoover, 2013).

More specifically, teachers use CBM to monitor student progress and use the data from these assessments to plan and modify instruction. One benefit of using CBM with ELs is that students are tested on material they are exposed to in the classroom. In addition, the use of CBM allows educators to create linguistically and culturally appropriate/relevant assessment tools for EL students (Hoover & Klingner, 2011). The use of CBM also allows teachers to monitor students' educational progress by directly assessing their reading skills. Although most research on CBM has been conducted with native English speakers, the use of CBM may also help determine how well ELs are acquiring English skills and content area material. In the contemporary structure of MTSS, the use of CBM is widely preferred due to its usefulness in ongoing monitoring of progress toward benchmarks adhering to standardized processes (Fuchs & Fuchs, 2006).

Dynamic Assessment (DA)

Dynamic assessment (DA) is a unique method for determining what students are learning, how they learn, and within what time frame they learn (Valle & Connor, 2011). The process of DA results in the increased understanding of how a student best learns and under what instructional conditions, or what it is that is necessary to move to the next level of skill development. Though many assessment approaches can be problematic when applied to the specific needs of second language learners suspected of having disabilities, Barrera (2004) suggests that dynamic assessment is a promising practice for distinguishing between disability-related learning difficulties and the normal process of acquiring a new language. Dynamic assessment examines students' learning ability as a function of what learners can do as they are being taught rather than of what students already know or do not know. Dynamic assessment (DA) procedures consist of teaching a new learning task to a student and collecting progress and procedural data as the student learns the new task (Grigorenko, 2009; Valle & Connor, 2011). Thus, dynamic assessment is less dependent on the student's previous opportunities to learn than other assessment procedures (e.g., standardized assessment tests).

Dynamic Assessment Features

DA represents an instructional-assessment set of procedures adjusted, as necessary, based on a learner's response to instruction. In the assessment process for special education eligibility, educators should be interested not only in where children are now given previous and most recent educational experiences but also to where their potential can lead them tomorrow, assuming they are provided culturally and linguistically responsive education. DA assessment and instruction are viewed as a single, interconnected activity that simultaneously diagnoses and clarifies a learner's development (Lantolf & Poehner, 2008). DA is an interactive process in which the educator uses best practice to enhance the child's performance within the testing situation for the purpose of identifying, selecting, and modifying effective instruction. In the case of an EL referred and being assessed for special education, DA provides an exceptional opportunity for educators to clarify culturally and linguistically responsive instruction.

Dynamic Assessment Process

The overall goal of DA is to modify a learner's performance during the assessment (Lantolf & Poehner, 2004), by altering tasks to identify the methods or prompts that achieve the best achievement results. One DA process that may be used is an assisted, three-step scaffolded process referred to as pretest-teach-posttest. The pretest-teach-posttest procedure measures an EL's ability to learn during and after delivery of a prescribed instructional opportunity, rather than assessing only previous and post-instruction knowledge. Key to DA is the *mediation* provided by the educator during the instruction-assessment process. An overview of one example of a DA process is provided in Table 6.4, developed from several sources including Grigorenko (2009), Grigorenko and Sternberg (1998), Lidz (2003), Lidz and Elliott (2000), and Valle and Connor (2011). For additional information about dynamic assessment, the reader is referred to these sources cited in this section.

Table 6.4 Dynamic Assessment Sample Process

Step 1: Pretest. Begin by administering a classroom-based CBM test, considered a pretest, which establishes the child's current performance. Record these results for future reference.

Step 2: Teach. A period of instruction follows the pretest. Instruct the child in an area of need identified through the pretest. The instructional sessions provide the EL with tasks relevant to the principles, concepts, or ideas measured by the pretest. For example, a teacher-led lesson that uses actual content from the learner's educational program is incorporated into a best practices structure of teaching, while providing the following supports as necessary: (a) educator actively intervenes during the course of the instruction-assessment process, intentionally attempting to induce positive change in the learner's current level of functioning; and (b) educator attempts to focus on the learner's problem-solving skills to determine how to best facilitate successful learning. Therefore, instructional tasks are modified and altered, based on learner response during the instruction-assessment process. This aspect of modifying tasks or instruction is referred to as *teacher mediation* and is essential to the DA process.

Teacher Mediation

Modification of instruction is provided during the instruction-assessment procedure. Through DA, assessment and instruction are integrated and connected tasks to best understand student knowledge, skills, and preferred ways of learning. To achieve this end, the educator introduces mediation, which may take many different forms such as

(a) training, providing resources, guiding peer discussions, responding to questioning, probing, or scaffolding;

(b) teacher and student work collaboratively, so the learner best succeeds and demonstrates under what conditions the learning occurs;

(c) items gradually increase in difficulty, so learning one task prepares student to perform a more advanced task;

(d) overall goal is to change EL's responses to improve learning while identifying and recording mediated supports used to create observed changes;

(e) active learner engagement is stressed within a challenging and mediated environment; and

(f) use learner responses as a platform for more challenging assessment activities requiring the student to employ a deeper and more systematic analysis of the learning process (Poehner & Lantolf, 2005).

Step 3: Posttest. Using a parallel yet different CBM, usually an alternate version of the pretest, administer a posttest following the teach phase. Compare results with the pretest, connecting to the methods and prompts that appeared to be most effective for the EL. Adjust classroom instruction accordingly.

When delivering DA it is essential to properly record results, documenting the methods or teacher-mediated prompts that were most effective in helping the EL understand and use knowledge and skills. Specifically, educators should (a) record the unique and relevant information in the assessment process thereby documenting EL's response to instruction, and (b) document intervention(s) or prompts that successfully promote change in the learner thereby connecting assessment with intervention. The Research to Practice example provides results from one project investigating use of dynamic assessment with diverse learners.

RESEARCH TO PRACTICE

Effectiveness of Dynamic Assessment With English Learners

To illustrate the effectiveness of dynamic assessment, Barrera (2004) conducted a study where thirty-eight teachers from general and special education were recruited to conduct assessments of 114 work samples from three groups of Mexican American students from two school districts in southwestern Minnesota and south Texas. The groups were designated as follows: (1) second language learners identified with LD, (2) second language learning peers not in special education, and (3) peers considered normal to high achieving bilingual or English-proficient. The dynamic assessment procedure consisted of using a two-entry *reflection and analysis journal* to have students write notes as they learned vocabulary terms. Students were taught to use the reflection side of the journal to engage in vocabulary building activities before, during, and after classroom discussions or lectures. In the analysis side of the journal, students wrote vocabulary definitions in their own words and constructed two sentences using the vocabulary words.

The process of dynamic assessment consisted of three steps. First, teachers asked students to take notes to determine if they had already acquired the skill to be taught. Second, students were provided continuous instruction on how to use the two-entry journal during a two-week period. Finally, a posttest on the new skill consisted of the last instance of journal note taking without instruction on the final day of the two-week period (Barrera, 2004). Teachers involved in the study conducted masked assessments of student work samples (i.e., they did not know in which group each student belonged). More specifically, a packet was given to each teacher that included three sets of student work samples previously coded by group (LEP with LD, LEP only, and bilingual/English-proficient). Further, four sets of scoring sheets were provided for each set of student notes. Teachers then reviewed the notes to see to what degree students followed directions for completing the dynamic assessment. Results from Barrera's study

(Continued)

(Continued)

indicate that learners with limited English proficiency and LD can be differentiated through data collected from dynamic assessments and assessed by classroom teachers. Furthermore, results indicate that high achieving learners had a higher percentage of key words with notes (in their journals) than LEP and LEP/LD groups, but general education students demonstrated the lowest percentage. However, high achieving learners were the least likely to complete the task of writing two sentences.

Results of Barrera's study also show that many of the measures used did not demonstrate statistically significant differences among students with limited English proficiency and their peers with limited English proficiency and LD. Barrera (2004) notes that differentiation among the student groups was clearest with quantitative measures (e.g., words and letters written, percentage of words spelled correctly, number of complete sentences). Barrera argues that this general outcome verifies the difficulties observed in the field for clearly differentiating low achieving learners from those with LD and reinforces the views of researchers and practitioners seeking more objective, quantifiable methods for assessing these learners. See Table 6.5 for a summary of key findings from this research.

Table 6.5 Summary of Dynamic Assessment Research Findings

1. Learners with limited English proficiency (LEP) and LD can be differentiated through data collected from dynamic assessments.
2. High achieving learners had a higher percentage of key words with notes than LEP and LEP/LD groups, but general education students demonstrated the lowest percentage.
3. High achieving learners completed the task to write two sentences with a lower percentage.
4. Many of the measures used did not demonstrate statistically significant differences among students with limited English proficiency and their peers with limited English proficiency and LD.
5. High achieving learners usually outperformed others despite their predilection to minimize their efforts in the writing of notes.
6. General education students showed minimal total writing.
7. Students with limited English proficiency and LD tended to write more total notes despite lower quality of results.

The DA model is viewed as an addition to the current, more traditional approaches and is not a substitute for existing procedures. Each type of assessment (CBM, norm-referenced, performance-based, dynamic, observations, etc.) provides different information used by educators to best understand the EL's knowledge, skills, and preferred ways of learning prior to making a special education eligibility decision. Overall, benefits exist for using curriculum-based measurement and dynamic assessment procedures to help distinguish between those students who have true disabilities and those who are struggling for other reasons. Results from these authentic assessment practices provide valuable supportive evidence to progress monitoring and formal assessment results when considering an EL for possible special education.

SUMMARY

Foundational to effective assessment for special education of ELs is an appropriate, culturally and linguistically responsive referral. The proper referral of an EL is a required precursor to proper special education eligibility assessment. Though a proper referral is essential, additional concerns arise as the EL is moved into the assessment process. A major source of measurement error in assessment leading to invalid results is produced by the interaction of the student with the test item and language, or the interaction of the student with the test item and dialect. Additionally, assessment features designed for native English speakers may pose significant problems for ELs. ELs often perform well on some items administered in one language or dialect (e.g., English) and well on other items administered in the other language or dialect (e.g., Spanish). The concept of dialect is relevant to addressing the tremendous linguistic and cultural diversity that may exist within broad linguistic groups of ELs who are users of the same given language. The concept of register is relevant to addressing academic language and the wide diversity of instructional and assessment contexts. Language factors that affect the dependability of achievement measures vary at the level of dialect. No matter what language any individual speaks (either a first or second language), that person is using a particular dialect (standard or nonstandard) of that language.

Regardless of whether ELs are tested in English or in their native language, linguistic misalignment occurs when the linguistic features of a test do not match their actual linguistic backgrounds and the contexts within which they have been instructed. This misalignment accounts for measurement error, due to dialect and/or register, and results in less valid assessment results. Linguistic features must be identified and accounted for to obtain accurate, valid, and reliable results for ELs, particularly those with suspected LD. The use of authentic assessment procedures, such as curriculum-based measurement and dynamic assessment, may assist practitioners in the implementation of a more culturally and linguistically appropriate assessment process as ELs are considered for possible special education due to continued lack of academic progress.

7

Data-Driven Decision Making

Distinguishing Language Acquisition and Cultural Behaviors From a Disability

John J. Hoover

As previously discussed in Chapter 2, a multi-tiered system of supports (MTSS) provides the contemporary structure of education for students who struggle with learning, moving away from the previous "wait to fail" model (i.e., continuum of prereferral, referral, assessment, placement). The emphasis in today's schools is on providing layers or tiers of interventions based on how well a learner responds to instruction, grounded in collected data (CCSSO, 2015; Fuchs & Fuchs, 2006). While one of the purported strengths of a multi-tiered system of supports is early identification of the needs of struggling learners, educators must ensure that problems experienced over the past decades associated with misinterpreting learning differences, or language acquisition, as disabilities are avoided. In addition, the continuing practice of misinterpreting culturally driven behaviors as disabilities must also be addressed to avoid overrepresentation of diverse learners in intensive intervention settings (e.g., Tier 3) and/or special education. One of the solutions to avoid previous instructional or placement decision errors is the use of data on which to base instructional decisions. This chapter discusses EL behaviors that educators should consider when making data-based decisions about why an EL might be struggling. The focus of the chapter is on what to do initially and during the early stages of providing data-driven interventions to an EL who does not seem to be progressing in reading.

Vignette: Culturally and Linguistically Responsive Data-Based Decision Making

Han is a seven-year-old, second-grade student who is struggling with reading in English. She is a child of an immigrant family from Vietnam whose primary home-spoken language is Vietnamese. Han's family moved to the United States when she was four years old. She has limited proficiency in English, being more fluent in Vietnamese. At home, Han speaks some English and Vietnamese, while at school English is the primary language of instruction. Language proficiency assessment results indicate that she is at the *developing* or *production* stage of English. At this time, she exhibits several behaviors consistent with the developing, production stage of second language acquisition including (a) increasing proficiency by speaking in short phrases and simple sentences, (b) writing that contains some grammatical errors, and (c) speech that contains some grammatical and pronunciation errors. In reading, Han is developing sight word vocabulary; able to sequence pictures, events, and processes; beginning to identify main ideas; and uses some context clues to determine word meanings. Han has been receiving Tier 2 instruction that emphasizes oral reading fluency (ORF) for an extended amount of time with little progress made based on an ORF test. The scores from the ORF progress monitoring are the only pieces of information the teacher uses to base instructional decisions on. However, the classroom teacher, who is not a native speaker and who is unfamiliar with Vietnamese culture and teachings, periodically gathers anecdotal evidence.

During a grade-level team meeting, Han's teachers report that she is very attentive in school, works well with others, and attends to literacy tasks in meaningful ways. However, she continues to struggle with curricula delivered in English, demonstrating lack of progress with high-frequency vocabulary and fluency. After several attempts at differentiating instruction, Han's second-grade teacher brought the situation to the school-wide multi-tiered system of supports (MTSS) team. The MTSS team addressed several aspects of the instructional situation and concluded that (a) fidelity of implementation of the curricula occurred (though it was delivered only in English), (b) extensive emphasis on whole class presentations provided much direct instruction, (c) some cooperative or paired learning existed, and (d) some student-student and teacher-student verbal interactions and discourse were periodically incorporated into the whole class direct instruction. However, instructional features not addressed by the MTSS team included cultural relevancy of the reading material, limited amount of time in US schools, use of home language in learning, limited use of methods that facilitated paired or cooperative learning, and home-school connections. Additionally, the progress monitoring was completed in English using an oral reading fluency test not specifically normed for students with limited English language proficiency. After consideration of the instructional body of evidence, the MTSS team recommended that Han be considered for special education for a learning disability in reading.

Reflection Items

1. Did the MTSS team reflect cultural and linguistic responsiveness? If not, why not?

2. What are the effects of ignoring the educational items identified above that were not discussed in the instructional decision-making or special education referral procedures?

3. What are the limitations of using only one set of data scores and sources when measuring the reading progress of an EL?

4. What recommendations should be made to this MTSS team to ensure that culturally and linguistically responsive data-driven decision making occurs to avoid misinterpreting language acquisition (i.e., stage of second language development) as a learning disability?

Within a multi-tiered model is the process of identifying effective interventions and determining progress toward established curricular benchmarks using data generated through ongoing progress monitoring (Brown-Chidsey & Steege, 2010; CCSSO, 2015). Therefore, as students begin to show signs of struggling with learning, the process to be followed includes these elements:

1. Determining whether initial efforts included the proper implementation and use of evidence-based practices with appropriate instructional differentiations

2. Determining needed supplemental support to complement the general class curriculum

3. Selecting appropriate supplemental evidence-based intervention

4. Implementing selected intervention with fidelity

5. Gathering data to determine effectiveness of the intervention in meeting student needs

6. Using collected data as the foundation for making culturally and linguistically responsive educational decisions

7. Gathering and incorporating relevant home and community information to ensure a cultural and linguistic responsive process (Hoover & Klingner, 2011).

Once an EL has been identified as struggling, the documentation using quantifiable data becomes essential for making informed multi-tiered instructional and/or special education referral and eligibility decisions.

DATA-DRIVEN DECISION MAKING

The foundation for making effective decisions for struggling learners throughout the multi-tier process is found in the evidence and data that illustrate level of progress (CCSSO, 2015; Hoover, 2013). As struggling learners are provided supplemental interventions and ongoing progress monitoring occurs, educators are collecting, charting, and analyzing data. For example, the specific number of times a learner uses a skill or the number of words read correctly within a two-minute time frame may be counted and charted by the teacher. This progress monitoring may continue for a few school weeks, at which time the problem-solving team would review the learner's progress using the charted or graphed data points (i.e., number of words read correctly). As a result, the team would be using the quantified data to base decisions on concerning the effectiveness of the instruction (e.g., Tier 1) and/or evidence-based intervention (e.g., Tier 2), regarding future adjustments, possible referral, or special education eligibility (i.e., data-driven decision making). In regard to decision making for diverse learners, when "interpreting assessment results teachers must recognize that norms regarding expected student performance may vary depending on students' cultural backgrounds and experiences" (Aceves & Orosco, 2014, p. 19).

Additionally, the types of documents and information used on which to base instructional decisions, noncompliance with various state and district laws or guidelines, as well as an indifference to using valid and appropriate information to make informed educational data-based decisions for ELs (Figueroa & Newsome, 2004; Klingner & Harry, 2004; Wilkinson, Ortiz, & Robertson-Courtney, 2004) must be addressed if ELs are to be effectively educated in today's instructional multi-tiered environments. For several decades, school systems have followed a prereferral intervention process for selecting and implementing instruction to meet the needs of struggling learners in the classroom. However, once potential problems were identified, extended periods of time often elapsed prior to beginning interventions. Additionally, the documentation of the effectiveness of prereferral interventions was less formal than we tend to see in the delivery of contemporary multi-tiered instructional models. As we deliver the more contemporary MTSS, we must ensure that similar problems, or barriers to effective education, are avoided. In order for a multi-tiered system of supports to build upon previous successes, the following, at minimum, should occur to be of benefit to ELs:

- Educators are properly trained to select and implement evidence-based practices designed for use with ELs.
- Educators receive training and support to implement appropriate classroom-based assessments delivered through a standard process to ensure reliability and validity.

- Educators require support to avoid misconceptions about ELs to properly implement evidence-based interventions in culturally and linguistically responsive ways. (See Chapter 3.)
- Multi-tier teams must include representation from all appropriate educators (e.g., EL teachers, special educator, general class teacher, bilingual educator, interventionist, etc.).
- Selected evidence-based practices must have research to support their use with the target population of students (e.g., English or second language learners). (See Chapter 5.)
- Progress-monitoring practices and instruments must be clearly understood by the teachers.
- Data related to student progress must, in part, be quantified, charted, and used as a foundation for making subsequent educational decisions, coupled with related cultural information.

These and similar skill sets are fundamental to avoiding problems previously experienced with prereferral intervention models and to generate successful implementation of multi-tiered instruction with data-driven decisions for ELs. When implemented effectively, the multi-tiered process could be of significant benefit to ELs as more formal and in-depth screening and monitoring are undertaken to determine whether cultural or linguistic factors contribute to suspected learning or behavioral problems. Along with this, a major issue for ELs is to ensure that the influence of language or cultural factors on suspected learning and behavioral problems is clarified and understood by all involved in the instructional process (Abedi, 2011; Hoover & Klingner, 2011). One of the more effective ways to ensure appropriate interpretation of struggling learner needs, and reduce bias when working with ELs, is to be knowledgeable of behaviors that may be more reflective of (a) second language acquisition and (b) culture-based teachings and values rather than indicators of disability. Hoover and Klingner (2011) wrote that ELs are often provided "Tier 2 instruction based on one screening score with little or no consideration for rate of progress and related cultural and linguistic factors" (p. 145). We discuss influences of linguistic and cultural factors on decision making in the following sections.

Second Language Acquisition (SLA) and Decision Making

Knowledge of expected SLA behaviors is critical to avoid misinterpreting language acquisition as a learning disability. Though much goes into effective data decision making for ELs, one of the most essential educational considerations pertains to the English language proficiency level of the struggling EL. Specifically, effective data-driven decisions for ELs must be made within the context of, What is the current language proficiency level of the EL who is struggling, and how might expected second language acquisition (SLA) behaviors relate to these struggles? The contemporary set of parameters for instructing, assessing, and examining progress of ELs is grounded, in part, in the WIDA: Can Do Descriptors (2014). These descriptors provide important suggested indicators of expected behaviors associated with the different English language proficiency levels measured by the WIDA ACCESS language proficiency test. The extent to which educational achievement data are interpreted relative to expected SLA behaviors reflects the extent that proper decision making occurs for ELs struggling in reading. Herrera et al. (2015) wrote that "the more a teacher knows about a student's particular stage of second language acquisition, the better able the teacher is to plan literacy lessons that support the student's comprehension and engagement in academic tasks" (p. 33).

Drawing upon literature-defining stages and proficiency levels of second language acquisition, I developed Table 7.1—as one tool to assist educators in decision making by considering the particular stage of second language acquisition an EL was most operating within at the time reading data were collected. The two-column table summarizes select behaviors as identified in (a) the WIDA proficiency levels (1–6) and (b) various second language acquisition development models (preproduction to advanced stages) often used within today's schools. The table, which is not designed to be all-inclusive, illustrates potential alignment between select WIDA Can Do descriptors and typical SLA stages of development behaviors. The reader is referred to the sources cited above for additional examples and discussion about items in the table.

As shown, descriptors associated with WIDA Level 1 may associate with behaviors typically found in the beginning, or Preproduction Stage, of SLA. WIDA Levels 2 and 3 and expected behaviors seen in ELs functioning within SLA Early Production and Production Stages, respectively, are connected. WIDA Levels 4 and 5 most associate with behaviors typically seen during the SLA Intermediate Stage. A working understanding of the general behaviors associated with one or more models of English language proficiency is critical to making certain that learning behaviors, appearing to be indicative of a reading or learning disability, are not in reality expected behaviors based on the EL's current second language proficiency stage or level of development. Consideration of the WIDA Can Do descriptors and behaviors most associated with second language acquisition allows educators to determine consistency in learner behaviors, those that rule out language proficiency level as the most plausible explanation for EL struggles in reading. That is, should the learner exhibit SLA stage of development behaviors in a manner consistent with expected Can Do descriptors based on WIDA ACCESS, then the learner is performing as expected, even if lower than other grade-level peers; therefore a disability does not appear evident.

In addition to considering alignment between the descriptors and SLA behaviors, decision-making team members require an understanding of how behaviors typical of a learning disability may in fact be expected behaviors due to the stage of second language acquisition within which

Table 7.1 Language Proficiency Descriptors and SLA Development Behaviors

Sample WIDA Can Do Descriptors	Sample Expected SLA Stage Behaviors
WIDA Level 1: Entering *Listening:* Learner is able to point to pictures, words, or phrases; follow one-step directions given orally; and match objects to oral statements *Speaking:* Learner is able to name objects, people, and pictures; and respond to who, what, when, where, which questions *Reading:* Learner is able to match symbols to words or phrases and identify print concepts and text features *Writing:* Learner is able to label objects and pictures, draw an illustration in response to a prompt, or produce symbols and words to convey messages	**SLA STAGE: Preproduction** *Silent Period* • Very little English spoken by learner: may respond nonverbally by nodding yes or no, drawing, and pointing • May not respond when spoken to • May have difficulty following directions • May have difficulty understanding questions • May have difficulty expressing needs • May experience confusion with locus of control • May be withdrawn/show low self-esteem • May seem to exhibit poor attention and concentration
WIDA Level 2: Beginning *Listening:* Learner is able to sort pictures and objects based on oral instructions, follow two-step oral directions, and match information from oral descriptions to objects *Speaking:* Learner is able to ask the five *Wh* questions, orally describe pictures or events, and restate facts *Reading:* Learner is able to find and classify information, identify facts, and determine language patterns connected to facts *Writing:* Learner is able to compile a list of items, develop drawings, generate short phrases, and provide responses to requested information	**SLA STAGE: Early Production** • Limited English spoken by learner: usually speaks in one- or two-word phrases • Uses present-tense verbs • May respond to who, what, where, and either/or questions with one-word answers • May complete sentences when given sentence starters • May participate using key words and familiar phrases • May memorize short language chunks (with or without errors)
WIDA Level 3: Developing *Listening:* Learner is able to locate and select information from oral discourse, complete several steps of instructions, and categorize/sequence orally presented material *Speaking:* Learner is able to predict, hypothesize, describe procedures, and retell stories *Reading:* Learner is able to sequence, identify main ideas, and use context clues appropriately in reading *Writing:* Learner is able to generate basic text, use compare-and-contrast statements, and describe in writing events, people and procedures	**SLA STAGE: Production Stage** *Speech Emergence* • Increasing proficiency: speaks in short phrases and simple sentences • Writing may contain grammatical errors • Speech may contain grammatical and pronunciation errors • Developing sight word vocabulary • May be able to describe, compare, and make predictions • Can answer how/why questions • May be withdrawn/show signs of frustration • May seem to have trouble concentrating • Limited participation in group discussions

(Continued)

Table 7.1   (Continued)

WIDA Level 4: Expanding	SLA STAGE: Intermediate Stage
Listening: Learner is able to compare/contrast functions and relationships from oral material, conduct analyses of oral information, and engage in cause and effect discussions *Speaking:* Learner is able to discuss issues and concepts, deliver a speech, present orally, and engage in creative problem solving and solutions generation *Reading:* Learner interprets material and data, locates details, supports main ideas, and identifies word families *Writing:* Learner is able to summarize, edit, revise, and create original ideas	• English is approaching age-appropriate levels, but learner still makes grammatical errors in writing and makes grammatical and pronunciation errors in speech • May engage in dialogue • Receptive and expressive language mismatch: learner may understand more than she/he is able to demonstrate or may seem more proficient than she/he is • May seem slow processing challenging language • May be confused by idioms/slang conveyed in English • May seem to have poor auditory memory
WIDA Level 5: Bridging *Listening:* Learner is able to draw conclusions from oral material, develop models reflecting oral discussions, and make connections to orally presented material and ideas *Speaking:* Learner debates, provides detailed examples and justifications for reasoning, and is able to defend viewpoint *Reading:* Learner conducts research, using multiple sources, and draws conclusions from different forms of text *Writing:* Learner is able to apply material in a new context and author multiple forms of writing	
WIDA Level 6: Reaching	**SLA STAGE: Advanced Stage** • Language usage, meaning, and fluency are age appropriate; learner has very good comprehension • Academic, behavioral, cultural, and social skills are L2 age appropriate

Sources: Developed from material found in Hill and Miller (2013); Hoover et al. (2008); Krashen and Terrell (1983); Lake and Pappamihiel (2003); WIDA (2014).

the learner is functioning. Table 7.2 provides an overview of selected behaviors often associated with disabilities as well as those typical of second language acquisition.

As shown, some of the same behaviors are seen as both typical disability behaviors and SLA expected behaviors, providing much opportunity for confusion about disability or acquisition. When considering the severity of

Table 7.2   Similarities Among Second Language Acquisition Behaviors and Suspected Learning Disabilities (LD)

Learning/Behavior Challenges Often Associated With LD	Expected Behaviors in Stages When Learning Second Language (English L2)
Preschool Children *Language* • Slow speech development • Pronunciation problems • Difficulty learning new words • Difficulty following simple directions • Difficulty understanding questions • Difficulty expressing needs • Difficulty rhyming words *Cognition* • Trouble memorizing • Difficulty with cause and effect • Difficulty with basic concepts *Attention* • High distractibility • Impulsive behavior • Unusually restless • Difficulty staying on task • Difficulty changing activities *Social* • Trouble interacting with others • Easily frustrated • Withdrawn • Poor self-control **Elementary School-Aged Language** • Slow learning sound-symbol correspondence • Difficulty remembering sight words • Difficulty retelling a story in sequence *Attention* • Difficulty concentrating • Difficulty following multiple directions • Difficulty finishing work on time • Difficulty following multiple directions *Social* • Difficulty interpreting facial expressions • Difficulty understanding social situations • Apparent lack of common sense • Misinterpreting behavior of peers	**The Silent Period Stage** • Difficulty following directions • Speaks very little English • May be silent, not respond when spoken to • Difficulty understanding questions • Difficulty expressing needs • May be withdrawn/show low self-esteem • May seem to exhibit poor attention and concentration • Pronunciation problems **The Early Production Stage** • May be withdrawn • Speaks in single words and phrases • May seem to have trouble concentrating • Phrases may contain notable grammatical errors • May be easily frustrated **The Intermediate Stage** • Learner is approaching age-appropriate levels • Still makes errors in speech, reading, and writing in English (academic, behavioral, cultural, social) • May seem more proficient than she is • May seem slow processing challenging language • May be confused by idioms, slang conveyed in English • May understand more than he is able to demonstrate • May seem to have poor auditory memory

Sources: Developed from material found in Baca and Cervantes (2004); Collier and Hoover (1987a, b); Cummins (2000); Hoover (2012); Hoover and Collier (1985); Hoover and Klingner (2011); Hoover et al. (2008); Klingner et al. (in press); Ortiz et al., (2011); Ortiz and Wilkinson (1991).

needs for ELs struggling in learning, behaviors must be put into a proper linguistic context to avoid misinterpreting acquisition as disability. Over the past several decades, many researchers have discussed alternative possible explanations for an EL's behaviors within the context of linguistic background, rather than learning disorders (Abedi, 2011; Adler, 1975; Baca & Cervantes, 2004; Collier, 1988; Collier & Hoover, 1987b; Donovan & Cross, 2002; Figueroa & Newsome, 2004; Grossman, 1995; Hoover & Collier, 2003; Hoover, Klingner et al., 2008; Klingner & Harry, 2004; Lachat, 2004; Loe & Miranda, 2002; Nazzaro, 1981; Ortiz et al., 2011; Wilkinson et al., 2004). Discussions in these and other sources emphasize the notion that educators must consider any suspected learning problem relative to the struggling student's linguistic needs, especially when using these behaviors as a basis for making multi-tiered instructional decisions (Hoover & Klingner, 2011).

Culture-Based Behaviors and Decision Making

Interconnected with our efforts to distinguish language acquisition from learning disabilities is the reality that different cultures hold unique teachings and values that become evident in classroom behaviors. That is, just as we must avoid misinterpreting behaviors typically associated with second language acquisition as learning disability behaviors, we also must make certain that we distinguish between cultural values and teachings and disability behaviors. To assist the reader, Table 7.3 provides select examples of possible cultural explanations, based on teachings or values, for behaviors that may be associated with ELs' struggles in school. These are not all-inclusive and may not apply to all ELs; however, in order to effectively and appropriately educate ELs in multi-tiered systems, alternative explanations based on cultural background must be explored to avoid misinterpreting cultural differences as indicators of disability characteristics.

As shown, a variety of plausible cultural explanations may account for ELs' behaviors as they experience formal school and associated expectations. These and similar explanations should be considered to make more informed instructional or eligibility decisions for ELs. Educators teaching struggling ELs must make every effort to determine if exhibited behaviors are typical and expected—due to various cultural teachings or values—and select appropriate evidence-based interventions accordingly to distinguish culturally learned behaviors from disability characteristics.

CULTURAL AND LINGUISTIC DIFFERENCES AND DISABILITY DECISION MAKING

In a study assessing educator perceptions about teaching ELs, de Oliveira and Burke (2015) wrote that educators "need to be able to provide best

Table 7.3   Cultural Explanations for ELs Who Struggle in Learning

Exhibited Behaviors	Plausible Cultural Explanations
Extended periods of silence	May be associated with cultural teaching and value (i.e., some cultures encourage children to be quiet as a sign of respect)
Confusion with locus of control	Some cultures teach that events are out of the control of individuals (i.e., external locus of control) and this should not be misinterpreted as not caring or requiring intervention
Indifference to time	The concept of time is often perceived differently in various cultures and may be significantly different than time emphasized in US schools (e.g., completion of tasks or the making of important decisions are more frequently based on when the individual[s] perceive that the time is right rather than on a specific time indicated by a clock)
Social withdrawal	Shy or withdrawn behavior may be associated with the process of adjusting or acculturating to a new environment (e.g., US schools/classrooms) and should not be misinterpreted as an indicator of a disability as the behavior will lessen over time
Acting out/aggressive behavior	Some cultures may teach that assertive behavior (e.g., standing up for oneself) is desirable social behavior; inexperience with US classroom rules may also account for acting out behaviors
Difficulty with independent work	Some cultures may value group performance over individual achievement; thus, students may be unfamiliar with independent, competitive learning and prefer cooperative group learning
Perceived lack of significance of school achievement	While education is highly valued across cultures, sometimes other priorities in that culture may take priority (e.g., family needs, spring harvest, etc.)
Poor performance on tests	Formal testing to which we subject students may be unfamiliar to ELs and therefore produce anxiety or confusion with assessment expectations leading to invalid results
Low self-esteem	Students from different cultures may initially experience difficulty while adjusting to new cultural expectations and/or learning a new language, which may temporarily negatively impact a child's self-concept
Differences in perception of everyday items	Different cultures may view everyday concepts differently from the mainstream culture (e.g., personal space, sharing of belongings, gender, meaning of color, directions), and knowledge of how cultures view these and related items is necessary to make informed decisions

(Continued)

Table 7.3   (Continued)

Exhibited Behaviors	Plausible Cultural Explanations
Increased anxiety	Stress associated with adjusting to a new culture and/or learning a new language often results in increased anxiety in learners until they feel more comfortable in the new environment with second language
Difficulty observing school/class expectations	Unfamiliarity with formal schooling, classroom expectations, testing, and routines is often experienced by children new to US schools; they require additional time and support to become more accustomed to US schools' behavioral and learning expectations
Learning preferences	Preferred styles of learning are reflective of cultural values; styles of ELs may be different than typically emphasized in school (e.g., more wait time, cooperative rather than competitive learning, different experiential backgrounds, etc.)
Instructional strategies	Teaching strategies typically used in today's classrooms may conflict with cultural views and/or be inappropriate for students' limited English language proficiency levels, erroneously leading to perceived learning or behavior problems

Sources: Developed from material found in several sources including Baca and Cervantes (2004); Collier and Hoover (1987a, b); Cummins (2000); Hoover (2012); Hoover and Collier (1985); Hoover and Klingner (2011); Hoover et al. (2008); Klingner et al. (in press); Ortiz et al. (2011); Ortiz and Wilkinson (1991).

practices for ELLs such as recognizing different linguistic and academic needs . . . instructing students in language learning strategies (specifically reading and writing strategies)" (p. 4). As discussed and illustrated in Tables 7.2 and 7.3, the possibility of misinterpreting linguistic and/or cultural behaviors as indicators of a disability is very high due to similarities among exhibited behaviors. As a result, during the decision-making process, one of the more fundamental issues confronting educators is determining whether an area of need for ELs is due to

1. a learning or behavior disability,

2. cultural teachings or second language acquisition, or

3. a combination of the above two.

The unique ways that individuals successfully acquire, process, integrate, and utilize knowledge and skills (which may deviate from what is typically accepted or preferred in schools or individual classrooms) reflect a learning *difference*, not a disability. Conversely, a learning *disability* or *disorder* is represented by a condition within the learner, which interferes with or limits the individual's ability to successfully acquire, process, integrate, and generalize knowledge and skills (Hoover & Klingner, 2011; Hoover, Klingner et al., 2008). Members of teams who receive, review, and act upon progress-monitoring data should bear in mind that a primary difference between a learning difference and a learning disability is that a disability is represented by characteristics that limit or interfere with one's learning, often regardless of the instructional method used, while cultural and linguistic diversity and qualities represent strengths that advance and support students' educational progress when students receive appropriate culturally and linguistically responsive instruction and assessment.

During the multilevel instructional process, educators should document the results of efforts undertaken to differentiate between acquisition or cultural values and a disability as it pertains to the educational needs of ELs:

1. Make certain that various evidence-based interventions have been tried.

2. Engage in culturally/linguistically appropriate interventions with ELs.

3. Develop and use effective decision-making strategies and practices to make team decisions.

4. Ensure that team members are sufficiently prepared to make informed data-driven decisions about ELs and their needs, using all available and relevant progress-monitoring data.

Central to distinguishing a learning difference from a disability is the quality of instruction provided to the learner. Table 7.4, developed from various sources cited in this chapter, provides a rating scale to assist educators in the process of distinguishing acquisition or difference from disability by examining the cultural and linguistic responsiveness of the reading instruction delivered to an EL showing signs of struggle. These items represent a sampling of the types of information required to ensure delivery of a culturally and linguistically responsive education specific to the topic of this book, and necessary to best understand assessment results to make informed decisions.

Responses to each of these twelve items contribute to a greater understanding about an EL's struggles in reading. Lower ratings suggest that classroom instruction may be central to the learner's academic problems and therefore less attributable to a disability. Conversely, strong responses suggest that culturally and linguistically responsive instruction exists, indicating that there may be more involved with the learner's struggles beyond quality of instruction, requiring additional evidence collection.

Table 7.4   Culturally/Linguistically Responsive Instructional Rating Scale

Instructions: Rate extent to which the following are evident in the teaching and learning of an EL showing signs of struggle in reading in the classroom:			
1 = None (Not at all)	2 = Little (Once per month)	3 = Some (Weekly)	4 = Extensive (Daily)
To what extent is each item evident in the reading instruction for the EL who is struggling?			

Instructional Feature	Rating			
1. Connections made to student's cultural and linguistic environments	1	2	3	4
2. Differentiate to reflect student's preferred ways of learning	1	2	3	4
3. Diverse cultural values incorporated in the delivery of curriculum	1	2	3	4
4. Acculturation needs (i.e., adjusting to new school/community environment) accommodated through relevant instruction	1	2	3	4
5. Functional, purposeful classroom dialogue	1	2	3	4
6. Background experiences and knowledge are built upon	1	2	3	4
7. Instruction scaffolded to help link new with existing knowledge	1	2	3	4
8. Learning context reflects student's home values/norms/teachings	1	2	3	4
9. Strategic use of student verbal interactions with less teacher talk	1	2	3	4
10. Curricula and learning experiences are cognitively challenging	1	2	3	4
11. Cooperative, joint learning occurs for all students	1	2	3	4
12. Academic language of instruction is commensurate with EL's proficiency	1	2	3	4

Gathering Relevant Student Data

Along with objective achievement and related data, information gathered on ELs' academic and social-emotional abilities and needs must be valid and corroborated. To highlight this important area of need, we share a previous study completed by Wilkinson et al. (2004), in which an expert panel reviewed documents and records of ELs identified as having a learning disability. These results are directly applicable to multi-tiered instructional decision making.

The expert panel reviewed the documents to determine if the identified students qualified as having learning disabilities, as recommended by the special education placement team. They considered various items within the records including language assessments, standardized test results, IQ and achievement test results, and statements describing discrepancies between potential and actual achievement. Results from the study revealed that the panel agreed that slightly over half of the ELs clearly qualified for special education, while the others did not qualify. Within the qualified group, the panel questioned the classification of some of the students as having a learning disability and suggested that more data were required to make a more informed disability decision. For those students who did not appear to qualify for special education, the panel found one or more of the following:

1. Significant events (e.g., divorce, death in family) in the child's life affecting education were not considered in eligibility decisions.

2. Records contained missing or incomplete data upon which eligibility decisions were made.

3. Inappropriate assessments, particularly assessing the students in their nondominant language, yielded invalid results.

4. Prereferral interventions were either not completed or results not documented for consideration in eligibility decisions.

Other studies also investigating EL decision making for special education have been recently published. Ortiz et al. (2011) found similar results to those summarized above, documenting that ELs are still misplaced in special education due to lack of appropriate interventions, limited or interrupted schooling, incomplete information, or misinterpretation of results through neglect to consider cultural and linguistic factors. In another related recent study previously discussed and presented in a Research to Practice box in Chapter 6, Hoover and Erickson (2015) found that a rural school system lacked a culturally and linguistically responsive referral decision-making process due to extensive use of assessments not designed or appropriate for use with ELs. However, results from their piloted project in the same school district, in which a culturally responsive referral guide was used, showed positive changes in the district's process for examining the body of evidence in the referral decision-making process for ELs.

EVIDENCE-BASED INTERVENTIONS AND MULTI-TIERED INSTRUCTION

Evidence-based interventions are instructional practices that have been researched and validated for their intended purposes and population of learners. As discussed, the use of evidence-based interventions is central to the effective implementation of multi-tiered instruction (CCSSO, 2015; Hoover, 2013), particularly in Tiers 2 and 3. Also emphasized is the idea that the interventions must be implemented the way they were designed and researched (i.e., implementation with fidelity). Effective decision making regarding the reading needs of ELs initially requires proper implementation of evidence-based interventions. The guide in Table 7.5, developed from various sources cited in this chapter, provides several items to consider during the selection and implementation process of evidence-based interventions. Similar to the other chapter guides, these items represent a sampling of the types of information required to select an appropriate intervention for an EL struggling in reading.

The purpose of the checklist is to assist educators to ensure selection of the most appropriate evidence-based interventions for ELs struggling with learning early in the process of identifying needs. In addition, other important information should be gathered to make the most informed decision. For example, parental/guardian perceptions of the child's suspected problem may help clarify cultural influences or values taught to the child at home. Also, classroom observations are necessary to determine how suspected problems are interrelated with various content areas and the extent to which different evidence-based interventions assist with promoting student achievement. Educators should discuss how each of these checklist items, and related information, are addressed prior to acting on gathered progress-monitoring data.

Table 7.5   Selecting Culturally/Linguistically Responsive Evidence-Based Interventions

To best select appropriate evidence-based interventions for an EL, *each* of the following should be addressed (*Check if evidence demonstrates consideration in intervention selection*):
___ Student's most proficient language for instruction is identified
___ Student's level of acculturation and adjustment to school environment is determined
___ Discrepancies between teaching and learning style differences are identified
___ Culturally and linguistically relevant instructional interventions are attempted and results documented
___ ESL and/or bilingual education instruction is implemented
___ Sufficient time and opportunity for student to make satisfactory progress are provided relative to acculturation and English proficiency levels
___ Authentic or other curriculum-based tests are used to assess student progress and socio-emotional development
___ One or more classroom observations are made to observe student interactions in the academic environment and to ensure fidelity of implementation of intervention
___ ELs' academic language is at a level consistent with the language required to use the intervention

In addition, as stressed throughout this book, all educators of ELs must ensure that they possess culturally and linguistically responsive assessment practices to minimize erroneous multi-tiered instructional decision making. Table 7.6, also developed from sources cited in this chapter, identifies several key knowledge and skill areas that all educators should possess to provide effective assessments for ELs in any tier of instruction.

Table 7.6   Knowledge and Skills Checklist for Effective Assessment of ELs

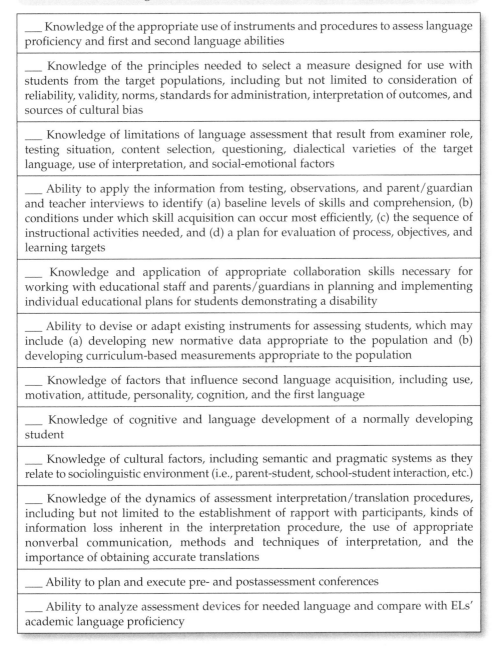

___ Knowledge of the appropriate use of instruments and procedures to assess language proficiency and first and second language abilities
___ Knowledge of the principles needed to select a measure designed for use with students from the target populations, including but not limited to consideration of reliability, validity, norms, standards for administration, interpretation of outcomes, and sources of cultural bias
___ Knowledge of limitations of language assessment that result from examiner role, testing situation, content selection, questioning, dialectical varieties of the target language, use of interpretation, and social-emotional factors
___ Ability to apply the information from testing, observations, and parent/guardian and teacher interviews to identify (a) baseline levels of skills and comprehension, (b) conditions under which skill acquisition can occur most efficiently, (c) the sequence of instructional activities needed, and (d) a plan for evaluation of process, objectives, and learning targets
___ Knowledge and application of appropriate collaboration skills necessary for working with educational staff and parents/guardians in planning and implementing individual educational plans for students demonstrating a disability
___ Ability to devise or adapt existing instruments for assessing students, which may include (a) developing new normative data appropriate to the population and (b) developing curriculum-based measurements appropriate to the population
___ Knowledge of factors that influence second language acquisition, including use, motivation, attitude, personality, cognition, and the first language
___ Knowledge of cognitive and language development of a normally developing student
___ Knowledge of cultural factors, including semantic and pragmatic systems as they relate to sociolinguistic environment (i.e., parent-student, school-student interaction, etc.)
___ Knowledge of the dynamics of assessment interpretation/translation procedures, including but not limited to the establishment of rapport with participants, kinds of information loss inherent in the interpretation procedure, the use of appropriate nonverbal communication, methods and techniques of interpretation, and the importance of obtaining accurate translations
___ Ability to plan and execute pre- and postassessment conferences
___ Ability to analyze assessment devices for needed language and compare with ELs' academic language proficiency

Practitioners should self-assess skills and abilities to ensure they possess these needed competencies and work to acquire skills in deficient areas.

MULTI-TIER TEAMS AND THE DECISION-MAKING PROCESS

As previously discussed, over the past couple of decades, researchers have investigated the effectiveness of educational team practices and decision making, particularly as they relate to referral and placement for special education. While decision-making teams continue to evolve as multi-tiered systems expand in our schools, it is crucial that the issues or mistakes made by previous problem-solving teams be minimized. To assist, two forms were developed and are presented in two subsequent tables. Table 7.7, developed from information found in several sources including Hoover and Klingner (2011), Klingner and Harry (2004), Meadows Center (2014), and Ortiz et al. (2011), includes several selected themes that all problem-solving teams must consider when addressing instructional intervention needs of struggling ELs.

As shown, nine specific themes are identified along with relevant considerations for ELs. Themes represent the core features addressed throughout the chapters of this book to best distinguish language acquisition and cultural teachings from learning or language disabilities. The second form developed, Table 7.8, is a checklist representing a sampling of essential items to be considered by the multi-tiered decision-making team to ensure that culturally and linguistically responsive assessment information has been gathered and examined.

As shown, the checklist contains nine critical items necessary to ensure the most appropriate multi-tiered process for ELs by assisting teams to make effective decisions concerning level and intensity of interventions.

Nondiscriminatory Progress Monitoring

As discussed in the previous chapter, one of the more controversial issues in the education of students from culturally and linguistically diverse backgrounds pertains to the use of biased assessment instruments and associated practices (Basterra et al., 2011). While advances have been made to ensure that assessment and progress-monitoring instruments have minimal bias, some assessment practices for ELs still contain a variety of biases that affect interpretation of progress-monitoring results (Basterra et al., 2011; Hoover & Klingner, 2011). In addition, as previously discussed, interventions and practices selected for use during Tiers 1 and 2 instructions may have a significant impact on future decisions within the multi-tiered process. As a result, attention to nondiscriminatory selection of teaching methods and associated progress-monitoring tools used with

Table 7.7   Culturally/Linguistically Responsive Themes in Multi-Tier Decision Making

Theme	Essential Consideration
1. Acquisition/Difference Versus Disability	Educators ensure that limited English proficiency or cultural teachings are not mistaken for a learning or language disability.
2. Proper Time for Formal Referral	Formal referral for special education evaluation should occur only after multi-tiered interventions have been implemented and progress documented.
3. Proper Language of Instruction/Assessment	Teams instruct/assess ELs in their most proficient language of instruction.
4. Limited English Proficiency and IQ	Teams are cognizant of the fact that limited proficiency in the use of English does not indicate low IQ or inability to use higher order thinking abilities.
5. Opportunities to Learn	Teams ensure that students with limited English proficiency are provided sufficient opportunities to learn by implementing necessary differentiations to address cultural and linguistic features.
6. Cross-Cultural Observations/ Interviews	Teams ensure that observations and interviews conducted with ELs are culturally and linguistically appropriate.
7. Proper Interpretation and Use of Progress-Monitoring Data	Teams corroborate progress with multiple forms of authentic, classroom-based assessments, observations, interviews, work samples, and other.
8. Home-School Connections	Teams confirm that reading instruction is connected to home and family in meaningful and responsive ways.
9. Matching Academic Language	Teams make certain that the ELs' academic language levels are consistent with the language levels necessary to be successful with selected curricula and interventions.

struggling ELs must begin during Tier 1 instruction and continue throughout the entire multi-tier decision making process.

Practitioners must be cognizant of the fact that some progress-monitoring procedures may be inappropriate for use with culturally and linguistically diverse students since they may yield unreliable and invalid results (Basterra et al., 2011). During the progress-monitoring process, two of the more important issues challenging ELs are (a) opportunities to learn and (b) academic language required to be successful with the evidence-based intervention. One way to ensure that progress monitoring with ELs is valid and reliable is to evaluate the process adhering to various nondiscriminatory practices. Several important

Table 7.8   Multi-Tier Team Checklist for English Learners

Instructions: Place a check next to each item, once evidence exists confirming it was addressed by the team for the EL. Record any related comments below each item:
___ Evidence-based interventions are implemented and progress is monitored.
Comments:
___ Culturally responsive team includes all key people in the decision process.
Comments:
___ Parent/guardian input was obtained, valued, and incorporated into the decision making.
Comments:
___ Cultural and linguistic factors relative to suspected problem area were addressed.
Comments:
___ Referral for special education made at appropriate time and only after evidence-based interventions have been attempted.
Comments:
___ Language/learning differences versus learning disabilities were discussed.
Comments:
___ Translator was used properly when necessary.
Comments:
___Classroom observations were completed by properly prepared culturally responsive observer.
Comments:
___ Level of English proficiency and expected academic language needed to be successful with the reading curriculum content, and skills were considered and determined to be consistent.
Comments:

considerations for nondiscriminatory practices have been identified for practitioners working with ELs and are presented in Table 7.9, developed from information found in several sources including Basterra et al. (2011), Figueroa and Newsome (2004), and Hoover and Klingner (2011). The checklist is recommended for use by practitioners in conjunction with other guides in this chapter as a means to provide appropriate progress monitoring and associated decision making for ELs. Adhering to these items will lead to more effective and accurate decision making within the multi-tiered support systems.

In summary, use of the various tools presented in this and the other chapters assist teams to make more informed decisions. A document from the University of Texas–Austin's Meadows Center published in 2014 posed several key questions concerning the educational decision making for ELs that ranged from types of administrative supports to use of evidence-based instructional and assessment practices. Many of the items found in the various guides, checklists, or rating scales in this book reflect the Meadows Center document as well as significant research completed by the many professionals cited. We summarize the decision-making process for ELs by emphasizing the importance of the following skills:

Table 7.9 Checklist for Nondiscriminatory Assessment and Decision Making

Tasks reflecting nondiscriminatory practices . . .
___ Cross-cultural interviews and classroom observations are conducted.
___ Cross validation of information from the home and family settings corroborates progress-monitored data.
___ Culturally responsive progress-monitoring methods are implemented.
___ Effects of environmental and cultural influences on suspected problem are documented.
___ Progress-monitoring tasks are completed by culturally and/or linguistically competent persons.
___ Linguistically appropriate goals and services are included in progress monitoring.
___ Previous instructional programs and student progress in those programs are considered.
___ Evidence-based adaptive behavior interventions are attempted and documented.
___ Home and family information are documented and accurate.
___ Student's language dominance, English proficiency, and needed academic language are determined.
___ Translators/interpreters are properly used if necessary in the progress monitoring.
___ Alternative and authentic forms of progress monitoring are included.

1. *Efficiently manage* large amounts of information on ELs prior to decision making

2. *Provide early intervening* services by differentiating general class curriculum and instruction to meet personalized reading needs

3. *Effectively problem solve* to best select culturally and linguistically responsive evidence-based interventions bearing in mind several critical aspects (e.g., type of intervention, academic language required, duration, home-community connections, appropriate methods for monitoring response to the intervention, etc.)

4. *Differentiate* instruction to provide cultural and linguistic supports, build background knowledge, engage learners, and assess in ongoing ways

5. *Interpret progress-monitoring* data by considering alternate reasons for suspected problems (e.g., acculturation; lack of sufficient opportunities to learn; level of English proficiency and required academic language on curriculum performance, etc.)

6. *Corroborate* progress monitoring and other assessment results by using culturally and linguistically relevant practices and devices, along with input from parents/guardians and colleagues

Overall, educator teams responsible for making intervention and eligibility decisions must use all relevant available information, making certain to gather necessary data to acquire a comprehensive understanding of the EL's reading needs, strengths, and qualities.

SUMMARY

The significance of effective multi-tiered, evidence-based interventions; appropriate progress monitoring; and effective data-driven decision-making practices cannot be overstated when addressing the needs of ELs struggling with learning. This chapter discussed many issues associated with the overall decision-making process for educating ELs who show signs of struggling with reading. Several guides and checklists were presented to assist practitioners to ensure that cultural and linguistic factors and issues are appropriately explored, discussed, and accounted for during the comprehensive implementation of and associated data decision making within multi-tiered support systems in school districts nationwide. The use and application of the information discussed in this chapter will assist problem-solving teams to make more informed decisions, based on appropriate and objective data, avoiding issues associated with misinterpreting language and cultural differences as language or learning disabilities in English learners.

8

Conclusion

Putting the Pieces Together

Leonard M. Baca, Todd Fletcher, and John J. Hoover

This practical book provides teachers of English learners who struggle with reading with a foundation to make more informed decisions pertaining to understanding English language acquisition and learning disabilities. This, in turn, provides educators with greater knowledge to draw upon to more accurately distinguish language differences from suspected learning disabilities. The intent of this final chapter is to summarize key ideas and practices discussed in the earlier chapters to assist educators of ELs to integrate information and skills as they move forward with the challenging task of effectively teaching culturally and linguistically diverse learners. The previous chapters discussed several key ideas and practices important to bear in mind to best understand language development and learning disabilities. We begin by summarizing several common themes among the interrelated topics discussed throughout this book.

SUMMARY OF THEMATIC PERSPECTIVES

Theme: Multi-Tiered System of Supports (MTSS)

The contemporary framework for educating all learners in today's schools is one that includes several tiers, or layers, of instruction to best meet academic and social/behavioral developmental needs. All students are provided Tier 1 instruction, and depending on how well they "respond" to that instruction, one or more intensive instructional levels may be provided.

Tier 2 instruction directly supplements the core, general classroom instruction and is provided to students who show signs of struggle, are at risk in learning, or fail to make adequate progress toward grade-level benchmarks. In addition to leveled instruction, a multi-tiered system of supports (MTSS) functions within a shared leadership philosophy, using evidence-based practice, multiple forms of assessment, and data-driven decision making. MTSS represents a highly promising teaching and learning framework for ELs who struggle in reading (Klingner & Hoover, 2014). And if implemented properly, MTSS provides safeguards against mistakenly perceiving language acquisition as a learning disability.

Theme: Universal Screening

All students are screened to determine those who are experiencing academic or behavioral difficulties. Universal screening generally occurs between one and three times per year (IRIS Center for Training Enhancements, n.d.). When implemented on a periodic basis throughout the academic year (e.g., three times per year, at the beginning, middle, and near end of the school year), students who begin to struggle during the school year who did not demonstrate problems at the beginning of the school year are more quickly identified. Students who fall below a specified cutoff score are identified as struggling learners and provided Tier 2 supplemental support. According to Brown-Chidsey and Steege (2010), many districts use the twenty-fifth percentile as the cutoff for determining students at risk who require additional support.

Theme: Progress Monitoring

Struggling learners identified through universal screening are provided supplemental (Tier 2) or intensive (Tier 3) support to address their needs. The implementation of this supplemental instruction must now also include ongoing progress monitoring, documenting the extent to which students make progress toward the achievement of defined goals and benchmarks. Progress data are gathered on a frequent basis (e.g., monthly, weekly) and should be charted to visually display student progress (Brown-Chidsey & Steege, 2010; Deno, 2005). These data are subsequently used to make informed data-driven decisions reflecting student response to instruction.

Theme: Formal Assessment

Formal diagnostic assessment should focus on strengths in both languages, or in the case of simultaneous bilinguals, assessment of the combined use of two languages, which often yields more accurate results than separate assessment within each language. Both curriculum-based measurement and dynamic assessment should be employed in the progress-monitoring and formal assessment stages. To best understand language acquisition, dialect and register need to be considered in instructional and assessment decisions (Basterra et al., 2011).

Theme: Evidence-Based Interventions

Evidence-based interventions must have been validated with ELs to be considered appropriate for this population. Effective instruction for ELs within a multi-tiered framework should include cultural responsiveness, language development beginning early when a student demonstrates a need, reading instruction that is systematic and explicit, and teachers able to craft respectful, reciprocal, and responsive interactions across diverse cultural settings. In addition, where possible and in accordance with district policies, primary language literacy instruction should be provided.

Theme: Teacher Preparation and Professional Development

Teacher preparation should (a) focus on the development of cultural and linguistic competence, (b) be interdisciplinary in nature and focus on the whole child including the affective domain, (c) strive to improve skills of all educators including general and special education classroom teachers, and (d) address diverse learners' needs within a system-wide approach that incorporates a culture of collaboration, shared leadership, and continual professional development. Hoover (2012) wrote that a "common practice that continues to exist in our schools is the misinterpretation of learning differences due to diversity as indicators of disabilities" (p. 40). Contemporary teacher preparation and professional development should continue to emphasize strategies for reducing the tendency of educators misinterpreting language acquisition as a learning disability to best educate all ELs.

PRACTICAL APPLICATIONS OF SUGGESTED INTERVENTIONS

Each of these themes stresses a critical aspect associated with the successful education of ELs. Collectively, these represent some of the most important features necessary to consider when discerning differences between language development and learning disabilities. As educators move forward in efforts to meet EL needs, the many practical suggestions discussed in previous chapters will assist to provide an integrated education to best reduce the misinterpretation of language difference needs as disability needs. Several of the practical application ideas previously discussed are summarized below.

Application: Learning Disabilities or English Language Development?

Learning disabilities and second language acquisition behaviors may appear similar, which, in turn, may lead to misidentification for special education. To best avoid misidentification, educators should bear in mind that language acquisition is a very complex process and is influenced by a variety of factors, including first language proficiency, cultural values/ norms, personality, and acculturation (Hoover & Klingner, 2011). These and related factors must be considered by practitioners with expertise in second language acquisition and skilled in the implementation of instruction and associated progress monitoring to obtain the most valid educational results for ELs.

Application: Avoiding Misconceptions About ELs

Interrelated with an understanding of language development and learning disabilities is the need to avoid misconceptions about ELs. From a practical perspective, educators should bear in mind the following as previously discussed:

1. Utilize explicit instruction and scaffolding as needed

2. Consider a variety of factors such as those discussed above to best understand behaviors

3. Examine and consider one's own cultural assumptions and linguistic knowledge when implementing instruction with ELs

4. Integrate language goals and objectives, in addition to content objectives, into instructional activities and expected outcomes

Overall, to best avoid misconceptions about ELs, educators must recognize that academic and behavioral outcomes are influenced significantly by the interaction between what the learner brings to the classroom and what the school attempts to offer the learner. An understanding of the compatibility or incompatibility between these is essential to best address EL needs and avoid misconceptions.

Application: Effective Implementation of MTSS With ELs

As previously discussed, the implementation of multi-tiered learning holds significant promise for ELs if certain precautions are addressed. These include the use of evidence-based interventions that have been researched with the target population (i.e., ELs) along with assurances that teachers implementing MTSS (a) are adequately trained, (b) receive necessary support to effectively implement evidence-based interventions, and

(c) develop the skills necessary for culturally responsive documentation of student responses to instruction. By incorporating these practices into the education of ELs, MTSS reduces the risk of experiencing a fate similar to that found in many of the previous prereferral intervention models (i.e., wait-to-fail models). The practical application of MTSS for ELs will be effective only if implemented in culturally and linguistically responsive ways by culturally competent educators.

Application: Putting Effective Literacy Instruction Into Practice

Fundamental to avoiding misinterpretations about language development and disabilities is a working knowledge of the practical application of literacy instruction for ELs. As previously presented, inadequate opportunities to learn often lead to the misrepresentation of learning differences as disabilities (Hoover, 2012; Klingner & Edwards, 2006). The most effective literacy instruction for ELs provides the learner with culturally relevant teaching, including recognition of the types of literacy instruction previously experienced by the student. While the greater concern is misinterpreting a learning difference as a disability, it is also important to recognize that some ELs may truly have a learning disability and require targeted instruction to meet their needs as well. To this end, practitioners should adhere to the following suggestions previously explored in this book:

- Build strong positive relationships with learners
- Value cultural diversity in teaching and learning
- Provide sufficient attention and opportunity to oral language development
- Differentiate instruction as necessary to account for diverse needs
- Provide explicit instruction, particularly when introducing new concepts
- Combine phonological awareness with other reading and English language development activities (whether instruction is in the student's first language or English)
- Provide explicit vocabulary instruction to facilitate reading comprehension in students' first language and English
- Teach and encourage the use of reading comprehension strategies
- Help students develop a strong foundation in their first language as a way to promote literacy in both the native language and English (Klingner, Artiles, & Barletta, 2006)

Overall, effective literacy instruction requires practitioners to understand, value, and account for diverse learners' cognitive, academic, and social-emotional backgrounds and experiences. This knowledge assists educators to best determine literacy needs and reduces tendencies to misinterpret language acquisition as learning disabilities.

Application: Role of Data-Driven Decision Making

The implementation of multi-tiered instruction in MTSS models includes provisions in teaching and learning that address one of the most basic principles of instructional decision making. Specifically, this refers to the use of data, directly reflective of instructional efforts, forming the foundation for making decisions concerning tiers and intensity of evidence-based interventions. While MTSS problem-solving teams may use several sources of information to make decisions (e.g., teacher ratings, classroom observations, interviews), the use of quantitative data, collected and charted over time, is essential to determining the extent to which a learner responds to instruction. Practitioners in today's classrooms must become more proficient with data collection and presentation, be provided the time to collect necessary data, and receive needed training to acquire the skills to efficiently and effectively gather progress data to be used in the overall decision-making process. Additionally, educators should become better prepared to make important instructional data-driven decisions through a strength-based lens (Valle & Connor, 2011). In regard to ELs, the data collected must reflect appropriate evidence-based instruction through the use of culturally responsive assessment techniques and devices. Effective data-driven decision making for ELs can occur only if the data reflect culturally competent teaching and learning.

Application: Problem-Solving Teams

Whether the team is called an intervention team, a problem-solving team, or by another name, it is important for a well-qualified, well-prepared team to examine screening, progress monitoring, and other data to determine the best course of action for a student who seems to be struggling. The team should include experts in language acquisition in all phases of instructional, referral, and assessment processes, particularly when students seem to be delayed in acquiring both their first language and English (Klingner et al., 2006). As noted previously, the team should consider contextual features, sociocultural factors, school and program characteristics, and students' opportunities to learn in all phases of instructional, referral, and assessment processes.

Application: Avoiding Assessment Pitfalls With ELs

Throughout this book, we have provided many examples and suggestions that relate to effective assessment of ELs. In particular, when dealing with language development and usage, the concepts of dialect and register must be considered by practitioners in order to ensure nonbiased assessment. Assessment personnel must keep in mind a few key points:

1. Assessment conducted in English with ELs who possess limited English proficiency becomes primarily an English test rather than a test of academic or social/behavioral proficiency.

2. Some form of dialect is used in any language spoken.

3. Diverse linguistic features (i.e., register) may create a situation where assessment does not accurately reflect the linguistic contexts within which the EL has been instructed, and in turn, this potentially yields invalid results.

Practitioners aware of these assessment concerns are more likely to use authentic assessment procedures and devices to form the basis for making effective decisions about ELs in today's classrooms. Authentic assessments, including curriculum-based measurement and dynamic assessment provide highly useful instructional information that is used to distinguish language acquisition from learning disability (Hoover, 2013; Valle & Connor, 2011). In addition, Klingner and colleagues (2006) developed the following recommendations based on their review of research related to distinguishing between language acquisition and learning disabilities:

*   Use alternative ways of assessing students' strengths to determine the upper limits of their potential.
*   Conduct observations of students in different settings as part of any evaluation.
*   Pay greater attention to cultural and affective considerations when evaluating students (e.g., sources of potential conflict, motivation).
*   Give greater attention to students' native language and the role of language acquisition when determining whether a student may have learning disabilities.
*   Consider that weak auditory processing skills could indicate language acquisition rather than a processing disorder or learning disabilities.
*   Evaluate students in their first language as well as English to determine predictors of reading achievement.

PUTTING THE PIECES TOGETHER

The following guide may be used when considering the integrated implementation of the practical ideas above within the classroom. Table 8.1 provides a checklist to use to ensure the development and implementation of the best learning environment possible for ELs, with one overall goal being to best understand language development needs as different from learning disability needs.

As shown, a variety of educational practices assist practitioners to provide effective instruction to diverse learners. Educators can make certain that their classrooms support the use of these practices by periodically completing this guide.

In addition, Baca and Cervantes (2004) and Hoover, Klingner et al. (2008) suggest that the following best practices should be an integral part of the education of ELs:

- Prevention is viewed as a priority through professional collaboration.
- An ongoing, broadly based, nonbiased assessment is provided.
- Early intervention is offered.
- Some of students' struggles are viewed as symptoms rather than disabilities.
- A gifted rather than a remedial approach is used.
- A broad range of special education services is offered in an inclusive environment.
- Instruction is provided in the student's primary language, with ESL in the content areas.
- General classroom teachers are involved in program planning and implementation.

Also, parents should be provided with maximum amounts of information in a language they understand and should be meaningfully involved in planning and reinforcing instruction for their children.

Table 8.1   Checklist of Components for Effective Learning Environments for ELs

Instructions: Check each item addressed in the learning environment and share with problem-solving teams to best distinguish language difference from reading disability. Summary comments may also be documented at the end.
Optimal Learning Environment (Klingner et al., in press; Ruiz, 1995) . . .
___ Takes into account the student's sociocultural background and its effect on oral language, reading, writing, and second language learning
___ Takes into account the student's possible learning disabilities and its effect on oral language, reading, writing, and second language learning
___ Provides curriculum in a meaningful context where the communicative purpose is clear and authentic
___ Connects curriculum with the student's personal experiences
___ Incorporates children's literature into reading, writing, and ESL lessons

___ Involves the parents as active partners in the instruction of their children
Explicit and Enhanced Literature Instruction (Gersten & Baker, 2000; Gersten, Brengelman, & Jiménez, 1994; Gersten & Jiménez, 1994; Klingner et al., in press) . . .
___ Provides frequent feedback on quality of performance and support
___ Provides adequate practice and activities that are interesting and engaging
___ Reinforces oral language with written cues and material
___ Pays attention to language: synonyms, idioms, and so on
___ Includes mediation and feedback: rephrasing and expanding responses
___ Promotes vocabulary development by modeling and explaining
Authentic Language Usage (Escamilla, 1999; Herrera et al., 2015) . . .
___ Uses best practices for ELs that focus on language acquisition through authentic language usage
___ Stresses the importance of ELs being active participants in, rather than passive recipients of, language
___ Integrates the concept that authentic language use does not take place when language acquisition is treated as a separate subject in the student's day
Summary Comments:

CONCLUDING THOUGHTS ON FUTURE DIRECTIONS

As documented throughout this book, schools and school personnel in the 21st century have a critical need for interdisciplinary-trained special and general educators with specialized skills necessary to address linguistic and cultural diversity. These professionals can provide appropriate instructional programs and services to EL students (Bos & Fletcher, 1997; Darling-Hammond, 2000; Dee, 2000). In a recent article, "Constructing 21st Century Teacher Education," Darling-Hammond (2006) stated that "schools of education must design programs that help prospective teachers to understand deeply a wide array of things about learning, social and cultural contexts, and teaching and be able to enact those understandings in complex classrooms serving increasingly diverse students" (p. 302). She suggests that the enterprise of teaching embark on a "mutual transformation agenda," in essence developing partnerships with schools and communities as a part of this agenda.

We urge that professional development emphasize cross disciplinary and collaborative training that incorporates the multiple dimensions of teaching and learning discussed in this book. This suggests the use of collaborative teacher education models, which foster collaborative practices in which professionals are prepared to perform shared roles. The focus of classroom practice becomes more of a systems approach to meeting the needs of all children based on professional preparation using standards such as those developed by the Interstate Teacher Assessment and Support Consortium (CCSSO, 2013).

So as we embark on the enterprise of teaching in the 21st century, we applaud legislative initiatives, such as the MTSS model. The model, when implemented early, systematically, precisely, and with fidelity using culturally responsive evidenced-based interventions, holds promise to increase the academic success of all students. Nevertheless, we would like to caution and reiterate that it is incumbent on us as professionals to weave sociocultural and psycho-cultural variables into the process to ensure that contextualization occurs at multiple levels (Tharp, 1989). As previously emphasized, the MTSS approach has the potential to become a more refined process with validated procedures to ensure academic success for all students. To this end, continued research and further validation of the MTSS process for all students is necessary, especially for use with ELs.

References

Abedi, J. (2004a, November). *Psychometric issues in ELL assessment and special education eligibility*. Paper presented at the NCCRESt Conference, English Language Learners Struggling to Learn: Emergent Research on Linguistic Differences and Learning Disabilities, Tempe, AZ.

Abedi, J. (2004b). The No Child Left Behind Act and English language learners: Assessment and accountability issues. *Educational Researcher, 33*(1), 4–14.

Abedi, J. (2011). Assessing English language learners: Critical issues. In M. Basterra, E. Trumbull, & G. Solano-Flores (Eds.), *Cultural validity in assessment: Addressing linguistic and cultural diversity* (pp. 49–71). New York, NY: Routledge.

Abedi, J., Lord, C., & Plummer, J. (1997). *Language background as a variable in NAEP mathematics performance* (CSE Tech. Rep. No. 429). Los Angeles: University of California, National Center for Research on Evaluation, Standards, and Student Testing.

Aceves, T. C., & Orosco, M. J. (2014). Culturally responsive teaching (Document No. IC-2). Retrieved from University of Florida, Collaboration for Effective Educator, Development, Accountability, and Reform Center website: http://ceedar.education.ufl.edu/tools/innovation-configurations/

Adams, M. J. (1990). *Beginning to read: Thinking and learning about print*. Cambridge, MA: MIT Press.

Adler, P. (1975). The transitional experiences: An alternative view of culture shock. *Journal of Humanistic Psychology, 15*(4), 13–23.

Al Otaiba, S., Connor, C. M., Folsom, J., Wanzek, J., Greulich, L., Schatschneider, C., & Wagner, R. K. (2014). To wait in Tier 1 or intervene immediately: A randomized experiment examining first-grade response to intervention in reading. *Exceptional Children, 81*(1), 11–27.

Albert Shanker Institute. (2015). *The state of teacher diversity in American education*. Retrieved from http://www.shankerinstitute.org/resource/teacherdiversity

Allen, R. V. (1979). *Language experiences in communication*. Boston, MA: Houghton Mifflin.

Allington, R. L., & Cunningham, P. M. (2002). *Schools that work: Where all children read and write*. Boston, MA: Allyn & Bacon.

Almasi, J. F., & Gambrell, L. B. (1994). *Sociocognitive conflict in peer-led and teacher-led discussions of literature*. College Park, MD: National Reading Research Center.

Alton-Lee, A., Westera, J., & Pulegatoa-Diggins, C. (2012). *BES Exemplar 4 NgāKete Raukura—He tauira 4: Reciprocal teaching*. Ministry of Education, New Zealand. Retrieved from http://www.educationcounts.govt.nz/__data/assets/pdf_file/0017/107108/BES-Exemplar4.pdf

Alvermann, D. E., Young, J. P., Weaver, D., Hinchman, K. A., Moore, D. W., Phelps, S. F., . . . Zalewski, P. Z. (1996). Middle and high school students' perceptions of how they experience text-based discussions: A multicase study. *Reading Research Quarterly, 31*(3), 244–267.

American Speech-Language-Hearing Association (ASHA). (2004). *Knowledge and skills needed by speech-language pathologists and audiologists to provide culturally and linguistically appropriate services* [Knowledge and Skills]. Retrieved from www.asha.org/policy

Anthony, J. L., Solari, E. J., Williams, J. M., Schoger, K. D., Zhang, Z., Branum-Martin, L., & Francis, D. J. (2009). Development of bilingual phonological awareness in Spanish-speaking English language learners: The roles of vocabulary, letter knowledge, and prior phonological awareness. *Scientific Studies of Reading, 13*, 535–564.

Antunez, B. (2002). Implementing reading first with English language learners. *Directions in Language and Education, 15.* Retrieved from http://www.ncela.gwu.edu/pubs/directions/15.pdf

Artiles, A., Kozleski, E., Trent, S., Osher, D., & Ortiz, A. (2010). Justifying and explaining disproportionality, 1968–2008: A critique of underlying views of culture. *Exceptional Children, 76*, 279–299.

Artiles, A. J., Rueda, R., Salazar, J., & Higareda, I. (2005). Within-group diversity in minority disproportionate representation: English language learners in urban school districts. *Exceptional Children, 71*, 283–300.

Artiles, A. J., & Trent, S. C. (2000). Representation of culturally/linguistically diverse students. In C. R. Reynolds & E. Fletcher-Jantzen (Eds.), *Encyclopedia of special education, Vol. 1* (2nd ed., pp. 513–517). New York, NY: Wiley.

Au, K. H. (1993). *Literacy instruction in multicultural settings.* Orlando, FL: Holt, Rinehart & Winston.

Au, K. H. (2011). *Literacy achievement and diversity: Keys to success for students, teachers, and schools. Multicultural Education Series.* New York, NY: Teachers College Press.

Aud, S., Hussar, F., Johnson, G., Kena, G., & Roth, E. (2013). *The condition of education 2013* (NCES 2013–037). Washington, DC: US Department of Education, National Center for Education Statistics. Retrieved from http://nces.ed.gov/pubs2013/2013037.pdf

August, D., & Hakuta, K. (1997). *Improving schooling for language minority children: A research agenda.* Washington, DC: National Research Council and Institute of Medicine, National Academy Press.

August, D., & Shanahan, T. (2006). *Developing literacy in second-language learners: Report of the National Literacy Panel on language-minority children and youth.* Mahwah, NJ: Erlbaum.

Baca, L., & Cervantes, H. (2004). *The bilingual special education interface.* Upper Saddle River, NJ: Pearson, Merrill, Prentice Hall.

Bailey, A. L., & Carroll, P. E. (2015). Assessment of English language learners in the era of new academic content standards. *Review of Research in Education, 39*(1), 253–294.

Ballantyne, K. G., Sanderman, A. R., & Levy, J. (2008). *Educating English language learners: Building teacher capacity.* Washington, DC: National Clearinghouse for English Language Acquisition.

Barrera, M. (2004, November). *Roles of definitional and assessment models in the identification of new or second language learners of English for special education.* Paper presented at the 2004 NCCRESt Conference, English Language Learners Struggling to Learn: Emergent Research on Linguistic Differences and Learning Disabilities, Tempe, AZ.

Basterra, M. D. R. (2011). Cognition, culture, language and assessment: How to select culturally valid assessments in the classroom. In M. Basterra, E. Trumbull,

& G. Solano-Flores (Eds.), *Cultural validity in assessment: Addressing linguistic and cultural diversity* (pp. 72–95). New York, NY: Routledge.

Basterra, M. D. R., Trumbull, E., & Solano-Flores, G. (2011). *Cultural validity in assessment: Addressing linguistic and cultural diversity.* New York, NY: Routledge.

Bateman, B. (1965). An educational view of a diagnostic approach to learning disorders. In J. Hellmuth (Ed.), *Learning disorders: Vol. 1* (pp. 219–239). Seattle, WA: Special Child.

Bernhard, J. K., Cummins, J., Campoy, F. I., & Ada, A. F. (2004, November). *Cognitive engagement and identity investment in literacy development among English language learners: Evidence from the Early Authors Program.* Paper presented at the 2004 NCCRESt Conference, English Language Learners Struggling to Learn: Emergent Research on Linguistic Differences and Learning Disabilities, Tempe, AZ.

Bernhard, J. K., Cummins, J., Campoy, F. I., Ada, A. F., Winsler, A., & Bleiker, C. (2006). Identity texts and literacy development among preschool English language learners: Enhancing learning opportunities for children at risk of learning disabilities. *Teachers College Record, 108*(11), 2380–2405.

Best, J. W., & Kahn, J. V. (2006). *Research in education* (8th ed.). Boston, MA: Allyn & Bacon.

Blackorby, J., Lenz, K., Campbell, A., Wei, X., Greene, S., Padilla, C., & Lawyer-Brook, D. (2014a). *Denver Public Schools CSR Colorado: Evaluation of the 2011–12 school year.* Menlo Park, CA: SRI.

Blackorby, J., Lenz, K., Campbell, A., Wei, X., Greene, S., Padilla, C., & Lawyer-Brook, D. (2014b). *Denver Public Schools CSR Colorado: Evaluation of the 2012–13 school year.* Menlo Park, CA: SRI.

Boardman, A. G., Moore, B. A., & Scornavacco, K. (2015). Disrupting the "norm" with collaborative strategic reading. *English Journal, 105*(1), 48–54.

Boelé, A. L., Boardman, A. G., & Klingner, J. K. (2013). Promoting high quality student talk about text. *Connecticut Reading Association Journal, 2*(1), 29–36.

Bos, C., & Fletcher, T. (1997). Sociocultural considerations in learning disabilities research: Knowledge gaps and future directions. *Learning Disabilities Research and Practice, 12,* 92–99.

Bronfenbrenner, U. (1995). Developmental ecology through space and time: A future perspective. In P. Moen, G. Elder, & K. Luescher (Eds.), *Examining lives in context: Perspectives on the ecology of human development* (pp. 619–647). Washington, DC: American Psychological Association.

Brophy, J. (2010). *Motivating students to learn* (3rd ed.). New York, NY: Routledge.

Brown-Chidsey, R., & Steege, M. W. (2010). *Response to intervention: Principles and strategies for effective practice* (2nd ed.). New York, NY: Guilford Press.

Buckley, P., Klingner, J., & Boardman, A. G. (2014, April). *The impact of collaborative strategic reading over time.* Paper presented at the American Educational Research Association Annual Meeting, Philadelphia, PA.

Buckley, P., & Moore, B. (2015, March). *The relation between fidelity of implementation to collaborative strategic reading and student achievement.* Paper presented to the Society for Research in Educational Effectiveness Annual Meeting, Washington, DC.

Burden, P. R., & Byrd, D. M. (2012). *Methods for effective teaching: Meeting the needs of all students* (6th ed.). Upper Saddle River, NJ: Pearson Education.

Burns, M. K., & Gibbons, K. A. (2008). *Implementing response-to-intervention in elementary and secondary schools: Procedures to assure scientific-based practices.* New York, NY: Taylor & Francis.

Calderón, M. (2008). Innovative policies and practices for developing teachers to work with English language learners. Retrieved from http://www.ets.org/Media/Conferences_and_Events/pdf/ELLsympsium/Calderon.pdf

Calderón, M., Hertz-Lazarowitz, R., Ivory, G., & Slavin, R. E. (1997). Effects of bilingual cooperative integrated reading and composition on students transitioning from Spanish to English reading. Center for Research on the Education of Students Placed At Risk (CRESPAR). Retrieved from http://www.csos.jhu.edu/crespar/techReports/report10.pdf

Camarota, S. A. (2012). *Immigrants in the United States: A profile of America's foreign-born population.* Washington, DC: The Center for Immigration Studies.

Canter, A. (2006). Problem solving and RTI: New roles for school psychologists. NASP *Communiqué, 34*(5). Retrieved from http://www.nasponline.org/publications/cq/cq345rti.aspx

Capp, R., Fix, M., Murray, J., Ost, J., Passel, J. S., & Herwantoro, S. (2005). *The new demography of America's schools: Immigration and the No Child Left Behind Act.* Washington, DC: Urban Institute.

Carlisle, J. F., Beeman, M. M., Davis, L. H., & Spharim, G. (1999). Relationship of metalinguistic capabilities and reading achievement for children who are becomming bilingual. *Applied Psycholinguistics, 20,* 459–478.

Cazden, C. (2001). *Classroom discourse: The language of teaching and learning.* Portsmouth, NH: Heinemann.

Celce-Murcia, M., & Larsen-Freeman, D. (1983). *The grammar book: An ESL/EFL teacher's book.* Rowley, MA: Newbury House.

Cha, K., & Goldenberg, C. (2015). The complex relationship between bilingual home language input and kindergarten children's Spanish and English oral proficiencies. *Journal of Educational Psychology, 107*(4), 935–953. http://dx.doi.org/10.1037/edu0000030

Chamot, A. U. (1995, Summer/Fall). Implementing the cognitive academic language learning approach: CALLA in Arlington, VA. *The Bilingual Research Journal, 19*(3 & 4), 379–394.

Chamot, A. U., & O'Malley, J. M. (1996). The cognitive academic language learning approach (CALLA): A model for linguistically diverse classrooms. *Elementary School Journal, 6*(3), 259–273.

Chandler, J. (2003). The efficiency of various kinds of error feedback for improvement in the accuracy and fluency of L2 student writing. *Journal of Second Language Writing, 12,* 267–296.

Chiappe, P., Siegel, L. A., & Gottardo, A. (2002). Reading-related skills of kindergartners from diverse linguistic backgrounds. *Applied Psycholinguistics, 23,* 95–116.

Child Trends. (2014). *Immigrant children.* Retrieved from http://www.childtrends.org/?indicators=immigrant-children

Chomsky, N. (1965). *Aspects of theory of syntax.* Cambridge, MA: MIT Press.

Christ, T. J., Burns, M. K., & Ysseldyke, J. E. (2005). Exploring RTI: Conceptual confusion within response-to-intervention vernacular: Clarifying meaningful differences. *NASP Communiqué, 34*(3). Retrieved from http://www.nasponline.org/publications/cq/cq343rti.aspx

Cloud, N., Genesee, F., & Hamayan, E. (2009). *Literacy instruction for English language learners: A teacher's guide to research-based practices.* Portsmouth, NH: Heinemann.

Cognitive Academic Language Learning Approach, The (CALLA). (2015). Overview. Retrieved from http://jillrobbins.com/calla/overview.html

Cohen, L. G., & Spenciner, L. J. (2015). *Assessment of children and youth with special needs.* Boston, MA: Pearson.

Collier, C. (1988). *Assessing minority students with learning and behavior problems.* Boulder, CO: Hamilton.

Collier, C. (2005). Separating language difference from disability. *NABE News, 28*(3), 13–17.

Collier, C., & Hoover, J. J. (1987a). *Cognitive learning styles for minority handicapped students.* Boulder, CO: Hamilton.

Collier, C., & Hoover, J. J. (1987b). Sociocultural considerations when referring diverse children for learning disabilities. *LD Focus, 3*(1), 39–45.

Colombo, M. (2012). *Teaching English language learners: 43 strategies for successful K–8 classrooms.* Thousand Oaks, CA: Sage.

Colorado Department of Education (CDE). (2015). Multi-tiered system of supports (MTSS). Colorado Department of Education website: http://www.cde.state.co.us/mtss/components.

Colorín Colorado (2007). Cooperative learning strategies. Retrieved from http://www.colorincolorado.org/educators/content/cooperative/

Commins, N. L. (2012). What are defining features of effective programs for English language learners? In E. Hamayan & R. Freeman (Eds.), *English language learners at school: A guide for administrators* (2nd ed., pp. 98–100). Philadelphia, PA: Caslon.

Compton, D. L., Fuchs, D., Fuchs, L. S., & Bryant, J. D. (2006). Selecting at-risk readers in first grade for early intervention: A two-year longitudinal study of decision rules and procedures. *Journal of Educational Psychology, 98,* 394–409.

Congressional Budget Office. (2013). Snapshot of the foreign-born population in the United States, 1860–2010. Washington, DC. Retrieved from https://www.cbo.gov/publication/44135?utm_source=feedblitz&utm_medium=FeedBlitzEmail&utm_content=812526&utm_campaign=0

Council for Exceptional Children (CEC). (2008). CEC's position on response to intervention (RTI): Unique role of special education and special educators. In *Council for Exceptional Children 2008 Policy Manual;* Section Four, Part 3; pp. 1–10. Retrieved from https://www.cec.sped.org/~/media/Files/Policy/CEC%20Professional%20Policies%20and%20Positions/RTI.pdf

Council of Chief State School Officers (CCSSO), Interstate Teacher Assessment and Support Consortium (InTASC). (2013, April). *Model core teaching standards and learning progressions for teachers 1.0: A resource for ongoing teacher development.* Washington, DC: Author.

Council of Chief State School Officers (CCSSO). (2015). *Promises to keep: Transforming educator preparation to better serve a diverse range of learners.* Washington, DC: Author.

Cramer, L. (2015). Inequities of intervention among culturally and linguistically diverse students. *Penn GSE Perspectives on Urban Education, 12*(1). Retrieved from http://files.eric.ed.gov/fulltext/EJ1056724.pdf

Crawford, J. (1999). *Bilingual education: History, politics, theory, and practice* (4th ed.). Los Angeles, CA: Bilingual Educational Services.

Crystal, D. (1997). *The Cambridge encyclopedia of language* (2nd ed.). Cambridge, UK: Cambridge University Press.

Cummins, D. D., Kintsch, W., Reusser, K., & Weimer, R. (1988). The role of understanding in solving word problems. *Cognitive Psychology, 20,* 405–438.

Cummins, J. (1979). Linguistic interdependence and the educational development of bilingual children. *Review of Educational Research, 49,* 221–251.

Cummins, J. (1981). The role of primary language development in promoting educational success for language minority students. In California State Department of Education (Ed.), *Schooling and language minority students: A theoretical framework* (pp. 3–50). Sacramento: California State Department of Education.

Cummins, J. (1984). *Bilingualism and special education: Issues in assessment and pedagogy.* Clevedon, England, UK: Multilingual Matters.

Cummins, J. (1986). Empowering minority students: A framework for intervention. *Harvard Educational Review, 56,* 18–36.

Cummins, J. (1989). A theoretical framework for bilingual special education. *Exceptional Children, 56*(3), 111–119.

Cummins, J. (2000). *Language, power and pedagogy: Bilingual children in the crossfire.* Clevedon, England, UK: Multilingual Matters.

Curtin, E. (2005). Teaching practices for ESL students. *Multicultural Education, 12*(3), 22–27.

Darling-Hammond, L. (2000). Teacher quality and student achievement: A review of state policy evidence. *Education Policy Analysis Archives, 8,* 1–67.

Darling-Hammond, L. (2006). Constructing 21st-century teacher education. *Journal of Teacher Education, 57,* 300–314.

de Oliveira, L., C., & Burke, A. M. (2015). Mainstream elementary teachers' perceptions about teaching English language learners. In L. C. de Oliveira & M. Yough (Eds.), *Preparing teachers to work with English language learners in mainstream classrooms* (pp. 3–15). Charlotte, NC: IAP and TESOL Press.

de Onís, C. (2005). The mismatch between teachers and students: Meeting the challenge of preparing teachers for diversity. In R. Hoosain & F. S. Farideh (Eds.), *Language in multicultural education* (pp. 205–229). Charlotte, NC: Information Age.

DeCapua, A., & Marshall, H. (2011). Reaching ELLs at risk: Instruction for students with limited or interrupted formal education. *Preventing School Failure, 55*(1), 35–41.

Dee, T. S. (2000). *Teachers, race and student achievement in a randomized experiment.* Unpublished manuscript, Swarthmore College, Pennsylvania.

Deno, S. L. (2005). Problem-solving assessment. In R. Brown-Chidsey (Ed.), *Assessment for intervention: A problem-solving approach* (pp. 10–40). New York, NY: Guilford Press.

Dole, J. A., Nokes, J. D., & Drits, D. (2009). Cognitive strategy instruction. In G. G. Duffy & S. E. Israel (Eds.), *Handbook of research on reading comprehension* (pp. 347–372). Mahwah, NJ: Erlbaum.

Donovan, M. S., & Cross, C. (Eds.). (2002). *Minority students in special and gifted education.* Washington, DC: National Academy Press.

Durgunoglu, A. (2002). Cross linguistic transfer in literacy development and implications for language learners. *Annals of Dyslexia, 52,* 189–204.

Durgunoglu, A. Y., Nagy, W. E., & Hancin-Bhatt, B. J. (1993). Cross-language transfer of phonological awareness. *Journal of Educational Psychology, 85,* 453–465.

Echevarria, J. (1995). Interactive reading instruction: A comparison of proximal and distal effects of instructional conversations. *Exceptional Children, 61*(6), 536–552.

Echevarria, J. J., Vogt, M. E., & Short, D. J. (2012). *Making content comprehensible for English learners: The SIOP model* (4th ed.). Boston, MA: Pearson.

Eeds, M., & Wells, D. (1989). Grand conversations: An exploration of meaning construction in literature study groups. *Research in the Teaching of English, 23*(1), 4–29.

Eppolito, A., Boardman, A., Jensen, C., & Wang, C. (2014). *Let's give them something to talk about: English learners' participation and academic language use in science and social studies.* Unpublished manuscript, School of Education, University of Colorado, Boulder, Colorado.

Escamilla, K. (1999). On educating culturally and linguistically diverse students: A professional development resource series. *Second Language Acquisition.* Boulder: University of Colorado, BUENO Center, School of Education.

Escamilla, K., & Escamilla, M. (2003). *Literature review: Best practices for Latino preschool children* (ALMAR Research Report). Boulder, CO: Boulder County Head Start, City of Boulder Children, Youth and Families Division.

Escamilla, K., & Hopewell, S. (2010). Transitions to biliteracy: Creating positive trajectories for emerging bilinguals in the U.S. In J. Petrovic (Ed.), *International perspectives on bilingual education: Policy, practice and controversy.* New York, NY: Information Age.

Escamilla, K., Ruiz-Figueroa, O. A., Hopewell, S., Butvilofsky, S., & Sparrow, W. (2010). *Transitions to biliteracy: Literacy squared 2004–2009* (Tech. Rep). Boulder: University of Colorado, Boulder School of Education, BUENO Center.

Fairbairn, S., & Jones-Vo, S. (2010). *Differentiating instruction and assessment for English language learners: A guide for K–12 teachers.* Philadelphia, PA: Caslon.

Farnia, F., & Geva, E. (2011). Cognitive correlates of vocabulary growth in English language learners. *Applied Psycholinguistics, 32,* 711–738. doi:10.1017/S0142716411000038

Farr, M., & Ball, A. F. (1999). Standard English. In B. Spolsky (Ed.), *Concise encyclopedia of educational linguistics* (pp. 205–208). Oxford, UK: Elsevier.

Fathman, A., & Whalley, E. (1990). Teacher response to student correction: Focus on form versus content. In Barbara Kroll (Ed.), *Second language writing: Research insights for the classroom* (pp. 178–185). Cambridge, UK: Cambridge University Press.

Ferris, D., & Hedgcock, J. S. (1998). *Teaching ESL composition: Purpose, process, and practice.* Mahwah, NJ: Erlbaum.

Ferris, D. R. (2002). *Treatment of error in second language student writing.* Ann Arbor, University of Michigan Press.

Figueroa, R. (1989). Psychological testing of linguistic-minority students: Knowledge gaps and regulations. *Exceptional Children, 56,* 145–153.

Figueroa, R. A., & Newsome, P. (2004, November). *The diagnosis of Learning Disabilities in English language learners: Is it nondiscriminatory?* Paper presented at the 2004 NCCRESt Conference, English Language Learners Struggling to Learn: Emergent Research on Linguistic Differences and Learning Disabilities, Tempe, AZ.

Fisher, D., & Frey, N. (2008). *Better learning through structured teaching: A framework for the gradual release of responsibility.* Alexandria, VA: Association for Supervision and Curriculum Development.

Flavell, J. H. (1979). Metacognition and cognitive monitoring: A new area of cognitive-developmental inquiry. *American Psychologist, 34,* pp. 906–911.

Ford, K. (2005). Fostering literacy development in English language learners. Retrieved from http://www.colorincolorado.org/article/12924/

Ford, K. (2012). ELLs and reading fluency in English. Retrieved from http://www.colorincolorado.org/educators/teaching/fluency/

Forman, E. A., & McPhail, J. (1993). Vygotskian perspective on children's collaborative problem-solving activities. In E. A. Forman, N. Minick, & C. A. Stone (Eds.), *Contexts for learning: Sociocultural dynamics in children's development* (pp. 213–229). New York, NY: Oxford University Press.

Francis, D. J., Rivera, M., Lesaux, N., Kieffer, M., & Rivera, H. (2006). *Research-based recommendations for instruction and academic interventions: Practical guidelines for the education of English language learners.* Houston, TX: Center on Instruction.

Freeman, G. G. (1978, June). *Interdisciplinary evaluation of children's primary language skills.* Paper presented at the World Congress on Future Special Education, First, Stirling, Scotland. (ERIC Document Reproduction Service No. ED157341.

Fry, R., & Taylor, P. (2012). *The rise of residential segregation by income.* Washington, DC: Pew Research Center.

Fuchs, D., & Fuchs, L. S. (2006). Introduction to response to intervention: What, why, and how valid is it? *Reading Research Quarterly, 41*(1), 93–99.

Fuchs, D., Mock, D., Morgan, P. L., & Young, C. (2003). Responsiveness-to-instruction intervention: Definitions, evidence, and implications for the learning disabilities construct. *Learning Disabilities: Research & Practice, 18*(3), 157–171.

Galland, P. A. (1995). *An evaluation of the cognitive academic language learning approach (CALLA) in the high intensity language training (HILT) science program in Arlington Public Schools* (Unpublished master's thesis), Washington, DC: Georgetown University.

Gallego, M., Zamora Durán, G., & Reyes, E. (2006). It depends: A sociohistorical account of the definition and methods of identification of learning disabilities. *The Teachers College Record, 108*(11), 2195–2219.

Galloway, E. P., & Lesaux, N. K. (2014). Leader, teacher, diagnostician, colleague, and change agent: A synthesis of the research on the role of the reading specialist in this era of RTI-based literacy reform. *The Reading Teacher, 67*(7), 517–526. doi:10.1002/trtr.1251.

Garcia, E. (2004, November). *Who are these linguistically and culturally diverse students?* Paper presented at the National Center for Culturally Responsive Educational Systems Research Conference on English Language Learners Struggling to Learn: Emergent Research on Linguistic Differences and Learning Disabilities, Scottsdale, AZ.

García, O. (2009). *Bilingual education in the 21st century: A global perspective.* West Sussex, UK: Wiley-Blackwell.

Garcia, S. B., & Ortiz, A. A. (2006). *Preventing disproportionate representation: Culturally and linguistically responsive prereferral interventions* (NCCRESt Brief). Tempe, AZ: National Center for Culturally Responsive Educational Systems.

Gascoigne, C. (2004). Examining the effect of feedback in beginning L2 composition. *Foreign Language Annals, 37*(1), 71–76.

Gay, G. (2010). *Culturally responsive teaching: Theory, research, and practice.* New York, NY: Teachers College Press.

Genesee, F. (Ed.). (1994). Introduction. In F. Genesee (Ed.), *Educating second language children: The whole child, the whole curriculum, the whole community* (pp. 1–11). Cambridge, UK: Cambridge University Press on Linguistic Differences and Learning.

Genesee, F., & Nicoladis, E. (2006). Bilingual first language acquisition. In E. Hoff & M. Shatz (Eds.), *Handbook of language development* (pp. 324–342). Oxford, UK: Blackwell.

Gentile, L. (2004). *The oracy instructional guide.* Carlsbad, CA: Dominie Press.

Gersten, R., & Baker, S. (2000). What we know about effective instructional practices for English-language learners. *Exceptional Children, 66,* 454–470.

Gersten, R., Brengelman, S., & Jimenez, R. (1994). Effective instruction for culturally and linguistically diverse students: A reconceptualization. *Focus on Exceptional Children, 27*(1), 1–16.

Gersten, R., & Jimenez, R. (1994). A delicate balance: Enhancing literacy instruction for students of English as a second language. *Reading Teacher, 47,* 438–449.

Gleitman, L., & Landau, B. (1994). *The acquisition of the lexicon.* Cambridge, MA: MIT Press.

Goldenberg, C. (1992–1993). Instructional conversations: Promoting comprehension through discussion, *The Reading Teacher, 46*(4), 316–326.

Goldenberg, C. (2006). *Improving achievement for English learners: Conclusions from 2 research reviews.* Retrieved from http://www.colorincolorado.org/article/12918

Goldenberg, C. (2008, Summer). Teaching English language learners: What the research does and does not say. *American Educator, 32*(2), 8–44.

Goldenberg, C. (2013). Unlocking the research on English Learners: What we know—and don't yet know—About effective instruction. *American Educator, 37*(2), 4–11, 38.

Goldenberg, C., Hicks, J., & Lit, I, (2013). Dual language learners: Effective instruction in early childhood. *American Educator, 37*(2), 26–29.

Good, R. H., & Kaminski, R. A. (Eds.). (2002). *Dynamic indicators of basic early literacy skills* (6th ed.). Eugene, OR: Institute for the Development of Educational Achievement.

Greene, J. (1997). A meta-analysis of the Rossell and Baker review of bilingual education research. *Bilingual Research Journal, 21,* 103–122.

Greenwood, C. R., Arreaga-Mayer, C., Utley, C. A., Gavin, K. M., & Terry, B. J. (2001). Classwide peer tutoring learning management system: Applications with elementary-level English language learners. *Remedial And Special Education, 22*(1), 34–47.

Greenwood, C. R., Terry, B., Utley, C. A., Montagna, D., & Walker, D. (1993). Achievement placement and services: Middle school benefits of classwide peer tutoring used at the elementary school. *School Psychology Review, 22*(3), 497–516.

Grigorenko, E. L. (2009). Dynamic assessment and response to intervention: Two sides of one coin. *Journal of Learning Disabilities, 42*(2), 111–132.

Grigorenko, E. L., & Sternberg, R. J. (1998). Dynamic testing. *Psychological Bulletin, 124,* 75–111.

Grossman, H. (1995). *Special education in a diverse society.* Boston, MA: Allyn & Bacon.

Gunn, B., Biglan, A., Smolkowski, K., & Ary, D. (2000). The efficacy of supplemental instruction in decoding skills for Hispanic and non-Hispanic students in early elementary school. *Journal of Special Education, 34*(2), 90–103.

Gunn, B., Smolkowski, K., Biglan, A., Black, C., & Blair, J. (2005). Fostering the development of reading skill through supplemental instruction: Results for Hispanic and non-Hispanic students. *Journal of Special Education, 39,* 66–85.

Haager, D. (2004, November). *Promoting reading achievement for English language learners learning in English: A case for explicit instruction.* Paper presented at the NCCRESt Conference, English Language Learners Struggling to Learn: Emergent Research on Linguistic Differences and Learning Disabilities, Tempe, AZ.

Hallahan, D. P., & Mercer, C. (2002). Learning disabilities: Historical perspectives. In R. Bradley, L. Danielson, & D. P. Hallahan (Eds.), *Identification of learning disabilities: Research to practice* (pp. 1–68). Mahwah, NJ: Erlbaum.

Halliday, M. A. K. (1978). *Language as social semiotic: The social interpretation of language and meaning.* London, UK: Edward Arnold.

Hamayan, E., Marler, B., Sanchez-Lopez, C., & Damico, J. (2013). *Special education considerations for English language learners: Delivering a continuum of services* (2nd ed.). Philadelphia, PA: Caslon.

Hammill, D., Leigh, F., McNutt, G., & Larsen, S. (1981). A new definition of learning disability. *Learning Disability Quarterly, 4,* 336–342.

Hanselman, E. (2015, February). *Multi-tiered system of supports: Uniting through one vision.* Beyond NCLB: Annual Statewide ESEA/NCLB Conference, February 3–5, Chicago, IL.

Harper, C. A., & de Jong, E. J. (2004). Misconceptions about teaching ELLs. *Journal of Adolescent and Adult Literacy, 48*(2), 152–162.

Harry, B., & Klingner, J. (2005). *Why are so many minority students in special education? Understanding race and disability in schools.* New York, NY: Teachers College Press.

Harry, B., & Klingner, J. (2014). *Why are so many minority students in special education?* New York, NY: Teachers College Press.

Hernandez, J. S. (1991). Assisted performance in reading comprehension strategies with non-English proficient students. *The Journal of Educational Issues of Language Minority Students, 8,* 91–112.

Herrell, A. L., & Jordan, M. (2008). *Fifty strategies for teaching English language learners.* Upper Saddle River, NJ: Pearson Education.

Herrera, S. G., Perez, D. R., & Escamilla, K. (2015). *Teaching reading to English language learners: Differentiated literacies* (2nd ed.). Boston, MA: Pearson.

Hidayah, T. (2009). Collaborative strategic reading (CSR) strategy and its significance for reading comprehension. Retrieved from http://www.academia.edu/4020740/Collaborative_Strategic_Reading_CSR_Strategy_and_Its_Significance_for_Reading_Comprehension

Hiebert, E. H., Pearson, P. D., Taylor, B. M., Richardson, V., & Paris, S. G. (1998). *Every child a reader: Applying reading research to the classroom.* Ann Arbor, MI: University of Michigan School of Education, Center for the Improvement of Early Reading Achievement.

Hill, J. D., & Miller, K. B. (2013). *Classroom instruction that works with English language learners* (2nd ed.). Alexandria, VA: ASCD.

Hite, C. E., & Evans, L. S. (2006). Mainstream first-grade teachers' understanding of strategies for accommodating the needs of English language learners. *Teacher Education Quarterly, 33*(2), 89–110.

Hoover, J. J. (2006, April). *Framework for culturally competent response to intervention.* Invited presentation delivered at the New York City Public Schools, Summit on Differentiated Instruction and Academic Interventions, New York, NY.

Hoover, J. J. (2010). Special education eligibility decision making in response to intervention models. *Theory into Practice, 49*(4), 289–296.

Hoover, J. J. (2012). Reducing unnecessary referrals: Guidelines for teachers or diverse learners. *Teaching Exceptional Children, 44*(4), 38–47.

Hoover, J. J. (2013). *Linking assessment to instruction in multi-tiered models: A teacher's guide to selecting reading, writing, and mathematics interventions.* Boston, MA: Pearson.

Hoover, J. J., & Collier, C. (1985). Referring culturally different children: Sociocultural considerations. *Academic Therapy, 20*(4), 503–509.

Hoover, J. J., & Collier, C. (2003). *Learning styles* [CD-ROM]. Boulder: University of Colorado, BUENO Center, School of Education.

Hoover, J. J., & Erickson, J. (2015). Culturally responsive special education referrals of English learners in one rural county school district: Pilot project. *Rural Special Education Quarterly, 34*(4), 18–28.

Hoover, J. J., & Klingner, J. (2011). Promoting cultural validity in the assessment of bilingual special education students. In M. Basterra, E. Trumbull, & G. Solano-Flores (Eds.), *Cultural validity in assessment: Addressing linguistic and cultural diversity* (pp. 143–167). New York, NY: Routledge.

Hoover, J. J., Klingner, J. K., Baca, L. M., & Patton, J. M. (2008). *Teaching culturally and linguistically diverse exceptional learners.* Columbus, OH: Merrill.

Hoover, J. J., & Love, E. (2011). Supporting school-based response to intervention: A practitioner's model. *Teaching Exceptional Children, 43*(3), 40–49.

Hoover, J. J., & Soltero-Gonzalez, L. (2014, April). *Examination of teaching abilities in the delivery of multilevel literacy instruction to ELs.* Conference presentation (of OSEP funded Model Demonstration Project), Council for Exceptional Children Convention, Philadelphia, PA, April 11, 2014.

Hosp, J. L., & Reschy, D. J. (2003). Referral rates for intervention or assessment: A meta-analysis of racial differences. *Journal of Special Education, 37*(2), 67–80.

Hunt, K. W. (1965). *Grammatical structures written at three grade levels* (Research Rep. No. 3). Urbana, IL: National Council of Teachers of English.

Individuals with Disabilities Education Act (IDEA) of 1991, Pub L. No. 102–119.

Individuals with Disabilities Education Act Amendments of 1997, Pub. L. No. 105–17, SS 601 *et seq.,* 111 Stat. 37 (1997).

Individuals with Disabilities Education Improvement Act (IDEIA, 2004) H.R. 1350. Retrieved from http://thomas.loc.gov/cgi-bin/query/z?c108:h.1350.enr

IRIS Center for Training Enhancements. (n.d.). *Star legacy module-RtI.* Retrieved from http://iris.peabody.vanderbilt.edu/resources.html

Irujo, S. (2004). Differentiated instruction: We can no longer just aim down the middle. *ELL Outlook.* Retrieved from http://coursecrafters.com/ELL-Outlook/index.html

Isik, A. (2000). The role of input in second language acquisition: More comprehensible input supported by grammar instruction or more grammar instruction? *ITL: Review of Applied Linguistics,* 129–130, 225–274.

Jiménez, R. T. (1997). The strategic reading abilities and potential of five low-literacy Latina/o readers in middle school. *Reading Research Quarterly, 32*(3), 224–243.

Jiménez, R. T., García, G., & Pearson, P. D. (1994). Three children, two languages, and strategic reading: Case studies in bilingual/monolingual reading. *American Educational Journal, 32,* 67–98.

Kendall, J., & Khuon, O. (2005). *Making sense: Small-group comprehension lessons for English language learners.* Portland, ME: Stenhouse.

Kirk, S. A. (1962). *Educating exceptional children.* Boston, MA: Houghton Mifflin.

Klassen, K., & Maune, M. (2015). Common Core State Standards in English language arts: Pedagogical implications of language analysis. In L. C. de Oliveira & M. Young (Eds.), *Preparing teachers to work with English language learners in mainstream classrooms* (pp. 77–92). Charlotte, NC: Information Age.

Klingner, J., Eppolito, A., Hoover, J. J., Soltero-González, L., Smith, C., K. White, & Cano-Rodriguez, E. (in press). Systemic issues in the implementation of RTI in culturally and linguistically diverse schools. In E. C. Lopez, S. G. Nahari, & S. L. Proctor (Eds.), *Handbook of multicultural school psychology: An interdisciplinary perspective* (2nd ed.). London, UK: Routledge.

Klingner, J., & Hoover, J. J. (2014). Challenges for implementing RTI for English learners. *Reading Today,* July/August, pp. 12–14.

Klingner, J., Vaughn, S., Boardman, A., & Swanson, E. (2012). *Now we get it! Boosting comprehension with collaborative strategic reading.* San Francisco, CA: Jossey-Bass.

Klingner, J. K., Artiles, A. J., & Barletta, L. M. (2006). English Language Learners Who Struggle With Reading Language Acquisition or LD? *Journal of Learning Disabilities, 39*(2), 108–128.

Klingner, J. K., Artiles, A. J., Kozleski, E., Harry, B., Zion, S., Tate, W., . . . Riley, D. (2005). Addressing the disproportionate representation of culturally and linguistically diverse students in special education through culturally responsive educational systems. *Education Policy Analysis Archives, 13*(38), 1–39. Retrieved from http://epaa.asu.edu/epaa/v13n38/

Klingner, J. K., Boelé, A. L., Linan-Thompson, S., & Rodriguez, D. (2014). Essential components of special education for English language learners with learning disabilities: Position statement of the Division for Learning Disabilities of the Council for Exceptional Children. *Learning Disabilities Research & Practice, 29*(3), 93–96.

Klingner, J. K., & Edwards, P. (2006). Cultural considerations with response to intervention models. *Reading Research Quarterly, 41,* 108–117.

Klingner, J. K., & Eppolito, A. (2014). *English language learners: Differentiating between language acquisition and learning disabilities.* Arlington, VA: Council for Exceptional Children.

Klingner, J. K., & Harry, B. (2004, November). *The special education referral and decision-making process for English language learners—Child study team meetings and staffings.* Paper presented at the 2004 NCCRESt Conference, English Language Learners Struggling to Learn: Emergent Research on Linguistic Differences and Learning Disabilities, Tempe, AZ.

Klingner, J. K., Soltero-Gonzalez, L., & Lesaux, N. (2010). Response to intervention for English language learners. In M. Lipson & K. Wixson (Eds.), *Successful approaches to response to intervention (RTI): Collaborative practices for improving K–12 literacy* (pp. 134–162). Newark, DE: International Reading Association.

Klingner, J. K., Urbach, J., Golos, D., Brownell, M., & Menon, S. (2010). Teaching reading in the 21st century: A glimpse at how special education teachers promote reading. *Learning Disabilities Quarterly, 33*(2), 59–74.

Klingner, J. K., & Vaughn, S. (1996). Reciprocal teaching of reading comprehension strategies for students with learning disabilities who use English as a second language. *The Elementary School Journal, 96,* 275–292.

Klingner, J. K., & Vaughn, S. (1998). Using collaborative strategic reading. *Teaching Exceptional Children, 30,* 32–37.

Klingner, J. K., & Vaughn, S. (2000). The helping behaviors of fifth-graders while using collaborative strategic reading (CSR) during ESL content classes. *TESOL Quarterly, 34,* pp. 69–98.

Kovaleski, J., VanDerHeyden, A., & Shapiro, E. (2013). *The RTI approach to evaluating learning disabilities.* New York, NY: Guilford Press.

Krashen, S. D. (1981). Bilingual education and second language acquisition theory. In Bilingual Education Office (Ed.), *Schooling and language-minority students: A theoretical framework,* pp. 51–79. Los Angeles, CA: Evaluation, Dissemination, and Assessment Center.

Krashen, S. D. (1982). *Principles and practice in second language acquisition.* Oxford, UK: Pergamon.

Krashen, S. D., & Terrell, T. D. (1983). *The natural approach: Language acquisition in the classroom.* London, UK: Prentice Hall Europe.

Lachat, M. A. (2004). *Standards-based instruction and assessment for English language learners.* Thousand Oaks, CA: Corwin.

Ladson-Billings, G. (2009). *The dreamkeepers: successful teaching for African American Students* (2nd ed.). San Francisco, CA: Jossey-Bass.

Lake, V. E., & Pappamihiel, N. E. (2003). Effective practices and principles to support English language learners in the early childhood classroom. *Childhood Education, 79*(4), 200–204.

Landis, D., Umolu, J., & Mancha, S. (2010). The power of language experience for cross-cultural reading and writing. *The Reading Teacher, 63*(7), 580–589.

Langdon, H. W. (1989). Language disorder or language difference? Assessing the language skills of Hispanic students. *Exceptional Children, 56,* 160–167.

Lantolf, J. P., & Poehner, M. E. (2004). *Dynamic assessment in the language classroom* (CALPER Professional Development Document CPDD-0411). University Park: The Pennsylvania State University, Center for Advanced Language Proficiency Education and Research.

Lantolf, J. P., & Poehner, M. E. (2008). *Sociocultural theory and the teaching of second languages.* London, UK: Equinox.

Lee, J. (2002). Racial and ethnic achievement gap trends: Reversing the progress towards equity. *Educational Researcher, 32,* 3–12.

Lesaux, N. (2013). Focus on higher-order literacy skills: How can schools best educate Hispanic students? *Education Next, 13*(2*).* Retrieved from http://educationnext.org

Lesaux, N., & Geva, E. (2006). Synthesis: Development of literacy in language-minority students. In D. August & T. Shanahan (Eds.), *Developing literacy in second-language learners: Report of the National Literacy Panel on Language Minority Children and Youth.* Mahwah, NJ: Erlbaum.

Li, X., & Zhang, M. (2004). Why Mei still cannot read and what can be done. *Journal of Adolescent and Adult Literacy, 48*(2), 92–101.

Lidz, C. (2003). The application of cognitive function scale: A dynamic assessment procedure for young children. In Tan O. S. & Seng A. S. H (Eds.), *Enhancing cognitive functions: Application across contexts.* Singapore, Republic of Singapore: McGraw Hill.

Lidz, C., & Elliott, J. (Eds.). (2000). *Dynamic assessment: Prevailing models and applications. Advances in cognition and educational practice* (Vol. 6). Philadelphia, PA: Elsevier Science.

Linan-Thompson, S. (2010). Response to instruction, English language learners and disproportionate representation: The role of assessment. *Psicothema, 22,* 970–974.

Linan-Thompson, S., Cirino, P. T., & Vaughn, S. (2007). Determining English language learners' Response to Intervention: Questions and some answers. *Learning Disability Quarterly, 30*(3), 185–195.

Linan-Thompson, S., & Vaughn, S. (2007). Research-based methods of reading instruction for English language learners, Grades K–4. Alexandria, VA: The Association for Supervision and Curriculum Development (ASCD).

Linan-Thompson, S., Vaughn, S., Prater, K., & Cirino, P. T. (2004, November). *The response to intervention of English language learners at-risk for reading problems.* Paper presented at the 2004 NCCRESt Conference, English Language Learners Struggling to Learn: Emergent Research on Linguistic Differences and Learning Disabilities, Tempe, AZ.

Lindsey, K. A., Manis, F. R., & Bailey, C. E. (2003). Prediction of first-grade reading in Spanish-speaking English-language learners. *Journal of Educational Psychology, 95,* 482–494.

Lloyd, J. W., & Hallahan, D. P. (2005). Going forward: How the field of learning disabilities has and will contribute to education. *Learning Disability Quarterly, 28*(2), 133–136.

Loe, S. A., & Miranda, A. H. (2002). Assessment of culturally and linguistically diverse learners with behavioral disorders. In G. Cartledge, K. Y. Tam, S. A. Loe, A. H. Miranda, M. C., Lamberts, C. D. Kea, & S. E. Simmons-Reed (Eds.), *Culturally and linguistically diverse students with behavioral disorders* (pp. 25–36). Arlington, VA: Council for Exceptional Children, Council for Children with Behavioral Disorders Division.

Macceca, S. (2007). *Reading strategies for science.* Huntington Beach, CA: Shell Education.

MacSwan, J. (2000). The threshold hypothesis, semilingualism, and other contributions to a deficit view of linguistic minorities. *Hispanic Journal of Behavioral Sciences, 22*(1), 3–45.

MacSwan, J. (2004, November). *The "Non-non" crisis: How language assessments mislead us about the native language ability of English Learners.* Paper presented at the 2004 NCCRESt Conference, English Language Learners Struggling to Learn: Emergent Research on Linguistic Differences and Learning Disabilities, Tempe, AZ.

MacSwan, J., & Rolstad, K. (2003). Linguistic diversity, schooling and social class: Rethinking our conception of language proficiency in language minority education. In C.B. Paulston & R. Tucker (Eds.), *Essential readings in sociolinguistics* (pp. 329–340). Oxford, UK: Blackwell.

MacSwan, J., & Rolstad, K. (2010). The role of language in theories of academic failure for linguistic minorities. In J. Petrovic (Ed.), *International perspectives on bilingual education: Policy, practice, and controversy* (pp. 173–195). Charlotte, NC: Information Age.

MacSwan, J., Rolstad, K., & Glass, G. (2002). Do some school-age children have no language? Some problems of construct validity in the Pre-LAS Espanol. *Bilingual Research Journal, 26*(2), 395–420.

Mahoney, K. S., & MacSwan, J. (2005). Re-examining identification and reclassification of English language learners: A critical discussion of select state practices. *Bilingual Research Journal, 29*(1), 31–42.

McAllum, R. (2014). Reciprocal teaching: Critical reflection on practice. *Kairaranga, 15*(1), 26–35.

McLaughlin, B. (1984). *Second language acquisition in childhood: Vol. 1. Preschool children* (2nd ed.). Hillsdale, NJ: Erlbaum.

Meadows Center. (2014). *Instructional decision-making procedures: Ensuring appropriate instruction for struggling students in grades K–12.* Austin: University of Texas Meadows Center, College of Education.

Mestre, J. P. (1988). The role of language comprehension in mathematics and problem solving. In R. R. Cocking & J. P. Mestre (Eds.), *Linguistic and cultural influences on learning mathematics* (pp. 200–220). Hillsdale, NJ: Erlbaum.

Moll, L. C., Amanti, C., Neff, D., & Gonzalez, N. (1992). Funds of knowledge for teaching: Using a qualitative approach to connect homes and classrooms. *Theory into Practice, 31*(2), 132–141.

Moll, L. C., & Greenberg, J. B. (1990). Creating zones of possibilities: Combining social contexts for instruction. In L. C. Moll (Ed.), *Vygotsky and education: Instructional implications and applications of sociohistorical psychology* (pp. 319–348). New York, NY: Cambridge University Press.

Moll, L. C., & Whitmore, K. F. (1993). Vygotsky in classroom practice: Moving from individual transmission to social transaction. In E. A. Forman, N. Minick, & C. A. Stone (Eds.), *Contexts for learning: Sociocultural dynamics in children's development,* pp. 19–42. New York, NY: Oxford University Press.

Montero, K., Newmaster, S., & Ledger, S. (2014). Exploring early reading instructional strategies to advance the print literacy development of adolescent SLIFE. *Journal of Adolescent and Adult Literacy, 58*(1), 59–69.

Moughamian, A. C., Rivera, M. O., & Francis, D. J. (2009). *Instructional models and strategies for teaching English language learners.* Portsmouth, NH: RMC Research Corporation, Center on Instruction. Retrieved from http://files.eric.ed.gov/fulltext/ED517794.pdf

National Association of State Directors of Special Education (NASDSE). (2005). *Response to intervention: Policy considerations and implementation.* Retrieved from NASDSE Publications website: http://www.nasdse.org

National Center for Education Statistics (NCES). (2013). *Digest of education statistics: 2013.* Washington, DC: US Department of Education.

National Center for Education Statistics (NCES). (2015). *The condition of education 2015: English language learners.* Washington, DC: US Department of Education. Retrieved from: http://nces.ed.gov/programs/coe/indicator_cgf.asp

National Center on Response to Intervention (NCRI). (n.d.). The essential components of RTI. Retrieved from http://www.rti4success.org

National Council of Teachers of English (NCTE). (2008). *English language learners* (Policy Research Brief). The James R. Squire Office for Policy Research. Retrieved from www.ncte.org/library/NCTEFiles/Resources/PolicyResearch/ELLResearchBrief.pdf

National Institute of Child Health and Human Development (NICHD). (2000). *Report of the National Reading Panel: Teaching children to read: An evidence-based assessment of scientific research literature on reading and its implications for reading instruction* (NIH Publication No. 00–4769). Washington, DC: US Government Printing Office.

National Reading Panel. (2000). *Teaching children to read: An evidence-based assessment of the scientific research literature on reading and its implications for reading instruction: Summary report.* Washington, DC: National Institute of Child Health and Development.

Nazarro, J. N. (Ed.). (1981). *Culturally diverse exceptional children in school.* Arlington, VA: Council for Exceptional Children.

Nguyen, H. T. (2012). General education and special education teachers collaborate to support English language learners with learning disabilities. *Issues in Teacher Education, 21*(1), 127–152.

Nicolopoulou, A., & Cole, M. (1993). Generation and transmission of shared knowledge in the culture of collaborative learning: The Fifth Dimension, its play-world, and its institutional contexts. In E. A. Forman, N. Minick & C. A. Stone (Eds.), *Contexts for learning: Sociocultural dynamics in children's development* (pp. 283–314). New York, NY: Oxford University Press.

No Child Left Behind Act (2001). Pub. L. 107–110, 115 Stat. 1425.

Ohta, A. S. (1995). Applying sociocultural theory to an analysis of learner discourse: Learner-learner collaborative interaction in the zone of proximal development. *Issues in Applied Linguistics, 6*(2), 93–121.

Olson, C. B., & Land, R. (2007). A cognitive strategies approach to reading and writing instruction for English language learners in secondary school. *NCTE's Research in the Teaching of English, 41*(3). Retrieved from http://www.nwp.org/cs/public/download/nwp_file/8538/Booth_Olson,_Carol,_et_al.pdf?x-r=pcfile_d

Orosco, M. (2007). *Response to intervention with Latino English language learners: A school-based study* (Unpublished doctoral dissertation). University of Colorado at Boulder.

Orosco, M. J. (2010). A sociocultural examination of response to intervention with Latino English language learners. *Theory into Practice, 49*(4), 265–272.

Orosco, M. J. (2014). A word problem strategy for Latino English language learners at risk for math disabilities. *Learning Disability Quarterly, 37*(1), 45–53.

Orosco, M. J., & Hoover, J. J. (2009). Characteristics of second language acquisition, cultural diversity and learning/behavior disabilities. In *Differentiating learning differences from disabilities: Meeting diverse needs through multi-tiered response to intervention* (pp. 39–64). New York, NY: Prentice Hall.

Orosco, M. J., & Klingner, J. (2010). One school's implementation of RTI with English language learners: "Referring into RTI." *Journal of Learning Disabilities, 43,* 269–288.

Orosco, M. J., & O'Connor, R. (2011). Cultural aspects of teaching reading with Latino English language learners. In R. O'Connor & P. Vadasy (Eds.), *Handbook of reading interventions* (pp. 356–379). New York, NY: Guilford Press.

Orosco, M. J., & O'Connor, R. E. (2014). Culturally responsive instruction for English language learners with learning disabilities. *Journal of Learning Disabilities 47*(6), 515–531.

Orosco, M. J., Swanson, H. L., O'Connor, R. E., & Lussier, C. (2013). The effects of dynamic strategic math on English language learners' word problem solving. *Journal of Special Education, 47*(2), 96–107.

Orr, E. W. (1987). *Twice as less: Black English and the performance of Black students in mathematics and science.* New York, NY: W. W. Norton.

Ortiz, A. A. (1997). LD occurring concomitantly with linguistic differences. *Journal of LD, 30,* 321–332.

Ortiz, A. A., & Maldonado-Colon, E. (1986). Recognizing learning disabilities in bilingual children: How to lessen inappropriate referrals of language minority students to special education. *Journal of Reading, Writing and Learning Disabilities International, 2*(1), 43–56.

Ortiz, A. A., Robertson, P. M., Wilkinson, C., Y., Liu, Y., McGhee, B. D., & Kushner, M. I. (2011). The role of bilingual education teachers in preventing inappropriate referrals of ELLs to special education: Implications for response to intervention. *Bilingual Research Journal: The Journal of the National Association for Bilingual Education, 34*(3), 316–333. doi: 10.1080/15235882.2011.628608

Ortiz, A., & Artiles, A. J. (2010). Meeting the needs of English language learners with disabilities: A linguistically and culturally responsive model. In G. Li & P. Edwards (Eds.). *Best practices in ELL instruction* (pp. 247–272). New York, NY: Guilford Press.

Ortiz, A., & Wilkinson, C. (1991). Assessment and intervention model for the bilingual exceptional student (AIM for the BEST). *Teacher Education and Special Education, 14*, pp. 35–42.

Ovando, O., Collier, V., & Combs, M. (2003). *Bilingual and ESL classrooms: Teaching in multicultural contexts.* Boston, MA: McGraw Hill.

Padron, Y. N. (1992). The effect of strategy instruction on bilingual students' cognitive strategy use in reading. *Bilingual Research Journal, 16*(3–4), 35–51.

Palincsar, A. S., & Brown, A. L. (1984). Reciprocal teaching of comprehension-fostering and comprehension-monitoring activities. *Cognition and Instruction, 1*(2), 117–175.

Palincsar, A. S., & David, Y. M. (1991). Promoting literacy through classroom dialogue. In E. Hiebert (Ed.), *Literacy for a diverse society: Perspectives, programs, and policies.* New York, NY: Teachers College Press.

Paradis, J., Genesse, F., & Crago, M. B. (2011). Dual language development & disorders: A handbook on bilingualism & second language learning (2nd ed.). Baltimore, MD: Paul H. Brooks.

Pearson. (2015). The SIOP Model. Retrieved from http://siop.pearson.com/about-siop/

Peregoy, S. F., & Boyle, O. F. (2012). *Reading, writing, and learning in ESL: A resource book for teaching K–12 English learners* (6th ed.). Boston, MA: Pearson.

Pew Research Center (2013). A nation of immigrants: A portrait of the 40 million, including 11 million unauthorized. Retrieved from http://www.pewhispanic.org/2013/01/29/a-nation-of-immigrants/

Pinker, S. (1994). *The language instinct: How the mind creates languages.* New York, NY: William Morrow.

Poehner, M. E., & Lantolf, J. P. (2005). Dynamic assessment in the language classroom. *Language Teaching Research, 9*(3), 233–265.

Polloway, E., A., Patton, J. R., & Serena, L. (in press). *Strategies for teaching students with special needs* (11th ed.). Columbus, OH: Merrill.

Portes, A., & Rumbaut, R. G. (2001). *Legacies: The story of the immigrant second generation.* Berkeley: University of California Press.

Preston, D. R. (2003). *American dialect research.* Philadelphia, PA: John Benjamins.

Proctor, C. P., Carlo, M., August, D., & Snow, C. E. (2005). Native Spanish-speaking children reading in English: Toward a model of comprehension. *Journal of Educational Psychology, 97*(2), 246–256.

Raphael, T. E. (1986). Teaching question-answer relationships. *The Reading Teacher, 39,* 516–520.

Richard-Amato, P. A. (2010). *Making it happen: From interactive to participatory language teaching: Evolving theory and practice* (4th ed.). White Plains, NY: Pearson Education.

Rinaldi, C., Ortiz, S. O., & Gamm, S., Esq. (n.d.). RTI-based SLD identification toolkit: Considerations for English language learners. Retrieved from RTI Action Network Website: http://rtinetwork.org/getstarted/sld-identification-toolkit/ld-identification-toolkit-considerations-for-ell?tmpl=component&print=1

Rodrigo, V., Krashen, S., & Gribbons, B. (2004). The effectiveness of two comprehensible-input approaches to foreign language instruction at the intermediate level. *System 32*(1), 53–60.

Rolstad, K., Mahoney, K., & Glass, G. (2005). The big picture: A meta-analysis of program effectiveness research on English language learners. *Educational Policy, 19,* 572–594.

Rosenshine, B., & Meister, C. (1994). Reciprocal teaching: A review of the research. *Review of Educational Research, 64*(4), 479–530.

Roskos, K., Boehlen, S., & Walker, B. J. (2000). Learning the art of instructional conversation: The influence of self-assessment on teachers' instructional discourse in a reading clinic. *The Elementary School Journal, 100*(3), 229–252.

Rueda, R., MacGillivray, L., Monzó, L., & Arzubiaga, A. (2001). *Engaged reading: A multilevel approach to considering sociocultural factors with diverse learners.* Ann Arbor, MI: Center for the Improvement of Early Reading Achievement.

Rueda, R., & Windmueller, M. P. (2006). English language learners, LD, and overrepresentation a multiple-level analysis. *Journal of Learning Disabilities, 39*(2), 99–107.

Ruiz, N. (1989). An optimal learning environment for Rosemary. *Exceptional Children, 56,* 29–41.

Ruiz, N. T. (1995). The social construction of ability and disability: Optimal and at-risk lessons in a bilingual special education classroom. *Journal of Learning Disabilities, 28,* 491–502.

Ruiz Soto, A. G., Hooker, S., & Batalova, J. (2015). *Top languages spoken by English language learners nationally and by state.* Washington, DC: Migration Policy Institute.

Rutter, M., & Yule, W. (1975). The concept of specific reading retardation. *Journal of Child Psychiatry, 16*(3), 181–197.

Ryan, C. (2013). *Language use in the United States: 2011.* Washington, DC: American Community Survey Reports.

Sable, J., Plotts, C., & Mitchell, L. (2010). *Characteristics of the 100 largest public elementary and secondary school districts in the United States: 2008–09* (NCES Rep. No. 2011–301). Washington, DC: U.S. Department of Education, National Center for Education Statistics.

Samson, J. F., & Collins, B. A. (2012). *Preparing all teachers to meet the needs of English language learners: Applying research to policy and practice for teacher effectiveness.* Washington, DC: Center for American Progress.

Samson, J. F., & Lesaux, N. K. (2009). Language-minority learners in special education: Rates and predictors of identification for services. *Journal of Learning Disabilities, 42,* 148–162. doi:10.1177/002221 9408326221

Santiago, I. C., & Alicea, Z. A., (2015). A conversation with Latino/Latina families and its implications for teacher beliefs about cultural and linguistic diversity. In L. C. de Oliveira & M. Yough (Eds.), *Preparing teachers to work with English language learners in mainstream classrooms* (pp. 59–74). Charlotte, NC: IAP and TESOL Press.

Saunders, W., O'Brien, G., Lennon, D., & McLean, J. (1998). Making the transition to English literacy successful: Effective strategies for studying literature with transition students. In R. Gersten & R. Jimenez (Eds.), *Effective strategies for teaching language minority students* (pp. 99–132). Belmont, CA: Wadsworth.

Saunders, W., Patthey-Chavez, G., & Goldenberg, C. (1997). Reflections on the relationship between language, curriculum content and instruction. *Language, Culture and Curriculum, 10*(1), 30–51.

Saunders, W. M., & Goldenberg, C. (1999). Effects of instructional conversations and literature logs on limited—and fluent—English-proficient students' story comprehension and thematic understanding. *The Elementary School Journal, 99*(4), 277–301.

Saville-Troike, M. (2006). *Introducing second language acquisition.* Cambridge, UK: Cambridge University Press.

Scornavacco, K., Boardman, A., & Klingner, J. (2014, April). *Leveraging teacher leadership in a district initiative to scale up and sustain an evidence based practice (EBP).* Paper presented at the American Educational Research Association Annual Meeting, Philadelphia, PA.

Scornavacco, K., Moore, B., Boardman, A., Lasser, C., Buckley, P. & Klingner, J. (2015). Using collaborative strategic reading to promote student discourse. In K. R. Harris & L. J. Meltzer (Eds.), *The power of peers: Enhancing learning, development and social skills* (pp. 102–142). New York, NY: Guilford Press.

Selinker, L., Swain, M., & Dumas, G. (1975). The interlanguage hypothesis extended to children. *Language Learning, 25*(1), 139–152.

Short, D. J., & Echevarria, J. (2004). Using multiple perspectives in observations of diverse classrooms: The sheltered instruction observation protocol (SIOP). In H. C. Waxman, R. G. Tharp, & R. S. Hilberg (Eds.), *Observational research in US classrooms: New approaches for understanding cultural and linguistic diversity* (pp. 21–47). New York, NY: Cambridge.

Slavin, R. E. (1995). *Cooperative learning: Theory, research and practice* (2nd ed.). Boston, MA: Allyn & Bacon.

Slavin, R. E. (2008). Cooperative learning, success for all, and evidence-based reform in education. *Education & Didactique, 2*(2), 151–159.

Slavin, R. E., & Cheung, A. (2004). How do English language learners learn to read? *Educational Leadership, 61*(6), 52–57.

Slavin, R. E., & Cheung, A. (2005). A synthesis of research on language of reading instruction for English language learners. *Review of Educational Research, 75,* 247–284.

Slobin, D. I. (1968). Recall of full and truncated passive sentences in connected discourse. *Journal of Verbal Learning and Verbal Behavior, 7,* 876–881.

Smith, T. E. C., Polloway, E. A., Patton, J. R., & Dowdy, C. A. (2012). *Teaching students with special needs in inclusive settings.* Boston, MA: Pearson.

Snow, C. (2002). *Reading for understanding: Toward an R&D program in reading comprehension.* Santa Monica, CA: RAND.

Snow, C. S., Burns, S. M., & Griffin, P. (1998). *Preventing reading difficulties in young children.* Washington, DC: National Academy Press.

Solano-Flores, G. (2004, November). *Language, dialect, and register: Sociolinguistics and the estimation of measurement error in the testing of English-language learners.* Paper presented at the NCCRESt Conference, English Language Learners Struggling to Learn: Emergent Research on Linguistic Differences and Learning Disabilities, Tempe, AZ.

Stuart, M. (1999). Getting ready for reading: Early phoneme awareness and phonics teaching improves reading and spelling in inner-city second language learners. *British Journal of Educational Psychology, 69*, 587–605.

Stuebing, K. K., Fletcher, J. M., LeDoux, J. M., Lyon, G. R., Shaywitz, S. E., & Shaywitz, B. A. (2002). Validity of IQ-discrepancy classifications of reading disabilities: A meta-analysis. *American Educational Research Journal, 39*, 469–518.

Swain, M. (1986). Communicative competence: Some roles of comprehensible input and comprehensible output in its development. In S. Gass & C. Madden (Eds.), *Input in second language acquisition*, 235–256. New York, NY: Newbury House.

Swain, M. (1995). Three functions of output in second language learning. In G. Cook & B. Seidlhofer (Eds.), *Principles and practice in the study of language.* Oxford, UK: Oxford University Press.

Swanson, H. L., Orosco, M. J., & Kudo, M. (in press). Does growth in the executive system of working memory underlie growth in literacy for bilingual children with and without reading disabilities? *Journal of Learning Disabilities.*

Swanson, H. L., Orosco, M., & Lussier, C. (2012). Cognition and literacy in English language learners at risk for reading disabilities. *Journal of Educational Psychology, 104*, 302–320. doi:10.1037/a0026225

Swanson, H. L., Orosco, M., Lussier, C., Gerber, M., & Guzman-Orth, D. (2011). The influence of working memory and phonological processing on English language learner children's bilingual reading and language processing. *Journal of Educational Psychology, 103*(4), 838–856. doi: 10.1037/a0024578

Swanson, H. L., Sáez, L., Gerber, M., & Leafstedt, J. (2004). Literacy and cognitive functioning in bilingual and nonbilingual children at or not at risk for reading disabilities. *Journal of Educational Psychology, 96*(1), 3–18.

Tharp, R. G. (1989). Psycho-cultural variables and constants: Effects on teaching and learning in schools. *American Psychologist, 44*, 349–359.

Tharp, R. G., & Gallimore, R. (1988). *Rousing minds to life: Teaching, learning, and schooling.* Cambridge, UK: Cambridge University Press.

Thomas, W. P., & Collier, V. P. (1997). *School effectiveness for language minority students.* Washington, DC: National Clearinghouse for Bilingual Education.

Thompson, L. W. (2004). Literacy development for English language learners: Classroom challenges in the NCLB age. *A Title I Communique Special Report,* 1–10.

Thorius, K. K., & Sullivan, A. L. (2013). Interrogating instruction and intervention in RTI research with students identified as English language learners. *Reading & Writing Quarterly, 29*(1), 64–88.

Thorn, E. A. (1969). Language experience approach to reading. *The Reading Teacher, 23*(1), 3–8.

Tikunoff, W. J. (1983). Compatibility of the SBIF features with other research instruction of LEP students. San Francisco, CA: Far West Laboratory.

Tomlinson, C. (1995). *Differentiating instruction for advanced learners in the mixed-ability middle school classroom.* Reston, VA: ERIC Clearinghouse on Handicapped and Gifted Children. (ERIC Document Reproduction Service No. ED389141)

Trumbull, E., & Solano-Flores, G. (2011). Addressing the language demands of mathematics assessments: Using a language framework and field research findings. In M. Basterra, E. Trumbull, & G. Solano-Flores (Eds.), *Cultural validity in assessment: Addressing linguistic and cultural diversity* (pp. 218–253). New York, NY: Routledge.

University of Texas Center for Reading and Language Arts. (2003). *3-tier reading model: Reducing reading difficulties for kindergarten through third grade students.* Austin: UT System/Texas Education Agency.

US Department of Education, National Center for Education Statistics. (2013). *Number and percentage distribution of teachers in public and private elementary and secondary schools, by selected teacher characteristics: Selected years, 1987–88 through 2011–12.* Retrieved from: http://nces.ed.gov/programs/digest/d13/tables/dt13_209.10.asp

US Office of Education. (1977). Definition and criteria for defining students as learning disabled. Federal Register, 42:250, p. 65083. Washington, DC: US Government Printing Office.

Valdés, G. (2001). *Learning and not learning English: Latino students in American schools.* New York, NY: Teachers College Press.

Valdés, G., & Figueroa, R. (1994). *Bilingualism and testing: A special case of bias.* Norwood, NJ: Ablex.

Valle, J. W., & Connor, D. J. (2011). *Rethinking disability: A disability studies approach to inclusive practices.* New York, NY: McGraw Hill.

Vaughn, S., & Bos, C. S. (2012). *Strategies for teaching students with learning and behavior problems* (8th ed.). Boston, MA: Pearson Allyn and Bacon.

Vaughn, S., & Fuchs, L. S. (2003). Redefining learning disabilities as inadequate response to treatment: The promise and potential problems. *Learning Disabilities Research and Practice, 18*(3), 137–146.

Vaughn, S., & Klingner, J. K. (2004). Strategies for struggling second-language readers. In T. L. Jetton & J. A. Dole (Eds.), *Adolescent literacy research and practice* (pp. 183–209). New York, NY: Guilford Press.

Vaughn, S., Klingner, J. K., Swanson, E., Boardman, A., Roberts, G., Mohammed, S., & Stillman-Spisak, S. (2011). Efficacy of collaborative strategic reading with middle school students. *American Educational Research Journal, 48,* 938–954.

Vygotsky, L. S. (1978a). Interaction between learning and development. In M. Cole, V. John-Steiner, S. Scribner, & E. Souberman (Eds.), *Mind in Society: The development of higher psychological processes* (Chapt. 6, pp. 79–91). Cambridge, MA: Harvard University Press.

Vygotsky, L. S. (1978b). *Mind in Society: The development of higher psychological processes.* Cambridge, MA: Harvard University Press.

Vygotsky, L. S. (1981). The instrumental method in psychology. In J. V. Wertsch (Ed.), The concept of activity in Soviet psychology (pp. 134–144). Armonk, NY: Sharpe.

Vygotsky, L. S. (1986). *Thought and language.* Cambridge, MA: MIT Press.

Wardhaugh, R. (2002). *An introduction to sociolinguistics* (4th ed.). Oxford, UK: Blackwell.

Waterman, D. C. (1969). The language experience approach in elementary language arts. *Contemporary Education, 40*(4), 206–211.

Watkins, N. M., & Lindahl, K. M. (2010). Targeting content area literacy instruction to meet the needs of adolescent English language learners. *Middle School Journal, 4*(3), 23–33.

Waxman, H. C., & Tellez, K. (2002). *Research synthesis on effective teaching practices for English language learners.* Washington, DC: Office of Educational Research and Improvement (ED). Retrieved from http://files.eric.ed.gov/fulltext/ED474821.pdf

What Works Clearinghouse (WWC). (2006). *Instructional Conversations and Literature Logs* (WWC Intervention Report). Washington, DC: Institute of Education Sciences.

What Works Clearinghouse (WWC). (2007). *Classwide peer tutoring* (WWC Intervention Report). Washington, DC: Institute of Education Sciences.

WIDA: Can Do Descriptors. (2014). Retrieved from www.wida.us/standards/CAN_DOs/

WIDA *Focus.* (2015, May). Focus on SLIFE: Students with limited or interrupted formal education. Retrieved from www.wida.us

Wilkinson, C. Y., Ortiz, A., & Robertson-Courtney, P. (2004, November). *Appropriate eligibility determination for English language learners suspected of having reading-related learning disabilities: Linking school history, prereferral, referral and assessment data.* Paper presented at the 2004 NCCRESt Conference, English Language Learners Struggling to Learn: Emergent Research on Linguistic Differences and Learning Disabilities, Tempe, AZ.

Willig, A. (1985). A meta-analysis of selected studies on the effectiveness of bilingual education. *Review of Educational Research, 55,* 269–317.

Wolfe, P., & Brandt, R. (1998). What do we know from brain research? *Educational Leadership, 56*(3), 8–13.

Wolfram, W. (2000). On the construction of vernacular dialect norms. In J. P. Boyle & A. Okrent (Eds.), *CLS 36: The 36th meeting of the Chicago Linguistic Society,* 2000. Chicago: Chicago Linguistic Society.

Wong Fillmore, L. (2000). Loss of family languages: Should educators be concerned? *Theory into Practice, 39*(4), 203–210.

Wong Fillmore, L. (2014). English language learners at the crossroads of educational reform. *TESOL Quarterly, 48*(3), 624–632.

Wood, K. D., & Blanton, W. E. (2009). *Literacy instruction for adolescents: Research based practice.* New York, NY: Guilford Press.

Xu, Y. (2014). Literacy 2.0: New literacies in culturally and linguistically diverse K–12 classrooms. Retrieved from https://discoverarchive.vanderbilt.edu/bitstream/handle/1803/6315/XuCapstone.pdf?sequence=1

Yell, M. (2004, February). *Understanding the three-tier model.* Presentation at the Colorado State Directors of Special Education Meeting, Denver, CO.

Yoon, B. (2008). Uninvited guests: The influence of teachers' roles and pedagogies on the positioning of English language learners in the regular classroom. *American Educational Research Journal, 45,* 495–522.

Zacarian, D. (2013). *Mastering academic language: A framework for supporting student achievement.* Thousand Oaks, CA: Corwin.

Zehler, A., Hopstock, P., Fleishman, H., & Greniuk, C. (1994). *An examination of assessment of limited English proficient students.* Arlington, VA: Special Issues Analysis Center.

Zepeda, M., & Rodriguez, J. L. (2015). Bilingual development in early childhood: Research and policy implications for Mexican American children. In Y. M. Caldera & E. W. Lindsey (Eds.), *Mexican American children and families: Multidisciplinary perspectives.* New York, NY: Routledge.

Index

Abedi, J., 120, 123, 124, 126, 126 (table), 131, 132, 133 (table), 145, 150
Academic achievement, 30
Aceves, T. C., 10, 119, 144
Acquisition-Learning Hypothesis, 59 (table)
Active/passive voice, 125 (table), 132 (table)
Ada, A. F., 97
    see also Bernhard, J. K.
Adams, M. J., 126 (table), 133 (table)
Additive bilingualism, 69
Adler, P., 150
Adults and Children with Learning and Developmental Disabilities Organization (ACLD), 17
Affective Filter Hypothesis, 60 (table)
African American students, 14
African American Vernacular English (AAVE), 129
Albert Shanker Institute, 10
Alicea, Z. A., 32
Allen, R. V., 103
Allington, R. L., 37 (table)
Almasi, J. F., 62 (table)
Al Otaiba, S., 33
Alphabetic principle instruction, 34 (table), 87 (table), 88–89
Alton-Lee, A., 107
Alvermann, D. E., 63 (table)
Amanti, C., 13
American Community Survey, 8
American Indian students, 14
American Speech-Language-Hearing Association (ASHA), 66–67
Anthony, J. L., 38 (table)
Antunez, B., 88, 89, 90
Arabic language speakers, 9 (table)
Argument construction, 129
Arizona State University, 5
Arreaga-Mayer, C., 115
Artiles, A. J., 14, 20, 57, 78, 101, 167
    see also Klingner, J. K.
Ary, D., 34 (table)
Arzubiaga, A., 95
Asian American students, 14
Assessment practices
    appropriate use, 117, 119–120, 168–169
    authentic assessment, 133–137, 136 (table), 169
    biases, 158
    cultural and linguistic responsiveness, 44–45, 118–123, 142, 157, 157 (table)
    dialects, 127–128, 129, 130, 168–169
    experiential backgrounds, 132–133 (table), 132–133

    linguistic features, 124, 125–126 (table), 126–127, 131 (table), 132–133 (table), 132–133, 168–169
    linguistic misalignment, 126–127, 130–131, 131 (table)
    nondiscriminatory progress monitoring, 161 (table), 161–162
    purpose, 119–120
    registers, 128–129, 130, 168–169
    validity and reliability challenges, 123–124, 126–127, 129, 131
    vignette, 118–119
    see also Data-driven decision making; Multi-tiered system of supports (MTSS)
Aud, S., 10
August, D., 37 (table), 41, 58, 72, 73, 75, 85, 86, 88, 89, 90, 91, 92
Au, K. H., 10, 36 (table)
Authentic assessment, 133–137, 136 (table), 156 (table), 169

Baca, L. M., 34 (table), 58, 149 (table), 150, 152 (table), 170
    see also Hoover, J. J.
Bailey, A. L., 71
Bailey, C. E., 88
Baker, S., 171 (table)
Ball, A. F., 128
Ballantyne, K. G., 10
Barletta, L. M., 20, 167
    see also Klingner, J. K.
Barrera, M., 40, 133, 134, 135, 137–138
Basterra, M. D. R., 21, 68, 71, 94, 115, 120, 123, 124, 126 (table), 127, 129, 133, 158, 159, 161, 165
Batalova, J., 8
    see also Ruiz Soto, A. G.
Bateman, B., 15, 16 (table)
Beeman, M. M., 37 (table)
Bernhard, J. K., 95, 97, 98
Best, J. W., 124
Bias, 158
Big Ideas, 86, 86–87 (table), 88–92
Biglan, A., 34 (table), 37 (table)
Bilingualism, 66–70, 67 (table), 72, 79–80
Black, C., 37 (table)
Blackorby, J., 111
Blair, J., 37 (table)
Blanton, W. E., 35 (table)
Bleiker, C.
    see Bernhard, J. K.
Boardman, A. G., 35 (table), 108, 111, 112
    see also Scornavacco, K.; Vaughn, S.

Boehlen, S., 112
  see also Roskos, K.
Boelé, A. L., 108, 115
Bos, C. S., 104, 171
Boyle, O. F., 38 (table), 90, 92
Brandt, R., 98
Branum-Martin, L.
  see Anthony, J. L.
Brengelman, S., 171 (table)
Bronfenbrenner, U., 21
Brophy, J., 94
Brown, A. L., 106
Brown-Chidsey, R., 143, 164
Brownell, M., 92
Bryant, J. D., 98
Buckley, P., 111
  see Scornavacco, K.
Burden, P. R., 94, 106
Burke, A. M., 150
Burns, M. K., 28, 134
Burns, S. M., 94
Butvilofsky, S., 116
Byrd, D. M., 94, 106
Calderón, M., 12, 13, 36 (table)
California, 8, 14, 27
Camarota, S. A., 8–9
Campbell, A.
  see Blackorby, J.
Campoy, F. I., 97
  see also Bernhard, J. K.
Cano-Rodriguez, E.
  see Klingner, J. K.
Canter, A., 28
Capp, R., 79
Carlisle, J. F., 37 (table)
Carlo, M., 37 (table)
Carroll, P. E., 71
Cazden, C., 92
Celce-Murcia, M., 126 (table), 133 (table)
Center for American Progress, 11
Center for Immigration Studies, 8
Cervantes, H., 58, 149 (table), 150,
  152 (table), 170
Cha, K., 66, 68, 73
Chamot, A. U., 34 (table)
Chandler, J., 60 (table)
Cheung, A., 38 (table), 74, 77
Chiappe, P., 88
Chicano/Latino students, 14
Child Trends, 8
Chinese language speakers, 9 (table)
Chomsky, N., 69
Christ, T. J., 28
Cirino, P. T., 40
Classroom environments, 41
Classwide peer tutoring (CWPT), 114–115
Cloud, N., 86
Code-switching, 79
Cognates, 90–91

Cognitive Academic Language Learning
  Approach (CALLA), 34 (table)
Cognitive Strategy Instruction (CSI), 34 (table)
Cohen, L. G., 124, 133
Cole, M., 61 (table)
Collaborative practices, 172
Collaborative Strategic Reading (CSR),
  35 (table), 107–112, 109 (table)
Collier, C., 58, 149 (table), 150, 152 (table)
Collier, V. P., 69, 75, 76
Collins, B. A., 11
Colombo, M., 107
Colorado, 8, 27
Colorado Department of Education (CDE), 25,
  28, 30
Colorín Colorado, 35 (table)
Combs, M., 70
Commins, N. L., 88, 91, 92, 94, 96, 98
Common Core State Standards (CCSS), 27, 85
Community-school partnerships, 29 (figure),
  32–33, 43
Comparative structures, 125 (table), 133 (table)
Composition index (CI), 23
Comprehensible Input Theory, 64–65 (table)
Comprehension Strategies Instruction, 35 (table)
Compton, D. L., 98
Concrete versus abstract/impersonal
  presentations, 126 (table), 133 (table)
Congressional Budget Office, 8
Connor, C. M.
  see Al Otaiba, S.
Connor, D. J., 134, 135, 136, 168, 169
Conventions, 129
Cooperative learning, 35 (table)
Council for Exceptional Children (CEC),
  5, 16 (table), 33, 42
Council for the Accreditation of Educator
  Preparation (CAEP), 42
Council of Chief State School Officers (CCSSO),
  21, 25, 29, 30, 31, 141, 143, 144, 155, 172
Crago, M. B., 58
  see also Paradis, J.
Cramer, L., 29
Crawford, J., 69
Cross, C., 14, 28, 29, 150
Crystal, D., 127
Cultural and linguistic responsiveness
  assessment practices, 118–123, 157, 157 (table)
  data-driven decision making, 142, 150,
    151–152 (table), 152–155, 154 (table),
    159 (table)
  evidence-based interventions, 156 (table), 165
  literacy instruction, 44–45
  multi-tiered system of supports (MTSS),
    159 (table)
Culturally and linguistically diverse teachers,
  10–11, 22, 165
Culture-based behaviors, 150, 151–152 (table)
Cummins, D. D., 126 (table), 133 (table)

Cummins, J., 38 (table), 58, 69, 75, 97,
        149 (table), 152 (table)
    see also Bernhard, J. K.
Cunningham, P. M., 37 (table)
Curriculum-Based Measurement (CBM),
        134, 164–165, 169
Curtin, E., 37 (table)
Damico, J., 83
    see also Hamayan, E.
Darling-Hammond, L., 171
Data-driven decision making
    appropriate use, 144–145
    cultural and linguistic responsiveness, 142,
        150, 151–152 (table), 152–155, 154 (table),
        156 (table), 157, 159 (table)
    culture-based behaviors, 150, 151–152 (table)
    evidence-based interventions, 155–158, 156
        (table), 157 (table), 160 (table), 168
    functional role, 168
    information gathering processes, 154–155
    intervention documentation, 143
    knowledge and skills checklist, 157 (table)
    multi-tiered system of supports (MTSS),
        29 (figure), 30, 43, 158–159, 159 (table),
        160 (table), 168
    nondiscriminatory progress monitoring,
        158–159, 161 (table), 161–162
    second language acquisition (SLA), 145–146,
        147–148 (table), 148, 149 (table), 150, 166
    vignette, 142–143
David, Y. M., 107
Davis, L. H., 37 (table)
DeCapua, A., 13
Dee, T. S., 171
de Jong, E. J., 72, 73, 77, 78, 80
Deno, S. L., 134, 164
de Oliveira, L., 150
de Onís, C., 10
Dialects, 88, 127–128, 130, 168–169
Differentiated instruction, 36 (table)
Discourse structure, 126 (table), 132 (table)
Discrepancy-based learning disability
        identification models
    see IQ discrepancy-based model
Disproportionate representation, 14–15, 22, 83
Dole, J. A., 34 (table), 35 (table)
Dominant bilingualism, 69
Donovan, M. S., 14, 28, 29, 150
Dowdy, C. A., 114
Drits, D., 34 (table)
    see also Dole, J. A.
Dumas, G., 78
Durgunoglu, A. Y., 34 (table), 88
Dynamic Assessment (DA), 134–139, 136 (table),
        138 (table), 165, 169
Dynamic Indicators of Basic Early Literacy
        Skills (DIBELS), 31 (table), 49, 50 (table)
Early Authors Program (EAP), 97–98
Echevarria, J. J., 39 (table), 40, 112, 114

Echo reading, 90
Education for All Handicapped Children Act
        (EAHCA, 1975), 17
Edwards, P., 40, 41, 42, 167
Eeds, M., 63 (table)
Effective learning environments checklist,
        169–170, 170–171 (table)
Effective reading instructional methods,
        33, 34–39 (table), 102–110, 109 (table),
        112–116, 167–168
Elementary and Secondary Education Act
        (ESEA, 1965), 2, 69–70
Elliott, J., 136
Emerging bilingualism, 70
English language development (ELD), 48, 120, 121
English learners (ELs)
    culturally and linguistically diverse teachers,
        10–11, 165
    demographic data, 8–10, 21–22
    disproportionate representation, 14–15, 22,
        83, 118
    effective reading instructional methods,
        33, 34–39 (table), 102–110, 109 (table),
        112–116, 167–168
    experiential backgrounds, 132–133 (table),
        132–133
    instructional challenges, 86, 86–87 (table),
        88–92
    linguistic diversity, 9 (table)
    literacy instruction, 67 (table), 71–73, 93
        (figure), 93–95, 98, 99–100 (table), 167–168
    standards-based instruction, 85
    students with limited/interrupted formal
        education (SLIFEs), 11–13, 22
    see also Assessment practices; Data-driven
        decision making; Learning disabilities;
        Reading skills; Second language
        acquisition (SLA)
Eppolito, A., 57, 58, 69, 75, 111
    see also Klingner, J. K.
Erickson, J., 21, 121, 155
Escamilla, K., 11, 32, 66, 68, 79, 85, 94, 98, 103,
        116, 171 (table)
    see also Herrera, S. G.
Escamilla, M., 66, 68
Essential teacher qualities/abilities, 42 (table),
        42–43
Evans, L. S., 37 (table)
Every Student Succeeds Act (ESSA, 2015), 2–3
Evidence-based instruction/intervention/
        assessment
    cultural and linguistic responsiveness,
        156 (table), 165
    data-driven decision making, 155–158,
        156 (table), 157 (table), 160 (table), 168
    definition, 100
    knowledge and skills checklist, 157 (table)
    multi-tiered system of supports (MTSS),
        29 (figure), 30, 31–32, 43, 119, 143

problematic assumptions, 40
vignette, 84–85
Explicit instruction, 36 (table), 77, 78, 89, 90, 93, 93 (figure)
Fairbairn, S., 36 (table)
False cognates, 91
Family-school partnerships, 29 (figure), 32–33, 43
Farnia, F., 20
Farr, M., 128
Fathman, A., 59 (table)
Feedback, 90
Ferris, D. R., 72, 78
Fifth Dimension, 61 (table)
Figueroa, R. A., 58, 66, 67, 68, 71, 128, 144, 150, 161
Filipino populations, 9 (table)
First language usage and support, 74, 75
Fisher, D., 72
Five Big Ideas, 86, 86–87 (table), 88–92
Fix, M.
    see Capp, R.
Flavell, J. H., 107
Fleishman, H., 120
Fletcher, J. M.
    see Stuebing, K. K.
Fletcher, T., 171
Florida, 8, 27
Fluency instruction, 37 (table), 87 (table), 89–90
Folsom, J.
    see Al Otaiba, S.
Ford, K., 37 (table)
Formal assessment, 164–165
    see also Assessment practices
Forman, E. A., 62 (table)
Francis, D. J., 94, 100
    see also Anthony, J. L.; Moughamian, A. C.
Free lunch program, 9
Freeman, G. G., 126 (table), 133 (table)
French language speakers, 9 (table)
Frey, N., 72
Fry, R., 9
Fuchs, D., 19, 25, 30, 31, 32, 33, 42, 98, 134, 141
Fuchs, L. S., 19, 25, 30, 31, 32, 33, 42, 98, 134, 141
Future directions, 171–172
Galland, P. A., 34 (table)
Gallego, M., 17, 18, 19, 21
Gallimore, R., 112
Galloway, E. P., 28
Gambrell, L. B., 62 (table)
Gamm, S., Esq., 123
Garcia, E., 75, 76
García, G., 34 (table)
García, O., 79
Garcia, S. B., 120
Gascoigne, C., 59 (table), 60 (table)
Gates MacGinitie standardized reading comprehension assessment (GMRT), 111
Gavin, K. M., 115

Gay, G., 10
Genesee, F., 58, 79, 86, 128
    see also Paradis, J.
Gentile, L., 93 (figure), 93–94
Gerber, M., 19, 20
    see also Swanson, H. L.
German language speakers, 9 (table)
Gersten, R., 115, 171 (table)
Geva, E., 20, 90
Gibbons, K. A., 134
Glass, G., 70, 74
    see also MacSwan, J.
Gleitman, L., 69
Goldenberg, C., 37 (table), 66, 68, 72, 73, 74, 77, 80, 112
Golos, D., 92
Gonzalez, N., 13
Good, R. H., 49
Gottardo, A., 88
Greenberg, J. B., 95
Greene, J., 74
Greene, S.
    see Blackorby, J.
Greenwood, C. R., 115
Greniuk, C., 120
Greulich, L.
    see Al Otaiba, S.
Gribbons, B., 64 (table)
Griffin, P., 94
Grigorenko, E. L., 135, 136
Grossman, H., 150
Guided reading, 37 (table)
Gunn, B., 34 (table), 37 (table)
Guzman-Orth, D., 19
    see also Swanson, H. L.
Haager, D., 40, 49, 94, 95–96
Haitian Creole language speakers, 9 (table)
Hakuta, K., 73, 75
Hallahan, D. P., 17, 19
Halliday, M. A. K., 128
Hamayan, E., 83, 84, 86, 88, 90, 92, 93, 94, 101
Hammill, D., 16 (table)
Hancin-Bhatt, B. J., 88
Hanselman, E., 28
Harper, C. A., 72, 73, 77, 78, 80
Harry, B., 11, 14, 15, 94, 98, 144, 150, 158
    see also Klingner, J. K.
Hedgcock, J. S., 72
Hernandez, J. S., 36 (table)
Herrell, A. L., 37 (table)
Herrera, S. G., 11, 32, 57, 58, 66, 72, 74, 75, 77, 79, 80, 85, 86, 88, 89, 90, 91, 92, 94, 96, 98, 103, 104, 105, 128, 131, 146, 171 (table)
Hertz-Lazarowitz, R., 36 (table)
Herwantoro, S.
    see Capp, R.
Hicks, J., 74
Hidayah, T., 35 (table)
Hiebert, E. H., 90

Higareda, I., 14
Hill, J. D., 148 (table)
Hinchman, K. A.
    see Alvermann, D. E.
Hispanic/Latino students, 14
Hite, C. E., 37 (table)
Hmong, 9 (table)
Home-community-school partnerships,
    29 (figure), 32–33, 43
Home language usage and support, 74
Hooker, S., 8
    see also Ruiz Soto, A. G.
Hoover, J. J., 11, 19, 21, 28, 30, 31, 32, 33,
    34 (table), 40, 41, 42, 43, 45, 57, 101, 107,
    115, 119, 120, 121, 123, 134, 143, 144, 145,
    148 (table), 149 (table), 150, 152 (table), 153,
    155, 158, 161, 164, 165, 166, 167, 169, 170
    see also Klingner, J. K.
Hopewell, S., 79, 116
Hopstock, P., 120
Hosp, J. L., 120
Hunt, K. W., 126 (table), 133 (table)
Hussar, F., 10
Idioms, 90, 129
Immigrant populations, 8–9
Impoverished populations, 9
Individuals with Disabilities Act (IDEA)
    Amendments (1997), 16 (table)
Individuals with Disabilities Education Act
    (IDEA, 1991), 17, 18
Individuals with Disabilities Education
    Improvement Act (IDEIA, 2004), 2, 3,
    16 (table), 17, 18, 19
Input Hypothesis, 60 (table)
Instructional conversations (IC), 112–114
Instructional decision-making questions, 96–98,
    99–100 (table)
Instructional responsiveness, 44–45
Intensive (Tier 3) intervention, 30–31, 31 (table),
    45, 47, 50 (table), 54–55 (table)
Interactive teaching, 37 (table)
Interlanguage stage, 67 (table), 78
Interrupted formal schooling, 11–13, 22
Interstate Teacher Assessment and Support
    Consortium (InTASC), 172
Intervention Central, 103
Intervention teams, 168
IQ discrepancy-based model, 15, 17–19, 21,
    22, 25
IRIS Center for Training Enhancements, 164
Irujo, S., 36 (table)
Isik, A., 65 (table)
Ivory, G., 36 (table)
Jensen, C., 111
Jewish populations, 9 (table)
Jiménez, R. T., 34 (table), 72, 115, 171 (table)
Johnson, G., 10
Jones-Vo, S., 36 (table)
Jordan, M., 37 (table)

Kahn, J. V., 124
Kaminski, R. A., 49
Kansas, 27
Kena, G., 10
Kendall, J., 35 (table)
Khuon, O., 35 (table)
Kieffer, M., 94
    see also Francis, D. J.
Kintsch, W., 126 (table)
    see also Cummins, D. D.
Kirk, S. A., 15, 16 (table)
Klassen, K., 85
Klingner, J. K., 11, 14, 15, 19, 20, 21, 28, 32,
    34 (table), 35 (table), 38 (table), 40, 41, 42,
    57, 58, 69, 75, 92, 94, 98, 101, 107, 108, 110,
    111, 112, 115, 119, 123, 134, 143, 144, 145,
    148 (table), 149 (table), 150, 152 (table),
    153, 158, 161, 164, 166, 167, 168, 169, 170,
    170 (table), 171 (table)
    see also Scornavacco, K.; Vaughn, S.
Korean language speakers, 9 (table)
Kovaleski, J., 16 (table), 19
Kozleski, E., 101
    see also Klingner, J. K.
Krashen, S. D., 59 (table), 60 (table), 64 (table),
    148 (table)
Kudo, M., 19
    see also Swanson, H. L.
Kushner, M. I.
    see Ortiz, A. A.
Lachat, M. A., 150
Ladson-Billings, G., 11
Lake, V. E., 148 (table)
Landau, B., 69
Landis, D., 104
Land, R., 34 (table)
Langdon, H. W., 131
Language
    acquisition rate, 67 (table), 75–76
    alphabetic principle, 87 (table), 88–89
    development behaviors, 58, 146,
        147–148 (table), 148, 149 (table), 150, 166
    dialects, 127–128, 129, 130, 168–169
    Early Authors Program (EAP), 97–98
    fluency, 87 (table), 89–90
    instructional practices and assessments,
        71–74, 80–81, 120, 166
    interlanguage errors, 67 (table), 78–79
    learning process, 67 (table), 76–78, 120, 146,
        147–148 (table)
    linguistic diversity, 9 (table)
    linguistic proficiency, 66–70, 67 (table),
        77, 79–80, 126–129, 146
    phonological awareness, 38 (table),
        86, 86 (table), 88
    reading comprehension, 87 (table), 91–92
    registers, 128–129, 130, 168–169
    vocabulary development, 87 (table), 90–91
    see also Learning disabilities; Native language

Language experience approach (LEA), 103–104
Lantolf, J. P., 135, 136 (table)
Larsen-Freeman, D., 126 (table), 133 (table)
Larsen, S., 16 (table)
Lasser, C.
    see Scornavacco, K.
Latino students, 14
Lawyer-Brook, D.
    see Blackorby, J.
Leafstedt, J., 20
Learning disabilities
    characteristics, 152–153
    contemporary perspective, 18 (table), 18–19
    cultural and linguistic responsiveness, 150,
        152–155, 154 (table), 156 (table), 157,
        159 (table)
    data-driven decision making, 143–145,
        147–148 (table), 148, 149 (table), 150,
        151–152 (table), 152–155
    disproportionate representation, 14–15, 22,
        83, 118
    historical perspective, 15, 16 (table), 17–18
    identification challenges, 21, 33,
        123–124, 143
    research background, 19–20
    second language acquisition behaviors,
        148, 149 (table), 150, 166
    see also Assessment practices
Learning Disability Initiative Summit,
    18, 18 (table), 19
Learning environments, 169–170,
    170–171 (table)
Learning theories, 59–65 (table)
Ledger, S., 12
LeDoux, J. M.
    see Stuebing, K. K.
Lee, J., 92
Leigh, F., 16 (table)
Lennon, D., 36 (table)
Lenz, K.
    see Blackorby, J.
Lesaux, N. K., 20, 21, 28, 90, 94, 98, 101
    see also Francis, D. J.
Level of performance, 30
Levy, J., 10
Lidz, C., 136
Limited bilingualism, 69
Limited English Proficient (LEP) students,
    69, 137–138, 138 (table)
Limited formal schooling, 11–13, 22
Linan-Thompson, S., 36 (table), 40, 101, 115
Lindahl, K. M., 39 (table)
Lindsey, K. A., 88
Linguistic diversity, 9 (table)
Linguistic features, 124, 125–126 (table),
    126–127, 131 (table), 132–133 (table),
    132–133, 168–169
Linguistic misalignment, 126–127, 130–131,
    131 (table)

Linguistic proficiency, 66–70, 67 (table), 77,
    79–80, 126–129, 146
Literacy instruction, 44–45, 67 (table), 71–73,
    93 (figure), 93–95, 98, 99–100 (table), 167–168
    see also Cultural and linguistic responsiveness
Lit, I., 74
Liu, Y.
    see Ortiz, A. A.
Li, X., 37 (table)
Lloyd, J. W., 19
Loe, S. A., 150
Long noun phrases, 125 (table), 132 (table)
Long question phrases, 125 (table), 132 (table)
Lord, C., 126 (table)
    see also Abedi, J.
Los Angeles Times, 70
Los Angeles Unified School District, 70
Love, E., 42, 45
Lussier, C., 19, 20
    see also Swanson, H. L.
Lyon, G. R.
    see Stuebing, K. K.
Macceca, S., 35 (table)
MacGillivray, L., 95
MacSwan, J., 68–69, 70, 71
Mahoney, K. S., 69, 71, 74
Maldonado-Colon, E., 58
Mancha, S., 104
Manis, F. R., 88
Marble Mountain Elementary School model,
    26, 45–49
Marler, B., 83
    see also Hamayan, E.
Marshall, H., 13
Massachusetts, 8
Maune, M., 85
McAllum, R., 106, 107
McGhee, B. D.
    see Ortiz, A. A.
McLaughlin, B., 66
McLean, J., 36 (table)
McNutt, G., 16 (table)
McPhail, J., 62 (table)
Meadows Center, 52 (table), 55 (table), 120,
    158, 161
Meaningful instruction, 94–95
Mediation, 135–136, 136 (table)
Meister, C., 107
Menon, S., 92
Mercer, C., 17
Mestre, J. P., 126 (table), 133 (table)
Metaphors, 90
Miller, K. B., 148 (table)
Miranda, A. H., 150
Mitchell, L., 9
Mock, D., 33
Mohammed, S.
    see Vaughn, S.
Moll, L. C., 13, 61 (table), 95

Monitor Hypothesis, 59–60 (table)
Monolingualism, 66, 67 (table), 68, 70
Montagna, D., 115
Montero, K., 12
Monzó, L., 95
Moore, B. A., 111
    see also Scornavacco, K.
Moore, D. W.
    see Alvermann, D. E.
Morgan, P. L., 33
Motivation, 94–95
Moughamian, A. C., 39 (table)
Multi-tiered continuum of supports, 29 (figure),
    30–31, 31 (table), 43
Multi-tiered system of supports (MTSS)
    authentic assessment, 134
    basic concepts, 25–26
    benefits, 141, 163–164, 172
    challenges, 43–49
    components and characteristics, 27–33,
        29 (figure), 31 (table), 42 (table), 43
    data-driven decision making, 29 (figure), 30,
        43, 158–159, 159 (table), 160 (table), 168
    definitions, 27
    effective reading instructional methods,
        33, 34–39 (table), 167–168
    evidence-based interventions, 29 (figure), 30,
        31–32, 43, 119, 143, 155–158, 156 (table)
    implementation readiness, 51–52 (table),
        166–167
    instruction planning guide, 53–55 (table)
    legislative mandates, 3
    lessons learned, 49–50
    Marble Mountain Elementary School, 45–49
    practical applications, 41–49
    problematic assumptions, 40–41
    Rural School District Model, 41–45, 42 (table)
    two-dimensional framework, 42 (table),
        42–43
    vignette, 26–27
    see also Cultural and linguistic
        responsiveness; Data-driven decision
        making
Multi-word sentences, 125 (table), 132 (table)
Murray, J.
    see Capp, R.
Nagy, W. E., 88
National Association for Bilingual Education
    (NABE), 5
National Association of School Psychologists, 28
National Association of State Directors of
    Special Education (NASDSE), 30, 31
    (table), 32, 33
National Center for Culturally Responsive
    Educational Systems (NCCRESt), 5, 95
National Center for Education Statistics
    (NCES), 7, 8, 9, 10
National Center on Response to Intervention
    (NCRI), 42, 120

National Council for Accreditation of Teacher
    Education (NCATE), 42
National Council of Teachers of English
    (NCTE), 38 (table)
National Institute of Child Health and Human
    Development (NICHD), 37 (table)
National Joint Committee on Learning
    Disabilities (NJCLD), 16 (table), 17–18
National Literacy Panel on Language Minority
    Children and Youth, 86, 92
National Reading Panel, 84, 86, 94
Native American students, 14
Native language
    instructional practices and assessments, 20,
        73–74, 80–81
    literacy instruction, 37–38 (table), 67 (table)
    proficiency assessments, 67 (table), 70–71
    see also Bilingualism
Natural Order Hypothesis, 59 (table)
Nazarro, J. N., 150
Neff, D., 13
Negations, 126 (table), 133 (table)
Newmaster, S., 12
Newsome, P., 144, 150, 161
New sounds, 88–89
New York, 8
Nguyen, H. T., 41, 57
Nicoladis, E., 79
Nicolopoulou, A., 61 (table)
No Child Left Behind Act (2001), 2, 28
Nokes, J. D., 34 (table)
    see also Dole, J. A.
Nondiscriminatory progress monitoring,
    158–159, 161 (table), 161–162
Non-non classifications, 70
Normal curve equivalent (NCE) measures,
    75–76
North Carolina, 8, 27
Notation, 129
Noun phrases, 125 (table), 132 (table)
O'Brien, G., 36 (table)
O'Connor, R. E., 10, 11, 20, 40
Odds ratio, 23
Ohta, A. S., 61 (table)
Olson, C. B., 34 (table)
O'Malley, J. M., 34 (table)
Oracy model, 93, 93 (figure)
Oral language proficiency and assessment,
    67 (table), 71, 77, 92–94, 93 (figure)
Orosco, M. J., 10, 11, 19, 20, 21, 40, 41, 42, 58,
    76, 84, 89, 119, 144
Orr, E. W., 126 (table), 133 (table)
Ortiz, A. A., 21, 57, 58, 78, 98, 101, 117, 119, 120,
    123, 131, 144, 149 (table), 150, 152 (table),
    155, 158
Ortiz, S. O., 123
Osher, D., 101
Ost, J.
    see Capp, R.

Ovando, O., 69
Overrepresented groups, 14–15, 83, 118
Pacific Islander students, 14
Padilla, C.
    see Blackorby, J.
Padron, Y. N., 39 (table)
Palincsar, A. S., 106, 107
Pappamihiel, N. E., 148 (table)
Paradis, J., 58, 66, 75, 78
Paris, S. G., 90
Partner reading, 90
Partnerships, 29 (figure), 32–33, 42, 43
Passel, J. S.
    see Capp, R.
Pathway Project, 34 (table)
Patthey-Chavez, G., 112
Patton, J. R., 34 (table), 91, 114
    see also Hoover, J. J.
Pearson, 39 (table)
Pearson, P. D., 34 (table), 90
Peer tutoring, 114–115
Peregoy, S. F., 38 (table), 90, 92
Perez, D. R., 11, 32, 85, 94, 98, 103
    see also Herrera, S. G.
Pew Research Center, 8
Phelps, S. F.
    see Alvermann, D. E.
Phonics and word recognition instruction,
    38 (table)
Phonological awareness, 38 (table),
    86, 86 (table), 88
Pinker, S., 69
Plotts, C., 9
Plummer, J., 126 (table)
    see also Abedi, J.
Poehner, M. E., 135, 136 (table)
Polloway, E. A., 91, 114
Poor populations, 9
Portes, A., 75
Positive behavioral interventions and supports
    (PBIS), 25
Prater, K., 40
Prepositional phrases, 125 (table), 132 (table)
Preston, D. R., 127
Pretest-teach-posttest procedure, 135,
    136 (table)
Problem-solving teams, 168
Proctor, C. P., 37 (table)
Professional development, 43–44, 165, 172
Progress monitoring, 29, 29 (figure), 43, 153,
    158–159, 161 (table), 161–162, 164
Project PLUS, 49, 50 (table)
Public Law 94–142, 17
Pulegatoa-Diggins, C., 107
Question phrases, 125 (table), 132 (table)
Raphael, T. E., 108
Reading skills
    alphabetic principle, 87 (table), 88–89
    challenges, 83–85

effective reading instructional methods, 33,
    34–39 (table), 40–41, 102–110, 109 (table),
    112–116, 167–168
fluency, 87 (table), 89–90
instructional decision-making questions,
    96–98, 99–100 (table)
motivating instruction, 94–95
multi-tiered system of supports (MTSS), 33
phonological awareness, 38 (table),
    86, 86 (table), 88
reading comprehension, 87 (table), 91–92
standards-based instruction, 85
vignette, 84, 101–102
vocabulary development, 87 (table), 90–91
Reciprocal teaching, 38–39 (table), 106–107
Reduced-price lunch program, 9
Reflective activities
    assessment practices, 118–119
    data-driven decision making, 143
    instructional decision-making questions,
        99–100 (table)
    multi-tiered system of supports (MTSS),
        27, 143
    reading skills, 84, 102
Registers, 128–129, 130, 168–169
Relative clauses, 126 (table), 132 (table)
Relevant instruction, 94–95
Repeated readings, 104–105
Reschy, D. J., 120
Research-based instruction, 40–41, 84–85, 100
Research to Practice
    Collaborative Strategic Reading (CSR), 110–112
    cultural and linguistic responsiveness, 121–123
    Dynamic Assessment (DA), 137–139,
        138 (table)
    Early Authors Program (EAP), 97–98
    reading achievement, 95–96
Response to intervention (RTI), 18 (table),
    22, 25, 45–49
Reusser, K., 126 (table)
    see also Cummins, D. D.
Reyes, E., 17
    see also Gallego, M.
Richard-Amato, P. A., 79, 91
Richardson, V, 90
Riley, D.
    see Klingner, J. K.
Rinaldi, C., 123
Risk index (RI), 23
Rivera, H., 94
    see also Francis, D. J.
Rivera, M. O., 94
    see also Francis, D. J.; Moughamian, A. C.
Roberts, G.
    see Vaughn, S.
Robertson-Courtney, P., 144
Robertson, P. M.
    see Ortiz, A. A.
Rodrigo, V., 64 (table)

Rodriguez, D., 115
Rodriguez, J. L., 79
Rolstad, K., 68, 69, 70, 74
    see also MacSwan, J.
Rosenshine, B., 107
Roskos, K., 112, 114
Roth, E., 10
Rueda, R., 14, 15, 95
Ruiz-Figueroa, O. A., 116
Ruiz, N. T., 58, 170 (table)
Ruiz Soto, A. G., 8
Rumbaut, R. G., 75
Rural School District Model, 26, 41–45,
    42 (table)
Rutter, M., 17
Ryan, C., 8
Sable, J., 9
Sáez, L., 20
Salazar, J., 14
Samson, J. F., 11, 101
Sanchez-Lopez, C., 83
    see also Hamayan, E.
Sanderman, A. R., 10
Santiago, I. C., 32
Saunders, W. M., 36 (table), 112
Saville-Troike, M., 78
Schatschneider, C.
    see Al Otaiba, S.
Schemas, 89
Schoger, K. D.
    see Anthony, J. L.
School environments, 41
School-family-community partnerships,
    29 (figure), 32–33, 43
Scornavacco, K., 108, 110, 111, 112
Second language acquisition (SLA)
    acquisition rate, 67 (table), 75–76
    alphabetic principle, 87 (table), 88–89
    challenges, 57–58, 83, 123–124
    data-driven decision making, 145–146,
        147–148 (table), 148, 149 (table), 150, 166
    development behaviors, 58, 146, 147–148
        (table), 148, 149 (table), 150, 166
    fluency, 87 (table), 89–90
    instructional practices and assessments,
        71–74, 80–81, 120, 166
    interlanguage errors, 67 (table), 78–79
    learning process, 67 (table), 76–78, 120, 146,
        147–148 (table)
    misconceptions, 66–80, 67 (table), 166
    phonological awareness, 38 (table),
        86, 86 (table), 88
    reading comprehension, 87 (table), 91–92
    reading skills, 40–41, 83
    theoretical perspectives, 58, 59–65 (table)
    vocabulary development, 87 (table), 90–91
Selinker, L., 78
Semantics, 129
Semilingualism, 67 (table), 68–70

Sentence length, 125 (table), 132 (table)
Sentence structure, 126 (table), 132 (table)
Sequential bilinguals, 66, 67 (table), 79–80
Serna, L., 91
Shanahan, T., 41, 58, 72, 73, 85, 86, 88, 89,
    90, 91, 92
Shapiro, E., 16 (table)
    see also Kovaleski, J.
Shared leadership, 29 (figure), 29–30, 43
Shaywitz, B. A.
    see Stuebing, K. K.
Shaywitz, S. E.
    see Stuebing, K. K.
Sheltered Instruction Observation Protocol
    (SIOP), 39 (table)
Short, D. J., 39 (table)
    see also Echevarria, J. J.
Siegel, L. A., 88
Similes, 90
Simultaneous bilinguals, 66, 67 (table), 79–80
Slavin, R. E., 35 (table), 36 (table),
    38 (table), 74, 77
Slobin, D. I., 126 (table), 133 (table)
Smith, C.
    see Klingner, J. K.
Smith, T. E. C., 114
Smolkowski, K., 34 (table), 37 (table)
Snow, C. E., 37 (table), 91, 94
Sociocultural Theory, 61–62 (table)
Sociolinguistic Theory, 62–63 (table)
Solano-Flores, G., 21, 68, 127, 128, 129,
    130, 131 (table)
    see also Basterra, M. D. R.
Solari, E. J.
    see Anthony, J. L.
Soltero-González, L., 40, 41, 42, 43, 98
    see also Klingner, J. K.
Spanish language speakers, 8–9, 9 (table), 22
Sparrow, W., 116
Special education assessment
    appropriate use, 117, 119–120, 168–169
    authentic assessment, 133–137, 136 (table), 169
    biases, 158
    cultural and linguistic responsiveness, 44–45,
        118–123, 142
    dialects, 127–128, 129, 130, 168–169
    experiential backgrounds, 132–133 (table),
        132–133
    linguistic features, 124, 125–126 (table),
        126–127, 131 (table), 132–133 (table),
        132–133, 168–169
    linguistic misalignment, 126–127, 130–131,
        131 (table)
    nondiscriminatory progress monitoring,
        161 (table), 161–162
    purpose, 119–120
    registers, 128–129, 130, 168–169
    validity and reliability challenges, 123–124,
        126–127, 129, 131

vignette, 118–119
see also Data-driven decision making; Multi-tiered system of supports (MTSS)
Special education placement patterns, 14–15
Spenciner, L. J., 124, 133
Spharim, G., 37 (table)
Standard English, 129
Standards-based instruction, 85
Steege, M. W., 143, 164
Sternberg, R. J., 136
Stillman-Spisak, S.
see Vaughn, S.
Struggling learners
see Assessment practices; Cultural and linguistic responsiveness; Data-driven decision making; Multi-tiered system of supports (MTSS); Reading skills
Stuart, M., 34 (table)
Students with limited/interrupted formal education (SLIFEs), 11–13, 22
Stuebing, K. K., 17
Subordinate clauses, 126 (table), 132 (table)
Sullivan, A. L., 40
Swain, M., 64 (table), 77, 78
Swanson, E., 35 (table)
see also Vaughn, S.
Swanson, H. L., 19, 20
Tagalog, 9 (table)
Targeted (Tier 2) instruction, 30, 31 (table), 45, 47–49, 50 (table), 53–54 (table), 158, 164
Tate, W
see Klingner, J. K.
Taylor, B. M., 90
Taylor, P., 9
Teacher diversity, 10–11, 22
Teacher mediation, 135–136, 136 (table)
Teacher preparation, 165
Teacher qualities/abilities, 42 (table), 42–43
Teacher shortages, 10–11
Teaching English to Speakers of Other Languages (TESOL) International Association, 42
Tellez, K., 38 (table)
Terrell, T. D., 60 (table), 148 (table)
Terry, B. J., 115
Texas, 8
Tharp, R. G., 112, 172
Thomas, W. P., 75, 76
Thompson, L. W., 37 (table)
Thorius, K. K., 40
Thorn, E. A., 103
Three-tiered support systems, 30–31, 31 (table), 45, 47–49, 50 (table), 53–55 (table), 120, 141, 158–159
see also Data-driven decision making; Multi-tiered system of supports (MTSS)
Tikunoff, W. J., 36 (table)
Time on tasks expectations, 67 (table), 73–74
Tomlinson, C., 36 (table)

Trent, S. C., 14, 101
Trumbull, E., 21, 68, 127, 128
see also Basterra, M. D. R.
Umolu, J., 104
Underrepresented minority teaching force, 10–11
Universal screening, 29, 29 (figure), 43, 164
Universal (Tier 1) instruction, 30, 31 (table), 45, 47–48, 50 (table), 53 (table), 120, 158–159, 163
University of Texas Center for Reading and Language Arts, 52 (table), 55 (table)
University-school district partnership, 42
Urbach, J., 92
US Census, 8
US Department of Education, 7, 10, 16 (table), 17–18
US Office of Education, 17
US Office of Special Education Programs (OSEP), 18
Utley, C. A., 115
Valdés, G., 66, 67, 68, 71, 75, 128
Valle, J. W., 134, 135, 136, 168, 169
VanDerHeyden, A., 16 (table)
see also Kovaleski, J.
Vaughn, S., 34 (table), 35 (table), 36 (table), 38 (table), 40, 104, 110
Vietnamese language speakers, 9 (table)
Virginia, 8
Vocabulary development, 87 (table), 90–91
Vocabulary enrichment method, 39 (table)
Vogt, M. E., 39 (table)
see also Echevarria, J. J.
Vygotsky, L. S., 61 (table), 62 (table), 64 (table), 106, 107
Wagner, R. K.
see Al Otaiba, S.
Walker, B. J., 112
see also Roskos, K.
Walker, D., 115
Wang, C., 111
Wanzek, J.
see Al Otaiba, S.
Wardhaugh, R., 128
Washington, 8
Waterman, D. C., 103
Watkins, N. M., 39 (table)
Waxman, H. C., 38 (table)
Weaver, D.
see Alvermann, D. E.
Weimer, R., 126 (table)
see also Cummins, D. D.
Wei, X.
see Blackorby, J.
Wells, D., 63 (table)
Westera, J., 107
Whalley, E., 59 (table)
What Works Clearinghouse (WWC), 112, 114
White, K.
see Klingner, J. K.

Whitmore, K. F., 61 (table)
WIDA: Can Do Descriptors, 58, 73, 146, 147–148 (table)
WIDA *Focus*, 11–12, 13
Wilkinson, C. Y., 144, 149 (table), 150, 152 (table), 154
    see also Ortiz, A. A.
Williams, J. M.
    see Anthony, J. L.
Willig, A., 74
Windmueller, M. P., 15
Winsler, A.
    see Bernhard, J. K.
Wolfe, P., 98
Wolfram, W., 128
Wong-Fillmore, L., 74, 77
Wood, K. D., 35 (table)
Word frequency/familiarity, 125 (table), 132 (table)
Word length, 125 (table), 132 (table)
Writing skills, 72–73
Written language proficiency and assessment, 71, 77

Xu, Y., 77
Yell, M., 31
Yiddish speakers, 9 (table)
Yoon, B., 11
Young, C., 33
Young, J. P.
    see Alvermann, D. E.
Ysseldyke, J. E., 28
Yule, W., 17
Zacarian, D., 90, 94, 98
Zalewski, P. Z.
    see Alvermann, D. E.
Zamora Durán, G., 17
    see also Gallego, M.
Zehler, A., 120
Zepeda, M., 79
Zhang, M., 37 (table)
Zhang, Z.
    see Anthony, J. L.
Zion, S.
    see Klingner, J. K.
Zone of proximal development (ZPD), 62 (table), 64 (table)

CORWIN

A SAGE Publishing Company

Helping educators make the greatest impact

CORWIN HAS ONE MISSION: to enhance education through intentional professional learning.

We build long-term relationships with our authors, educators, clients, and associations who partner with us to develop and continuously improve the best evidence-based practices that establish and support lifelong learning.

Solutions you want. Experts you trust. Results you need.